Ten Years' Captivation with the Mahdi's Camps: Essays on Muslim Eschatology, 2005-2015

Timothy R. Furnish, Ph.D.

Ten Years' Captivation with the Mahdi's Camps: Essays on Muslim Eschatology, 2005-2015

Copyright © 2015 by Timothy R. Furnish, Ph.D.

Acknowledgments

This book (and its companion, *Sects, Lies, and the Caliphate: 10 Years of Observations on Islam*) came about because one much wiser than me–my wife, Davina–suggested that I compile ten years' writings on one topic (Islamic eschatology and Islam in general, respectively) and publish them. Thanks, dear, for pointing out what should have been obvious to me–but wasn't; and for your support in pulling it together. She also suggested I ask Gail Tyler to edit both manuscripts–and I thank Gail for plunging into work on a manuscript covering material far outside her usual area of expertise. I want to thank Rick Shenkman, editor of *History News Network* [HNN], for granting me permission to use several dozen pieces which had originally appeared on HNN; "Drdael," whose Mahdi from *deviantart.com* he allowed me to use for the cover; and my dear friend for over 40 years, Tony Arrasmith, for the excellent cover artwork–done with a little help from his friend John Doubét.

Preface

The title of this volume is adapted from a famous book about Mahdism (Islamic messianism), *Ten Years' Captivity in the Mahdi's Camp 1882-1892*, by F.R. Wingate, published in 1892. Major Wingate was a British Army intelligence officer in Cairo whose source was Father Joseph Ohrwalder, an Austrian priest and missionary to Sudan captured by the forces of the Sudanese Mahdi, Muhammad Ahmad, and held for a decade.

Unlike poor Fr. Ohrwalder, I have only been under the virtual, not real, thrall of the Mahdi, since taking a graduate class on African jihads at Ohio State University in 1995 and first learning of the aforementioned Muhammad Ahmad (portrayed so idiosyncratically by Sir Laurence Olivier in the 1966 movie *Khartoum*). I eventually wrote my doctoral dissertation "Eschatology as Politics, Eschatology as Theory: Modern Sunni Arab Mahdism in Historical Perspective" (Ohio State, 2001) on the topic; and this was transformed into my first book, *Holiest Wars: Islamic Mahdis, their Jihads, and Osama bin Laden* (Praeger, 2005).

The Mahdi is "the rightly-guided one" of Islamic traditions who, it is believed, will appear before the End of Time to usher in an age of global Muslim rule. Once believed to be the province only of the Shi`is, particularly the Twelvers, recent research (Pew, 2012) has empirically demonstrated what I had learned anecdotally from my own historical studies: that many Sunnis, not just Shi`is, expect the coming of this eschatological figure in the near future. I have tracked, analyzed and written on such beliefs and related movements for two decades: *Holiest Wars* summarized the results of that research, 1995-2005; the present work does so for the period 2005-2015, drawing upon my blogposts, articles, lectures and media interviews over that time. But whereas my first book was academic in nature, *Ten Years' Captivation with the Mahdi's Camps*, while grounded in solid historical and theological scholarship, is intended as a much more user-friendly, popular work on Mahdism and related topics. It will allow readers to learn about such important topics as: why the Islamic State calls its magazine *Dabiq* and beheads captives; whether Iran wants nuclear weapons to hotwire the apocalypse by attacking Israel; and how the US government can be so inept at dealing with both.

I was the first commentator to point out Islamic State's apocalyptic bent—long before *The Atlantic* "broke" the story in March, 2015; and I've not only studied, but visited, the Islamic Republic of Iran. While I am a Christian, I analyze the topic at hand in terms of its Islamic roots and manifestations, not how well I think it meshes with the book of Revelation; and unlike many media commentators and self-styled "experts," I've read the Qur'an and relevant sources in Arabic. My goal for the last decade has been to use that expertise and make the topic of Islamic eschatology, so easily misunderstood or hyperbolized, accessible to non-experts. I leave it to you, dear reader, to judge for yourself whether I've succeeded.

How to Use This Book

Ten Years' Captivation is, thus, a tool for non-experts on Islam, and not a reference or text book. There are 13 chapters arranged topically (and, I hope, logically), with essays in each chapter placed in reverse chronological order based on their original publication date. While every essay has been edited and, as needed, updated, each is still clearly embedded in its original context–but also quite relevant to current events in the Islamic world. The reader can thus skip around from topic to topic, and indeed from essay to essay, and still have the subject matter make sense. For anyone who wishes to trace the development of various facets of Mahdism over the last decade–as, for example, the explosion of claimants to the position of Mahd–then he or she can go to the last entry in that section and work forward in time. Most of the book is in essay, or at least analytical commentary, form–but do keep in mind that there are also entries referring to my relevant TV and radio interviews, or lectures. Such in the e-book version will have appropriate links.

Allow me some needed explanation of key terms: ***Mahdism*** refers to a belief or movement centered around a particular Muslim claiming to be said Mahdi; ***eschatological*** refers to "End of Time" matters that may or may not include the Mahdi; and ***apocalyptic***, while often used as a synonym for "eschatological," is most often employed here in contexts speaking of violent, End Time conflict (following its common understanding in the modern Western world).

One final caveat: while this book is chock-full of astute analysis, it is also heavily laced with flippant (and sometimes mordant) references to classic rock music, *The Simpsons*, science-fiction, and movies, notably *The Lord of the Rings*. So by all means, read and learn about the Mahdi– while also being, perhaps better than Maximus' audience, entertained.

Table of Contents

Background on Mahdism

June 26, 2015: It's Not Easy Being Green—Unless You're Discussing the Mahdi.

Yesterday, I was a guest on Tom Trento's excellent *The United West* radio/TV show. For almost 40 minutes Tom and I discussed Mahdism in general and the Iranian Twelver Shi`i variant thereof in particular. For much of the time, Skype—or perhaps the Hidden Imam—caused me to appear in green. Personally, I think it's a sign from God; but don't quote me on that.

May 7, 2013: The Mahdi under African Skies—A Primer on (African) Mahdism.

As a newly-minted fellow at RIMA, "Research on Islam and Muslims in Africa," I recently completed a brief Q & A on the topic of Mahdism in Africa as part of RIMA's "Ask the Expert" series. Please take a few minutes to check it out, if you're interested in Mahdism in general, Islam in Africa, Sufism, and/or jihad!

1. What is Madism in Islam and why is it important?

Mahdism is the belief in al-Mahdi, "the rightly/divinely-guided one" who will come before the end of time, along with the returned prophet `Isa, Jesus, to make the entire world Muslim (via conquest, persuasion—or both). This is according to hadiths, "sayings" attributed to Muhammad (in the Sunni view) and to the Imams (in the Twelver Shi`i view). It is important because Islamic history is rife with individuals claiming to be the Mahdi and leading, often, bloody rebellions or revolutions against established states (usually Islamic ones); prominent examples include Ibn Tumart and (the) *al-Muwahhidun* ("Almohads") in the medieval Maghrib; Shah Isma'il and the Safavids, who forcibly converted Iran to Twelver Shi`ism starting in 1501; the Sudanese Mahdi, Muhammad Ahmad, who took over that country in 1885 and ended the career–and life–of General Charles Gordon; and the abortive Mahdist movement in Saudi Arabia, 1979, led by Juhayman al-Utaybi in the name of the Mahdi Muhammad al-Qahtani.

2. What differentiates Mahdist movements and groups from other Islamic movements and groups?

They are defined, first and foremost, by a charismatic leader claiming to be this eschatological figure and by followers who accept this claim. Mahdist movements tend to emerge from Sufi milieux, as the mystical orders are prone to both producing charismatic shaykhs, and also provide a ready-made cadre of followers/soldiers. What sets them apart from more conventional Islamic groups is their absolute certainty that they are preparing the world (or at least their part of it, initially) for eschatological time–which does *not* mean the destruction of the world but, rather, its total conversion (or at least submission) to Islamic rule and norms. And since the Mahdi is, by definition, Allah's appointed ruler, he is free to interpret Qur'an, Hadith and *shari`a* as he sees fit, disregarding any previous *ijma`*, or scholarly Muslim "consensus." This means the Mahdi has, in effect, no brakes on his behavior other than his own intellect, personality and piety.

3. Have there been Mahdist movements or groups active in Africa? If so, please describe their activities?

Historically, Mahdism has been very prominent in Africa, particularly in the past several centuries. Shaykh Usman don Fodio (d. 1817), a shaykh of three different *tariqat*, founded the Sokoto Caliphate prior to British conquest and was thought by many Hausa to be the Mahdi–although he never claimed, openly, to be more than a *mujaddid*, "renewer" of Islam. Muhammad al-Mahdi al-Sanusi (d. 1902) was deemed by many adherents of the Sanusi order to be the Mahdi. The jihad of Salihi Shaykh Muhammad b. Abd Allah Hassan (d. 1920), of Somaliland, against the British and Italians led many to consider him the

Mahdi. And of course, there is the aforementioned Muhammad Ahmad, immortalized in the 1966 film *Khartoum*. In the 1970s and early 1980s, the Nigerian group Yan Tatsine or Maitatsine could certainly be labelled a Mahdist one, since its founder Muhammad Marwa Maitatsine (d. 1980) was thought by his followers—and perhaps by himself—to be the Mahdi. After his demise, his disciple Musa Makiniki led the group until his arrest in 2004. The current violent Islamic group Boko Haram, in northern Nigeria, is considered by some to either be an offshoot of, or heavily influenced by, Maitatsine. Considering the great percentages of adherence to Sufism in sub-Saharan Africa (huge minorities in Nigeria, Niger and Cameroon; over half in Chad; almost all in Senegal), and the nexus between Sufism and Mahdism, Mahdist claims in Africa are to be expected going forward.

4. Is Mahdism an important aspect of Islam particularly in Africa?

Yes, because as aforementioned the great numbers and influences of Sufis and Sufism in Africa—particularly (but not only) sub-Saharan parts of the continent—have tended to produce, in the past, jihads and/or Mahdism. Ironically, in the last several decades, Sufis and Mahdists have tended to coalesce around joint opposition to Salafis, who are seen as foreign in terms of being primarily Arab, and in terms of promoting a brand of Islam that is "unAfrican" in its intolerance for non-Muslims and for Muslim mystical spirituality. However, Sufis, while peaceful, are not pacifist and have not only waged jihad in the past but are doing so currently—most notably, in Africa, the Sufi organization *Ahl al-Sunna wa-al-Jama`a* in Somalia, which has been battling the Salafi, al-Qa`ida-oriented al-Shabab for several years in Somalia. Mahdism, in Africa and elsewhere in the *ummah*, could quite plausibly emerge again—even in a violent form—out of these Sufi contexts.

As a companion piece, I suggest reading my History News Network article "Mahdism (and Sectarianism and Superstition) Rises in the

Islamic World" (Aug. 13, 2012), which unpacks the Pew data on just how many Muslims–particularly in Africa–believe in the imminent coming of the Mahdi.

March 18, 2015: A Radio Primer on Mahdism.

I was on the *Peter Boyles Show*, KNUS AM 710, Denver, this morning ostensibly to discuss the Israeli election–but I wound up speaking for most of the 30 minutes on Mahdism. This is a good primer for those wishing to learn about the topic.

August 22, 2012: Up with the Mahdi and the Radio.*

Here's the hour-long archived clip of me on Dr. Jamie Glazov's radio show last night (August 21, 2012), discussing at some length Mahdism, eschatology (both Muslim and Christian), the latest Pew study on Islamic beliefs and U.S. policy toward the Muslim world. *Paraphrasing (slightly) U2's "Stay (Faraway, So Close)".

August 13, 2012: Mahdism (and Sectarianism and Superstition) Rises in the Islamic World.

Last week the prestigious and non-partisan Pew Forum on Religion and Public Life released a new study on beliefs and attitudes in the Islamic world, entitled "The World's Muslims: Unity and Diversity." Surveying over 28,000 Muslims in 24 countries, this massive report is not only statistically sound and extensive in geographic scope–it's the first to examine a number of topics of profound importance to U.S. foreign, defense and intelligence policy which have heretofore been largely off the radar screen of analysts as well as pollsters. Clearly the most fascinating–and disturbing–data in the Pew study is that revealing the great depth of belief in the "imminent return" [sic] of the Mahdi, the Islamic messianic figure who according to both Sunni and Shi`i traditions will make the entire world Muslim.[1] ("Sic" because the good Pew folks don't seem to totally understand Mahdism, in which the Mahdi only returns for Twelver Shi`is; for Sunnis, the Mahdi has yet to step onto the historical stage, despite the plethora of *mutamahdi*s, or "false Mahdis," who have declared themselves over the centuries.) This has been my academic specialty, upon which I wrote my doctoral dissertation and first book, *Holiest Wars*, as well as many articles; I also maintain a website following Mahdism. But while I have long suspected, based on anecdotal and qualitative research, that Mahdism was and still is endemic in the Islamic world, I was nonetheless taken aback by Pew's quantitative data which clearly shows the breadth and depth of such belief:

In South Asia, Southeast Asia and the Middle East and North Africa, clear majorities of Muslims expect the Mahdi's coming in the next few decades. Almost a third in Central Asia does so, as well. Only in Southern and Eastern Europe is the figure below 20%. (Pew, for some reason, did not ask this question in the sub-Saharan African Muslim region—but if it had, I would wager that the percentage would be even higher than anywhere else, knowing what I do of historical Mahdism in Africa.) Looking at specific countries, the highest percentage of the population expecting the Mahdi's near-term appearance is found in Afghanistan (83%), followed by Iraq (72%), Turkey (68%) and Tunisia (67%). Sixty percent of Pakistanis, 51% of Moroccans, 46% of Palestinians and 40% of Egyptians are looking for the Mahdi in their lifetimes. The conventional wisdom in recent decades

---

[1] For an overview of Mahdism and the differing views of it in Sunnism and Shi`ism, see the first four pages of my article "A Western View on Iran's WMD Goal: Nuclearizing the Eschaton, or Pre-Stocking the Mahdi's Arsenal?," Institute for Near East and Gulf Military Analysis, Special Report No. 12, January 2011.

among many journalists, and not a few area "experts," has been that Mahdism is an eccentric outlier belief held mainly by (Twelver) Shi`is and the uneducated on the fringes of the Sunni world. This Pew data, among other things, shows the intellectual vacuity of such biases. **The average for the 23 countries Pew surveyed on this issue of Mahdism comes out to 42%, and extrapolating from that to the entire Muslim world means there are over 670 million Muslims who believe the Mahdi will return here in the first half of the twenty-first century.**

What does this Pew information on Mahdism mean? First and foremost, Mahdism must be taken seriously as an intellectual, sociological and even political strain within the entire Islamic world–not dismissed as archaic, mythical nonsense. In addition, the good, the bad and the ugly faces of Mahdism throughout history need to be considered–political correctness be damned. The good is that Mahdism (mainly Shi`i, but also Sunni) does have peaceful social justice elements, akin to Catholic Christian "liberation theology," that can be harnessed to improve Muslims' lives (as is done on a regular basis by the Isma'ili, or Sevener, Shi`is, who define jihad as nonviolent benevolence) and ecumenical proclivities toward other "People of the Book" (as preached by the Turkish Mahdist Adnan Oktar and his followers). The bad is that Mahdism has often manifested as a political movement, against not just occupying non-Muslim (generally Christian) powers, but in point of fact far more often as a counter-Islamic-establishment revolutionary program. And the ugly truth about belief in the Mahdi is that Islamic history is rife with violent jihads led by self-styled Muslim messiahs and waged by their followers–from Ibn Tumart in medieval Morocco to nineteenth-century Sudan's Muhammad Ahmad (of *Khartoum* fame) and, more recently, 1979's attempted Mahdist putsch in Saudi Arabia as well as the flare-ups of Mahdist violence against U.S. and Iraqi government forces in Iraq in 2007, led by *Jund al-Sama'* ("Army of Heaven"). If even 1% of the 672 million Muslims who believe in the Mahdi take the jihad route, that provides the AQN (al-Qaʿida Network) with a pool of almost seven million jihadists. In terms of specific countries: the stratospheric Mahdist belief rate in Afghanistan is very likely connected to the fact that that country is occupied by "infidel" Christians; Turkey's very high eschatological proclivities might be attributable to the influence of the aforementioned Adnan Oktar, as well as to another neo-Mahdist strain of thought coming from the followers of Fethullah Gülen;[2] and Mahdist expectations in Tunisia could very well be due to the still-lingering legacy of Ibn Tumart and other Mahdist movements in the Maghrib in centuries past. In terms of policy ramifications, it is worth considering that: Mahdist fervor in Afghanistan could very possibly be contributing to the opposition to the continued presence of U.S. forces there; we should be thankful that the predominant strain of Islamic messianism in NATO's only majority-Muslim nation is, at least so far, pacific–while at the same time wary of what appears to be a burgeoning alliance between Turkish Mahdists and the neo-Ottomanists in the AK party in power; and such high levels of Mahdist belief in the vanguard country of the "Arab Spring" might very well be a harbinger of this political movement transmogrifying from an Arab "liberation" one into a more violent eschatological register, as at least one prominent Muslim intellectual is already preaching. One might also observe that when over half of the Lebanese, almost half of the Palestinians, millions of Egyptians and a large plurality of Jordanians expect the Mahdi soon, the Israelis might have good reason to fear the Arab eschatological pot being brought to boil by the those arch-Mahdists in the Islamic Republic of Iran (a

---

[2] On Oktar and Gülen and their joint intellectual descent from the 20th c. Turkish Mahdist Said Nursi, see subsequent sections on Ottoman and Turkish Mahdism..

country which, curiously, was not included in Pew's polling on this or
other issues). As for Pakistan, the fact that six in ten of its people are
looking for eschatological deliverance in the near-term means that even
Deobandi fundamentalism–the South Asian equivalent of (Saudi) Arab
Wahhabism–is far from immune to Islamic messianism.

Pew also reports that significant minorities of Muslims believe in
Jesus's imminent return. In both Sunni and Shi`i *hadith*s (alleged sayings
of Muhammad), the prophet "Isa [Jesus] will return from heaven, having
been taken up there before he died on the cross,"[3] and once back will
work with the Mahdi to defeat the forces of evil led by *al-Dajjal*, "the
Deceiver" (or Antichrist). Across the 22 countries Pew surveyed on this
issue, an average of 35% of the Muslim population believes Jesus is
coming back soon–with the strongest expectations in Tunisia (67%),
Turkey (65%), Iraq (64%), Lebanon (52%) and among Thailand's
Muslims (51%). This pales in comparison to the 79% of Christians who
look for Christ's Second Coming (as per Pew, from a 2009 study),
especially considering there are 2.2 billion Christians (far more than
there are Muslims); but Christian history is **not** replete with violent
crusades led by men claiming to be the returned Jesus, whereas Islamic
history has witnessed legions of Mahdist claimants, many militant–as
explained previously. The import of some 435 million Muslims looking
for Jesus's return in the early 21st century would seem to be mainly as
another apocalyptic signifier, reinforcing the more primary Islamic
eschatological expectation of the Mahdi. The Pew data on Muslim
interpretations of Islam, and views of Islamic sects, are two sides of the
same coin.

Interestingly, Pew included 16 sub-Saharan African countries in this
survey question, as well as 23 in other parts of Eurasia. The overall

---

[3] As per Sura al-Nisa' [IV]:157-158.

average for all 39 countries is just at 61%–meaning over six in ten Muslims "say there is only one interpretation of Islam," ranging from a high of 78% in Muslim Brotherhood-ruled Egypt to a mere 34% in Morocco. Pew also asked, separately, whether Ahmadis,[4] Alawis[5] or members of Jaringan Islam Liberal[6] are Muslims. An average of 41% of respondents said Ahmadis were not; 38% (of Lebanese, the only nationality polled on this sect) said Alawis were not; and 58% of Indonesians rejected Islam Liberal members as Muslims. Relatedly, Muslims in 23 countries were asked whether Sufis[7] were Muslims; on average, 21% said they most decidedly were NOT Muslims–ranging from a high of 44% in Egypt and Indonesia to a low of 6% in Thailand's Muslim provinces. However, large percentages in each of these 23 countries also said that they either "had never heard" of Sufis, or "didn't know" whether they were Muslims; and since Pew didn't break that data out further, it's safe to conclude that the percentage of Muslims who suspect Sufis are not really within the Islamic fold is much higher than 21%. This is important because Sufis still exist in large numbers in the Islamic world: majorities of Muslims in Senegal and Chad belong to Sufi order, as does over 25% of the Muslim population in nine other African countries; 26% of Bangladeshi, 17% of Pakistani, and 9% of Egyptian

---

[4] An Islamic offshoot group founded on the belief that Mirza Ghulam Ahmad (d. 1908) of India was both the Mahdi and the returned Jesus.

[5] A pseudo-Shi`i sect in Syria which believes that the 10th Shi`i Imam, Ali al-Hadi (d. 868 AD) was Allah Incarnate.

[6] An Indonesian Islamic moderate/modernist group that is trying to resurrect the Islamic rationalism of the *Mu`tazilah*, a movement in the early history of Islam that was quashed, over against Islamic militants and jihadists.

[7] Sufis are Islamic mystics whose devotional practices–all-night meditative prayer, visits to saints' tombs/shrines, reverence (bordering on worship) for the shaykhs of their orders, attempts to achieve union with Allah, etc.–often have been deemed not just excessive but heretical by other Muslims, mainly Sunnis.

Muslims claims to be Sufis, as well. Thus, that would mean there are some 38 million Sufis in Bangladesh, 30 million in Pakistan and well over 6 million in Egypt. Historically, and still to this day, Salafists—Islamic fundamentalists who strive to emulate the "ancestors" of Muhammad's time–dislike Sufis, and vice-versa. The daily news reports are rife with accounts of Islamic sects like the Ahmadis being persecuted by Muslims, as well as of Sufis and their beliefs being attacked by Salafists, Wahhabis, and/or jihadists, and sometimes fighting back. Yes, Christianity is divided into even more denominations and sects than is Islam–but since the Thirty Years War and the Enlightenment, Christians have abandoned killing each other in the name of their religion and, in fact, Western Christian civilization is the one among the world's cultures that developed the idea of religious tolerance. Southern Baptists may doubt that Roman Catholics are true Christians, but they certainly don't plant IEDs on the Catholics' cars during Mass. Muslims and the Islamic cultural zone, however, are still mired in religious intolerance and, far too often, violence against their own sects–a sad reality which no amount of American occupation and constitution-writing will change. As I argued three years ago on HNN, the reigning Qur'anic exegetical paradigm in Islam is a literalist, fundamentalist one–and until that changes (something only Muslims can do), Muslim sectarian minorities have every reason to fear the (usually Sunni) majority far more than they do Christians, Hindus, Buddhists or even Jews.

Pew also asked Muslims in 23 countries whether they believed in *jinn*[8] and witchcraft. Fifty percent of Muslims are convinced the former exist; while 33% feel the same way about witchcraft. Regarding jinn, belief is highest in Morocco and Bangladesh (each over 80%); Malaysia,

---

[8] Jinn are in Islamic tradition spiritual beings mid-way between humans and angels which, although they can possess humans, are not always evil or demonic.

10

Tunisia, Pakistan and Lebanon (each over 70%); Egypt, Palestinian territories and Turkey (each over 60%). Furthermore, some 16% of Muslims overall claim that "they have experienced evil spirits [being] driven out of a person"–ranging from almost half of Ethiopian Muslims, to over 20% of Indonesians, Bangladeshis and Afghanis and 11% of Palestinians, arguably the most Westernized of all the Arabs. As with Mahdism, the lowest percentages of belief on this issue were found in the former Soviet Central Asian republics: Uzbekistan, Kazakhstan, Kyrgyzstan. Did eight decades of Marxist occupation and indoctrination inoculate Central Asian Muslims against such beliefs? Or is some other factor at play in the 'stans? Pew finished the study with a few questions aimed at U.S. Muslims–the results of which hold some good news. Whereas six in ten of Muslims outside the U.S. say there is only one true interpretation of Islam, only 37% of American Muslims believe that. While 80% of global Muslims believe that the Qur'an should be read literally, only half of Muslims in the U.S. agree. The first bit of data indicates that Muslims in America seem to have imbibed at the well of American religious tolerance far more than their foreign co-religionists. The latter information, while positive, is not all that reassuring, however; what it means is that while eight in ten of the world's Muslims believe that a literal reading must be made of passages such as "behead the unbelievers,"[9] "beat your wives,"[10] and the infamous "Sword verse" of the Quran, "fight and slay the infidels wherever you find them,"[11] only half of the Muslims in America would go that far–not exactly a reason to celebrate.

---

[9] Sura al-Anfal [VIII]:12
[10] Sura al-Nisa'[IV]:34
[11] Sura al-Tawbah [IX]:5

Several real-world policy ramifications for the U.S. State and Defense departments, as well as the IC (Intelligence Community), can be drawn from this Pew study. First, a civilization laden with eschatological expectations AND a historical track record of militant movements motivated by messianic leaders, infused with intolerance toward its own schismatics, convinced of ongoing problems with demonic entities and witches and in thrall to a literalist reading of a violent religious text might not be amenable to rational actor theory in international relations. Second, political consolidation and/or jihadist movements led by self-styled Mahdis should be considered as real possibilities in the 21st century, especially as we approach key dates such as the hundred year mark from the dissolution of the Ottoman caliphate (2024) or the year 1500 of the Muslim calendar (2076)—since Mahdism, historically, clusters around such important dates which spark attempts to create rival caliphates, often violently. The vast geographic breadth, and surprising depth, of Mahdist belief in the Islamic ummah evidenced in this Pew data makes Mahdi-inspired movements, including jihads, quite plausible in the near future. Third, the Islamic Republic of Iran may not be pursuing a pipe dream by seeking *de facto* leadership of the Islamic world—especially once it has nuclear weapons (and short of U.S. Army and Marine boots on the ground, it is hard to see how Tehran's quest for them can be stopped). An Atomic Ayatollah-ate will not only be seen as the strong horse in the region; it will thus be all that more convincing, as the self-styled "Mahdist state in microcosm," in its appeals to the almost 700 million Muslims who are waiting on the Mahdi. Finally, the fact that Afghanistan and Iraq have the highest levels of Mahdist beliefs in the Islamic world tells us, very likely, that U.S.–"Christian, Crusader"–invasion and occupation, while ameliorating some problems (better roads, schools and hospitals, for example), greatly exacerbates another one: Muslim messianism and attendant

12

jihadism. What does it profit an occupier if it gains new infrastructure, but loses the eschatological war?

February 16, 2008: Enter the Mahdi.

My review of Yaroslav Trofimov's excellent book *The Siege of Mecca: The Forgotten Uprising in Islam's Holiest Shrine and the Birth of Al Qaeda* is running in the February 25, 2008, edition of *The Weekly Standard*. It is entitled "Enter the Mahdi: Was this the Opening Shot that Led to 9/11?" For those of you new to Mahdism Studies, that 1979 abortive coup against the al-Sa`ud regime was led by a man claiming that his brother-in-law was the Mahdi.

November 14, 2007: May the Schwartz Be With You.

Stephen Schwartz reviewed my first book in *Middle East Quarterly*. I appreciate the overall positive take; and I totally agree with Mr. Schwartz that "a serious, detailed, and comprehensible look at Shi'i beliefs about the 12th imam and his occultation and how they play out in the speeches of Ahmadinejad as well as the armed intrigues and depredations of the Sadrists, would be extremely useful to Westerners right now." But so far Ahmadinejad has yet to put his money where his Mahdist mouth is— whereas Sunni Mahdis have cropped up as far afield as Bangladesh, India, Gaza and Indonesia just this year alone. Plus, there's that little matter of that violent, Shi`i-Sunni combination, Soldiers of Heaven Mahdist movement that erupted in southern Iraq in January 2007. I'm not sure Mr. Schwartz is right that Shi`i Mahdism is more threatening, or important, than the Sunni brand.

February 6, 2007: Anti-Semitism in Islam: Israel Didn't Start the Fire [includes info on *al-Dajjal*, the Islamic "antichrist"].

Conventional wisdom among many American citizens, as well as numerous journalists, politicians and media anchors, has it that anti-

Semitism[12] in the Islamic world constitutes a not unreasonable reaction
to the late 19th c. Zionist movement which led to the creation of the
state of Israel right after World War II. In this view, were Israel to
totally withdraw from the West Bank (and other disputed Arab
territories), as well as enact the "right of return" and/or compensate
displaced Palestinians; anti-Semitism in the Islamic world would
dissipate like a mirage.

Unfortunately, hatred of Jews runs much deeper than a century or so
into the past. In fact, it originates not only in the actions of the founder
of Islam himself, but also in the eschatological belief-system of the
world's second-largest religion. In 622 CE the nascent Muslim
community under Muhammad, the prophet of Islam, left Mecca in
Arabia and headed north to the city of Yathrib. Part forced emigration,
part prearranged political move, this *hijrah* not only marked the
beginning of the Muslim calendar but the transition of the Muslims
from oppressed minority to ruling majority. The newly-renamed
Madinat al-Nabi, "city of the prophet," became–in its shortened form,
Madinah (Medina)–the capital of an expanding religious, political and
military movement that would encompass the entire Arabian Peninsula,
including Mecca itself, within eight years and then, of course, after
another century conquer from Iberia to the borders of India.

In the process of the Islamization of Arabia, and a few years before
Mecca fell to the Muslims in 630, a paradigm of Muslim-Jewish conflict
was established.[13] Several of the tribes of Madinah were Jewish, and
refused to accept the prophet hood of Muhammad. In fact the leaders

---

[12] While broadly-speaking "anti-Semitic" would refer to any ethnolinguistic group speaking a
Semitic language–amongst whom Arabs are, ironically, the vast majority –I use the term here in
it conventional, narrow sense are meaning "anti-Jewish."
[13] See `Abd al-Malik Ibn Hisham, *Life of Muhammad. A Translation of Ishaq's Sirat Rasul
Allah*, Introduction and Notes by A. Guillaume (Oxford: Oxford University Press, 1955), pp.
459-466.

of one tribe, the Banu Qurayzah, were reported to have been plotting to have Muhammad killed. After some negotiations and inter-tribal machinations–which included, portentously, Muhammad branding the Qurayzah "brothers of monkeys"[14]–Muhammad allowed "one of [their] own number," one Sa`d bin Mu'adh, to pronounce judgment on them. His verdict: "the men should be killed, the property divided, and the women and children taken as captives."

The narrative continues: "Then the apostle went out to the market of Medina … and dug trenches in it. Then he sent for them and struck off their heads in those trenches as they were brought out to him in batches…. There were 600 or 700 in all, though some put the figure as high as 800 or 900…. This went on until the apostle made an end of them.[…] Then the apostle divided the property, wives, and children of B. Qurayza among the Muslims…."[15] Now, this was a brutal time and a brutal society, in many ways. And in his treatment of "unbelievers" Muhammad is not unlike some of the divinely-sanctioned rulers in the Hebrew Scriptures, such as Joshua or David. (He is, however, most unlike the Jesus of the New Testament.)   Nonetheless, there is no getting around the fact that the man whom Muslims believe to have been God's last spokesman on Earth not only denigrated, but ordered the slaughter of, his fellow monotheists–and this long before Theodore Herzl, David Ben-Gurion or Ariel Sharon ever existed.

This pattern set by God's alleged prophet is particularly influential upon the jihadist wing of world Islam, for whom the example of the early Islamic community is supremely normative. However, there is a powerful eschatological motif in Islam which also contributes immensely

---

[14] *Ibid.*, p. 461
[15] *Ibid.*, p. 464, 466.

to the acrimony that too many Muslims feel towards the Jews: that of *al-Dajjal.*

The Dajjal, or "The Deceiver," is one of five major end times actors according to Islamic teachings, and the chief embodiment of evil.[16] In the anti-God camp with him will be the rapacious hordes of *Yajuj* and *Majuj*,[17] as well as *al-Dabbah*, the "Beast."[18] Opposing these will be the returned *'Isa*, or Jesus,[19] and *al-Mahdi*, the "rightly-guided one." Jesus, Yajaj and Majuj, and the Dabbah have both Qur'anic and hadith sourcing (hadiths are extra-Qur'anic sayings attributed to Muhammad); however, the Dajjal and the Mahdi appear nowhere in the Qur'an, but only in hadiths—curious, considering that in many ways they are the two most important eschatological figures in Islam[20].

What has this to do with anti-Semitism in Islam? The main role of the returned (Muslim) prophet Jesus and the Mahdi will be to defeat the evil forces of unbelief and usher in a global Islamic caliphate. And the forces that the Dajjal will lead forth to battle the Muslims will be…Jewish!![21] The Dajjal himself is usually described, drawing upon relevant hadiths, as corpulent and/or tall, frizzy- (perhaps red-) haired, one-eyed, able to perform sham miracles, having the Arabic linguistic

---

[16] See A. Abel, "al-Dadjdjal," *Encyclopedia of Islam, New Edition*, pp. 76-77.

[17] Surah al-Kahf [XVIII]:92ff; Surah al-Anbiya'[XXI]:96; and compare to the descriptions of Gog and Magog in the Bible at Ezekiel 38 and 39, as well as Revelation: 20.

[18] Surah al-Naml [XXVII}:82ff; also, compare this Beast to that of Christianity, Revelation 13 and 17

[19] Surah al-Ahzab [XXXIII]:7ff; Surah al-Ma'idah [V]:44ff, 75ff, 109ff; Surah al-Imran [III]:46ff; Surah al-Nisa' [IV]:156ff; Surah al-Saff [LXI]:15ff

[20] And in fact even there the Dajjal is more legitimately sourced than his counterpart the Mahdi, because the former is mentioned not only in dozens of hadiths but in the two most authoritative collections—those of al-Bukhari and Muslim. The Mahdi shows up only in lesser collections, such as those of Abu Da'ud, al-Tirmidhi and Ibn Majah—which, as I have written about extensively elsewhere, has not diminished belief in the Mahdi in any phase of Islamic history, including our own.

[21] For a complete list of relevant hadith cites, as well as exegesis thereof, see Usamah Yusuf Rahmah, *Iqtabarat al-Sa`ah* [The Approach of the Hour] (Damascus/Beirut: Dar Qutayba, 2001), pp. 164-208.

root for "unbelief"–K-F-R–tattooed on his forehead. And while he is actually not described as Jewish himself, the hadith accounts of his Jewish supporters have provided plenty of ammunition for Muslim exegetes to assume that he, too, will be Jewish and–of course–linked to Israel. For example, the K-F-R on the Dajjal's brow is said to be the same symbol used on the tail fins of Israeli fighter jets.[22] But the Jewish component is not the only one of the "Dajjal system," for that system is truly the one of unbelief–a rubric under which both science and Christianity should be subsumed.[23] While the hadiths suggesting that the Dajjal will be Jewish go back, in some cases, to the 9th century CE/3rd century AH, the recent upsurge in eschatological anti-Semitism probably dates to about 20 years ago, when the Egyptian writer Sayyid Ayyub began publishing works in Arabic claiming that the Dajjal was already active on Earth and that he was Jewish.[24] And this view is not active only in the Arab Muslim world, in the "front-line" states bordering Israel. A recent Indian Muslim writer[25] is convinced that "the Jews are waiting impatiently for the coming of Dajjal, their beloved king,"[26] for "Zionists in their bloodthirsty lust for power are not satisfied with Palestine. In their arrogance, they openly admit that they want all Syria...Lebanon...Jordan...Iraq...Iskenderun[27] ...the Sinai...the Delta area of Egypt and the Upper Hejaz[28] and Najd[29] ....They even want the

---

[22] Ahmad Thompson, Dajjal: *The King Who Had No Clothes* (London: Ta-ha Publishers, Ltd., 1986), p. 3.
[23] Ibid., pp. 6, 9, 80, and infra.
[24] See David Cook, "Muslim Fears of the Year 2000," *Middle East Quarterly*, V, 2 (June 1998), pp. 51-62.
[25] Mohamad Yasin Owadally, *Emergence of Dajjal. The Jewish King* (Delhi: Rightway Publications, 2001).
[26] Ibid., p. 12.
[27] The former Alexandretta, on Turkey's southwestern Mediterranean coast, of Indiana Jones fame.
[28] The Hijaz is the western coastal region of the Arabian peninsula.
[29] The Najd is central Arabia.

holy Madinah [sic][30] ....Their main aim is to **exterminate Islam**" [emphasis added].[31] This writer goes on to repeat the hadith that the Jews will get their comeuppance before the end, when in the final battles "they will not be able to hide behind any stone, wall, or animal or tree without it saying 'O Muslim, servant of Allah, here is a Jew, come and kill him.'"[32] The Dajjal will actually be killed by Jesus, and the Dajjal's dispirited army of Jews, unbelievers and "Magians" will then be defeated by the Mahdi and his army of Muslims. Afterwards peace will reign under the global rule of the Mahdi and/or Jesus for some time (the hadiths are not harmonious on just who will be superior and who will live longer), before both great Muslim leaders die and unbelief again proliferates. Thereafter, at some point, will come the true end of time and the Judgment.

Islamic eschatology has seen a resurgence in recent years, owing to the turn of the (Christian) millennium, the inability of the Islamic world to deal effectively with modernity and the perception among many Muslims that the ummah, the Islamic "nation," is not only in dire straits but is under attack from the West in general and the U.S. in particular. A powerful yearning for the Mahdi to come and deliver the ummah has grown among both Sunni and Shi`i Muslims, and the eschatological play cannot be acted out until the Dajjal comes, as well. Hugo Chavez may see President Bush as "El Diablo," but for many in the Muslim world this figure of evil is "the Jew," particularly in his armed-and-dangerous

---

[30] Owadally, p. 35.

[31] *Ibid.*, p. 36.

[32] *Ibid.*, p. 68. The actual hadith cite is found in the Sahih of al-Bukhari: Book 041, Number 6985: Abu Huraira reported Allah's Messenger (may peace be upon him) as saying: "The last hour would not come unless the Muslims will fight against the Jews and the Muslims would kill them until the Jews would hide themselves behind a stone or a tree and a stone or a tree would say: Muslim, or the servant of Allah, there is a Jew behind me; come and kill him; but the tree Gharqad would not say, for it is the tree of the Jews."

incarnation as "the Zionist entity"–Israel. If even a small percentage of the world's 1.3 billion Muslims are influenced by such a belief, as well as by the undeniable anti-Semitic example of their own founder (and all indications are that this is indeed the case), then it's naïve at best and dangerous at worst to expect that any sort of political or territorial concessions on the part of the Israelis will enervate such rancor.

March 11, 2007: In Response to Timothy Furnish's "Anti-Semitism in Islam: Israel Didn't Start the Fire" by David H Slavin, adjunct at Emory University.

HNN is a valuable resource and provocative opinion pieces that it publishes are useful in classes and discussion groups I teach or facilitate. However, by repeatedly running articles by someone as tendentious as Timothy Furnish, HNN legitimates his position and at the same time advertises his book. This is unfair. The time and effort required to refute his observations precludes a response from anyone who is knowledgeable enough to counter his seemingly well-documented arguments. The puerile remarks dumped in the "Comments" string in response to his recent column (and his own puerile responses) are a case in point. Few people read them, and what can be gleaned from them is slim pickings. Furnish's other contributions to HNN gave me a similar impression to this essay. Using his detailed acquaintance with Islam he imposes an interpretation that does violence to the larger historical context and that promotes and rests on assumptions rooted in the "clash of civilizations" world view.

Furnish's argument about the "deep roots" of Muslim anti-semitism (a rhetorical absurdity, Furnish admits in his first footnote, unless we are talking about "self-hating Arabs") ignores the entire history of dhimmi status, protection for "people of the book" (although they were subject to additional taxes). And while he turns to the dajjal in medieval Islamic mytho-history and eschatology, he ignores a wealth of sources from Sufi and falaysuf traditions that allow for and encourage many paths to knowledge of the divine. The distortions in Furnish's perspective are compounded by his use of contemporary or post-1948 interpretations of haditha and then attributing these recent perspectives to the original sources.

The specific incident of the massacre of 700 men of the Qurayzah clan occurred in the midst of the Battle of the Trench 627 CE in which the Meccan pagans had besieged Medina and the Qurayzah, within the walls of Medina, sided with the Meccans and their allied pagan clans within Medina and in the surrounding area. The conflict with the three Jewish Arab clans, the Qaynuqah, the Nadir, and the Qurayzah, was in part no doubt based on the competition with a new revelation of monotheism. Nevertheless it was primarily a political and military struggle with those clans allied with the Meccan pagans in which the survival of the Muslim ummah or community was at stake.

Furnish asserts that the standard interpretation of historians of this incident is common knowledge and conventional wisdom. This assertion is doubtful since it conflates public opinion, news commentators, and politicians with the consensus of those who have done some reading, teaching, and writing in the field. Karen Armstrong certainly represents that informed consensus, but to say informed views such as hers hold sway over U.S. or British or European public opinion ignores the widespread acceptance of propaganda promoting Muslim fanaticism. About the massacre of the Qurayzah, Armstrong writes in *Islam: A Short History* (Modern Library/ Random House, NY: 2000, 2002 p. 21). "Th[is] struggle did not indicate any hostility towards Jews in general, but only towards the three rebel tribes. The Quran continued to revere Jewish prophets and to urge Muslims to respect the People of the Book. Smaller Jewish groups continued to live in Medina, and later Jews, like Christians, enjoyed full religious liberty in the Islamic empires [i.e. the medieval caliphates]. Anti-semitism is a Christian vice. Hatred of the Jews became marked in the Muslim world only after the creation of the state of Israel in 1948 and the subsequent loss of Arab Palestine. It is significant that Muslims were compelled to import anti-Jewish myths from Europe, and translate into Arabic such virulently anti-semitic texts as the Protocols of the Elders of Zion, because they had no such traditions of their own."

Armstrong concludes by saying that nowadays the passages of the Quran referring to the struggle with the three Jewish "tribes" (clans would be a more accurate term) are used to justify anti-Jewish prejudices that are conflated with anti-Zionism. But what Furnish takes as common knowledge, or the dominant discourse, is far from it. Repeatedly the print and electronic media express the idea that fanaticism and "ancient tribal conflicts" are the source of the problems of the Middle East, and these are really the dominant views of a considerable portion of the U.S. public. The Sunni vs. Shi'a conflicts in Iraq (only a segment of the multiple dimensions of what has happened to Iraqi society under the U.S. occupation) are now being attributed to old "tribal" animosities, and are extrapolated into a world view, the "clash of civilizations." My own research traces the immediate ancestry of the clash of civilizations viewpoint to a trans-Atlantic counter-Enlightenment of the 1920s which nakedly described the future of humankind as race war. (I have looked at the writings of Lothrop Stoddard, Madison Grant, Henri Massis, Maurice Muret, Pierre Taittinger, and Charles Josey. The first four were translated into French and English respectively and exercised influence over a broad spectrum of conservative to liberal opinion in France and the U.S.) These white, European supremacists used the term race whereas today's cultural essentialists have discarded the tarnished word in favor of "civilizations." But in my view the race war theorists are the intellectual forbears of

Samuel Huntington, Timothy Furnish, or Daniel Pipes, who modifies the clash as one of civilization versus "ideological.barbarians" while ignoring that political Islam is as much a product of U.S. proxy wars against the Soviet Union as an indigenous movement—but a challenge to Pipes' views require another essay.

It would be reasonable to compare the treatment of Jews in the Islamic world from 622 CE to 1948 CE with Christendom's treatment of the Jews, since Jewish settlement was concentrated in these two regions. There is no comparison in the Muslim world to the frequent expulsions, confiscations of Jewish property and wealth, confinement to ghettos, pogroms and mass murders of Jews that besmirch European history. It was Catholic Spain which in 1492 expelled all Jews who refused to convert. They escaped to Islamic North Africa for the most part, although many also settled in Portugal and the Low Countries. Modern anti-semitism has its ideological roots in the poisonous writings of 19th century European public intellectuals such as Gobineau, Edouard Drumont, just to name its French purveyors, and anti-Jewish parties emerged in Vienna, Germany, along with terrorist groups such as the "Black Hundreds" in Russia. The 20th century opened in the wake of the Dreyfus Affair in France and mass emigration of Jews from the Pale of Settlement to escape the Tsarist Empire, and European anti-Jewish violence culminated in the Holocaust, in which tens of thousands of European anti-semites helped round up Jews for the Nazi extermination camps (see Theodore Hamerow's "The Hidden Holocaust" in Commentary [1978] as well as numerous other accounts from Raoul Hilberg et al).

Ignorance about Islam abounds in academic circles, not to mention the general public, and it behooves HNN to provide equal time and space in its forum for rebuttal of these seemingly (because they are footnoted) scholarly estimations of Furnish and others who are trying to prove the "clash of civilizations" world view. Historians who do world history, not to mention history of the Islamic world, have repeatedly demolished these notions only to have them rise up because there is powerful ideological aid and comfort and an important political stake in maintaining them (as was the case for anti-Judaism in 19th and 20th century Europe). If any analogy applies to "clash of civilizations" thinking, it is anti-Darwinism or refusal to accept human sources of global climate crisis. I am not asking that you stop publishing this stuff, but only to provide for a responsible rebuttal that addresses the specific arguments raised.

If you are interested in an article that I found thoughtful about anti-Jewish and anti-Muslim anti-semitisms, see Maleiha Malik's "Muslims are now getting the same treatment Jews had a century ago" (Guardian).

Response by Timothy Furnish, Ph.D.

Mr. Slavin's "critique" of my article says more about him than about me, frankly. (And I will largely ignore, except to note, his inability to employ normal academic civility by referring to me as "Mr." or, more properly, "Dr.") Nowhere do I mention the "clash of civilizations," with which he seems obsessed. I simply use Islamic and Arabic sources and demonstrate that strife between Muslims and Jews did not begin in 1948. Mr. Slavin may not like that, but it hardly qualifies as "puerile." I'd be happy to talk about *dhimmi*s, which Slavin whitewashes to mean only that "they were subject to additional taxes." Well, that plus not being able to build new churches or synagogues; being forced to wear distinctive clothing; being prevented from certain jobs; being prevented from marrying Muslims; etc. If one were to take Slavin's approach in discussing the oppression of black Americans prior to the 1960s one could say that they were subject to additional (poll) taxes and leave it at that. True, but not exactly an accurate portrayal of the second-class citizenship involved.

Slavin can, again, whitewash the slaughter and dissolution of the Banu Qurayzah, but facts are stubborn things, and the historical fact— again, related in the ISLAMIC sources–is that an entire Jewish tribe was liquidated. Slavin's ignorance comes to the fore by admitting that he relies on Karen Armstrong, a "scholar" who cannot even use Arabic sources. And Slavin is just flat-out wrong in several of his historical assertions, most notably that "hatred of Jews became marked in the Islamic world only after the creation of the state of Israel...." This is what happens when a European specialist wades into a field of which he is largely ignorant. The *al-Muwahhids*, who ruled the Maghrib and much of Iberia for over a century (1130-1269 CE), forcibly converted Jews to Islam (and, coincidentally, killed members of any Catholic religious order whom they could get their hands on). Slavin's slavish devotion to this myth of Islamic tolerance is laughable. Perhaps if he read some Arabic Muslim sources, rather than the likes of Armstrong or the litany of 20th century Europeans he mentions, he'd know a bit more about Islamic history. But by all indications, he is incapable of actually doing so–forcing him to simply repeat outmoded argument from secondary sources and make himself appear silly in the process.

July 25, 2005: What's Worse than Violent Jihadists?

Islamist terrorist bombings in the London subways. Buddhists beheaded by fanatical Muslims in Thailand. Hurricanes and Live 8 aside, the global event horizon these days seems to encompass little else but revolutionary (actually reactionary) Islamic violence. How much worse could it get? Much worse.

So far the bombings, attacks, murders and beheadings have been the province of mere jihadis–basically mundane, albeit dangerous, Islamic fundamentalists. Islamic fundamentalists, in a nutshell, reject modernity;[33] that is, they anathematize the mainstream of Western–and, by now, global–thought which has predominated since the Enlightenment, predicated upon: a Cartesian cleavage between reason and revelation, politically-enforced separation of religion and state and optimistic (well-nigh utopian) faith in science and technology. Many Christian fundamentalists share this antipathy for modernity. But jihadis (perhaps somewhere between 1 and 10% of the world's 1.3 billion Muslims) differ from Jerry Falwell in that, for them, history has taken a horrible wrong turn. The religion of the final and perfect revelation of Allah to mankind still lags, in number of adherents, to that superseded tritheism known as Christianity (with its 2 billion members). Islamic political power, regnant from Morocco to Indonesia and from the Hungarian forests to the African savanna in 1491, was first eclipsed by Europeans and now is dwarfed by the American imperium and its Cowboy Christian Caesar (triply galling to Usamah bin Ladin, as well as to Democrats and the French) and betrayed internally by faux Muslim leaders like Mubarak, Musharraf and the Saudi princes.

The cure for Islamic religious, political and cultural malaise, according to jihadi fundamentalism, is simple (albeit easier said than done): replacing fake Muslim rulers and governments with truly Islamic ones that impose and enforce shari`ah, or Islamic law. (Of course, "that depends on what your definition of 'Islamic law,' is." Wahhabi? Turkish? Nigerian? Iranian?) And of course the preferred way to get such leadership in place is through regime change, whether violent (the former Taliban in Afghanistan) or more populist (the Islamic Revolution in Iran). Jihadi ideology also calls for an end to outside "imperialism"– i.e., American influence and intervention–in the Muslim world in general

---

[33] See my article "Islamic Fundamentalism," *Encyclopedia of Fundamentalism* (New York and London: Routledge, 2001), pp. 235-240.

and the Middle East in particular (especially Arabia, the site of the two holy cities of Mecca and Medina).

There is another strain of fundamentalist ideology, however, that may not be willing to wait for jihadi governments to come to power: Mahdism. Al-Mahdi is "the rightly-guided one" who, in Islamic traditions allegedly going back to Muhammad (and nowhere to be found in the Qur'an), will come before The End of time to usher in a worldwide Islamic state with a little help from his returned prophet friend Jesus.[34] Mahdism is believed by many (including scholars, who should know better) to be the province only of the Shi`is, but many of the most successful Mahdist movements in history have been Sunni. Most prominent here would be Ibn Tumart's *al-Muwahhids* (Almohads) who ruled from Portugal to Tunisia, 1130-1269 CE, and Muhammad Ahmad's Sudanese Mahdists—about whom the movie *Khartoum*, starring Charlton Heston and Sir Laurence Olivier was made—who ruled Sudan from 1885-1898. Another famous Mahdist movement, albeit ultimately unsuccessful, was the attempt to overthrow the Saudi regime in 1979: one Juhayman al-Utaybi declared his brother-in-law Muhammad al-Qahtani to be the Mahdi and led several hundred armed followers to occupy the main mosque in Mecca (eventually all were either killed or captured and then executed). Scores of other self-styled Mahdis have arisen over the last millennium of Islamic history. If nothing else, Mahdism is certainly a powerful means of expressing dissatisfaction with extant Islamic government.

True, Mahdism shares many characteristics with mere jihadism, the most important of which are: a yearning (indeed demand) for Islamic law and a burning desire to restore Islamic rule to its former environs

---

[34] Mahdism and Madhist movements are the focus of my book *Holiest Wars: Islamic Mahdis, their Jihads and Osama bin Laden* (Westport, CT: Praeger, 2005).

and, in fact, to engineer the creation of a global caliphate. But Mahdist movements "are to fundamentalist uprisings what nuclear weapons are to conventional ones: triggered by the same detonating agents[35] yet far more powerful in scope and effect."[36] Once a charismatic Muslim leader becomes convinced he is the Mahdi, all bets are off. The Mahdi (and each one is of course convinced he is THE, not simply a, Mahdi) will, according to the Islamic traditions, be directed by Allah to restore the Prophetic caliphate and, as such, is not bound by the letter of the Islamic law. For example, both Ibn Tumart and Muhammad Ahmad declared that they alone were capable of interpreting the Qur'an, so any previous opinions and commentaries were relegated to irrelevance. And of course the opposition to them by establishment religious figures–for both of these men, as do most Mahdis, led revolutions against existing Islamic governments[37]–only served to reinforce their Mahdist claims, since true Muslims could recognize the Mahdi. Anyone claiming to be the Mahdi, then, is largely unfettered by any norms, Islamic or otherwise. Ibn Tumart and his leadership, for example, killed tens of thousands OF THEIR OWN FOLLOWERS deemed lukewarm in their support. And Muhammad Ahmad, who had Charles Gordon decapitated and his head displayed, may have proved just as bloodthirsty had he not died of malaria some six months after taking Khartoum.

There is, today, no one claiming to be the Mahdi–at least not yet. A number of Arabic books and websites have begun speculating whether

---

[35] Such as perceived illegitimate "Islamic" governments; alleged diminution of Islamic norms; moral laxity of rulers and/or society; interference by foreign powers (usually, but not always, non-Islamic ones; the Sudanese Mahdi, for instance, despised the Ottoman Turks although they were Muslims).

[36] *Ibid.*, p. 1.

[37] Ibn Tumart led the overthrow of the previous *al-Murabit* (Almoravid) sultanate, while Muhammad Ahmad and his followers ejected the Ottoman Turks and Egyptians, as well as British, from Sudan.

Usamah bin Ladin might be him.[38] Certainly no one else in the Islamic world has the stature to even attempt such a claim. Bin Ladin's charisma, mysterious whereabouts, ability to strike and hurt even the American imperium and ongoing criticism of existing (illegitimate) Islamic rulers may not quite qualify him for the Mahdi's ring of power–but they get him closer, certainly, than anyone else. What if he were to seize it? No doubt the vast majority of the world's Muslims would reject such a claim out of hand. Many who see Bin Ladin now as something of a Muslim Che Guevara would certainly renounce him as Mahdi, but the small percentage that would accept such a claim would be intensely devoted and fanatical. If that amounts to only 1% of the world's Muslims, the Mahdi would have 13 million potential suicide bombers.

And make no mistake: Mahdists would have even fewer constraints on their behavior than do jihadis. Since the end result of the Mahdi's plans would be, they believe, a global caliphate nothing would he asked would be beyond his followers: detonating a nuke in Vegas or Manhattan, intentionally infecting oneself with plague or smallpox and then crisscrossing American airports, suicide-bombing Christian day care centers in the Midwest. Helping the Mahdi restore Islam to planetary predominance would obtain one even more glory than the promised 72 huris in Paradise. And were Bin Ladin (or anyone else) to take power in, say, Arabia as the Mahdi, the entire world (even the French) would soon be waxing nostalgic about the Saudis.

Even if Bin Ladin eschews a Mahdi claim, someone eventually will make it. The Mahdi is often associated with a *mujaddid*, a "renewer" that according to other Islamic traditions will come every 100 years to reinvigorate Islam. And considering that the 16th Muslim century

---

[38] *Holiest Wars*, especially chapter 6: "Who will be the next Mahdi?", pp. 150ff.

begins in 2076, the American tercentenary may be met with more than normal fireworks.

"Gordon's Death" by George W. Joy (Wikipedia public domain). Will Mahdist history repeat itself?

Islamic State's Apocalyptic Agenda

February 21, 2015: Jihad, Apocalypse and Terrorism–Is ISIS Acting as Lucifer's Hands?

As most purveyors of my writings know by now, the mainstream media has (finally) discovered that Islamic apocalyptic thought drives ISIS: Graeme Wood wrote an excellent piece covering this in *The Atlantic*, and Peter Bergen did the same for CNN.

Apocalyptic traditions and movements, led by a Muslim claiming to be the End Time Mahdi ("rightly-guided one"), are not new with ISIS or *Jabhat al-Nusrah* or any of the other modern groups proclaiming belief in such. They go back to the early days of Islam, and are intrinsically connected to the more general Muslim practice of jihad, or holy war against "infidels."

As someone who's studied this topic for almost two decades now, I was asked to put together a three-day seminar on it for the Monterey Institute of International Studies, and I taught this class via 17 hours of contact time over Super Bowl weekend, 2015. Thirty MA students signed up (including many Muslims), and it went very well.

Here is how I organized the material:

I) Jihad

A Brief History of the Islamic World

Qur'an and Hadiths: Basic Teachings

Pew Data on Key Modern Muslim Beliefs

Moderate Islamic Actors

II) Apocalyptic

Acting Like it's the End of the World: Islamic Eschatology

Christian and Muslim Eschatology since 9/11

Twelver Shi`i Eschatology and the Iranian Vision

III) Terrorism

Terrorism: A History of Violence

4GW, 4th Terrorism Wave, or Forthcoming War? Sunni and Shi`i Jihad Analyzed

Fighting for the End of the (Christian) World: ISIS's Jihad Eschatology.

(This seminar is intended for a secular audience, but much of it can easily be adapted to a more religious venue, Christian, Jewish or even Muslim—if the latter are willing to be intellectually honest and open-minded.)

One major aspect of this seminar, reflecting my own well-researched opinion, is that ISIS and its ilk (like the "moderate" [sic] Jabhat al-Nusrah) **are** legitimately Islamic in waging jihad and hoping for the apocalyptic defeat of Western Christian forces. **BUT** I also firmly believe that such Islamic violence and triumphalism are predicated on a literal reading of the Qur'an and Hadiths, as well as a slavish following of Muhammad's more unsavory practices; and that Islamic sects and movements which interpret the religion non-literally can, eventually, perhaps pry Islam out of Lucifer's hands (to use a song title from U2's latest album).

February 20, 2015: The Media (Like Wizards) Are Never Late: They Discover Islamic Apocalyptic Precisely When They Mean To!

Since this is Lent, I must choose charity over envy: it is, indeed, a net positive for the world that *The Atlantic* and CNN have discovered that ISIS is Islamic, and that eschatological belief is one of its major drivers. However, as someone whose very doctorate is in Islamic End Times movements ("Eschatology as Politics, Eschatology as Theory: Modern Sunni Arab Mahdism in Historical Perspective;" 290 pp., The Ohio State University, 2001), who has published numerous articles and delivered a legion of lectures on this topic as well as advised the U.S. military on same–I do have to say: "what took you so bloody long?"

My take on Graeme Wood's excellent *Atlantic* piece has just yesterday been written up at WND; but I do have some further observations on Wood, as well as on Peter Bergen's CNN piece:

- Wood's description of ISIS's worldview as being that of "medieval Islam" is not entirely accurate, as it comes from the 7th-9th c. AD/1-3rd c. AH; "early Islamic" would be better. (My historian's distaste for automatically equating "medieval" with barbaric is showing, I freely confess.)

- "Quietist Salafism" as the antidote to ISIS's brutally literalist Islam is a stretch, since that approach is also one of Sunni fundamentalism. What's needed is a brand of Islam that eschews Qur'anic/hadith literalism, and that is found, rather, in sects such as the Ahmadis, Isma'ilis, and some Sufi orders.

- Bergen's labeling of ISIS as a non-rational actor implies that its members are, well, crazy–which they are not. They are entirely rational, once you accept their eschatological premises–which, according to Pew data, hundreds of millions of Muslims actually do.

Still and all, I am glad that Wood and Bergen, and their respective outlets, are interested–FINALLY–in this important issue.

But at the risk of hubris: is it too much to ask that, in future, said news entities cut out the (journalistic) middle men and go straight to a chap who's been studying this topic since (and like it's) 1999?

February 15, 2015:   ISIS Beheadings: Hotwiring the Apocalypse One Christian Martyr At A Time.

Major news outlets are reporting, today, the mass beheadings of 21 Coptic Christians by the Islamic State affiliate in Libya.

In my 2005 *Middle East Quarterly* article, "Beheading in the Name of Islam," I wrote that "the purpose of terrorism is to strike fear into the hearts of opponents in order to win political concession[s]." Then I went on to spend much of the article explicating the legitimately Islamic roots (Qur'anic rubrics, precedents by Muhammad, examples from Islamic history, exegesis by Muslim scholars) of decapitating "non-believers"–especially Christians, the primary political and military adversaries of Islamic expansion over the last 14 centuries.

The Islamic State has upped the ante with its regular beheadings of Christians by IS central and, now, its far-flung branches. Seen in light of incessant calls for recruits, and even more vociferous citations of apocalyptic hadiths–both of which are clearly explained in the many issues of *Dabiq* magazine–I now think that ISIS cares not one whit about political concessions. Rather, it chops off Christians' heads for three primary reasons: 1) to reinforce its literalist Islamic credentials; 2) to win over young Muslims, particularly men, and persuade them of Islamic State's power and dedication; and 3) to provoke the "Christian" West, particularly the United States (the world's most populous Christian nation), into deploying ground troops–which ISIS is certain it will defeat, based on the group's adherence to such eschatological hadith.

Metrics indicate that Christians, despite being the world's largest religious group, are the most-persecuted–and particularly in majority-Muslim areas. This should come as no surprise to anyone who had read the Qur'an, the biographies of Muhammad, or studied much Islamic history, because all three are rife with bitter condemnations of Christianity, as well as examples of deadly attacks upon Christians.

And Islamic civilization is unique today in that it is the only one on the planet in which violence against non-adherents (or, sometimes, even differing brands of its own devotees) is justified by both state (Sunni and Shi`i) and non-state actors (ISIS, al-Qa`idah, Boko Haram, Tehrik-i

Taliban Pakistan, Kata'ib Hizbullah, etc.).   Beheading, which seemed so horrifically novel 13 years ago when AQ used it to kill Daniel Pearl, is now a rather routine instrument in the Islamic terrorist toolbox of horrors.   Muslim authorities, for all their condemnations thereof, will find it difficult to lock this dreadful chest, considering its hallowed tradition in Islamic thought and praxis.   That leaves the option of sending beheaders to meet Allah–or, much more likely, Iblis. President Obama seems content to simply, gradually "degrade" the Islamic State. At least we might take some solace in thinking that this minimalist approach will allow Islamic beheadings to create more Christian martyrs. But they, and we, would probably be better off if the most powerful man in the world were less loathe to wield the sword of punishment.

November 26, 2014: *Dabiq* Issue 5:   Prepare Ye the Way of the Mahdi.

In the U.S., tomorrow, we will celebrate Thanksgiving–some as a secular holiday, but most as a quasi-religious one commemorating the 17th century English Protestants who fled Europe for the New World in order to establish their version of a Christian community. After reading the fifth issue of the Islamic State's *Dabiq* magazine, I'm convinced the Thanksgiving pantheon should be extended to famous political and military leaders who helped Christian civilization stave off Islamic conquest–such as Constantine IV, Charles Martel, Don John of Austria and Prince Eugene of Savoy. Thank God, and these men, that Islamic law never came to rule in Europe and, by extension, America.

Expanding, they hope, way down south—to Mecca-town and its Ka`bah!

Make no mistake, the Islamic State (formerly ISIS or ISIL), *contra* its apologists, is profoundly Muslim: the fifth issue of *Dabiq* adduces 22 Qur'anic passages, 31 Hadiths (alleged sayings of Muhammad), and a legion of quotations and commentaries from other Islamic scholars, living and dead. Even allowing for Shaytan's ability to quote "scripture," it's willfully ignorant to deny the ideological basis of the ISLAMIC State.

Herein the Islamic State [IS] follows the pattern of each previous publication [examined likewise, below]: explication of a major Qur'anic figure and application thereof to modern times; reports of success (unbridled, of course!) against its enemies on the battlefield and in the political realm; shrewd analysis of Western, particularly U.S., policy makers' and media positions; and, pulling all of those together, an eschatological narrative aimed at persuading Muslims to take the road to

Dabiq, where the "coalition of the cross," or the "Crusader armies," will burn in defeat.

This time, the personality adduced is John the Baptist–called "Yahya" in the confused Qur'anic version (which conflates separate Old and New Testament data, such as identifying John's father). The Islamic version is that John "was sent to the rebellious children of Isra'il to guide them back to Allah"–after being shamed by Jesus ('Isa) for his tardiness in doing so–who eventually killed, and thus martyred, him. "[T]he seriousness and attention given to the commands of Allah and the need to fulfill them, as well as the sense of urgency and haste in fulfilling them is a means of strength that can push a Muslim beyond hesitation and cause him to carry out the most difficult tasks in the path of Allah."

Continuing, the magazine trumpets (alleged) victories over Kurdish forces, mockingly propagandizing that "the only thing the kuffar [Christian Americans] are likely to find more impressively baffling than the incompetence of the PKK, is Obama's decision to keep relying on the incompetence of the PKK."

The publication also adduces its plan to start minting its own coins, and the many loyalty oaths sworn to Caliph al-Baghdadi by groups in Arabia, Yemen, Sinai, Libya and Algeria, as proof of its not just "remaining" but "expanding" as a state. With the help of these loyal new troops, the IS will reach Indonesia, China, Spain and Rome.

"Crusader experts" [sic] at RAND are shown and quoted to the effect that IS is winning. And a long section purportedly written by British hostage John Cantlie mocks not just Western experts but "Robo-Obama" who commits "the same mistakes over and over again," is powerless to prevent pro-IS jihadist attacks in his own country, and who should stick to playing golf. IS gloats over the assaults in Australia, Quebec and New York City, claiming that "all of these attacks were the direct result of the Shaykh's [al-Baghdadi's] call to action...."

Dabiq #5 ends with a hadith from Abu Dawud about the Mahdi: "If there were not left except a day from the dunya [world], Allah would lengthen that day to send forth on it a man from my family whose name matches my name [Muhammad] and whose father's name matches my father's name ['Abdullah]. He will fill the Earth with justice and fairness as it was filled with oppression and tyranny."

Observation: There is little new or noteworthy in this latest IS magazine—except for two things:

1. *The ramped-up eschatological fervor demonstrated by the Yahya/John exegesis and that final Mahdi reference.* I have been asked in radio interviews whether al-Baghdadi or his followers consider him the Mahdi. Based on this latest magazine, I think it more likely he sees himself as preparing the way for the Mahdi—similar to the role Yahya/John played to `Isa/Jesus; a leader who, like the Qur'anic Yahya, follows "the legacy of the Prophets…a legacy of…the confrontation between the Prophets and the disbelievers [which] continued to escalate until it reached either a point of physical battle, or a point of wholesale annihilation as the punishment of Allah descended upon the disbelievers…." Caliph al-Baghdadi probably expects that he will lead Muslim forces to a great military victory over American (Christian/"Crusader") forces at Dabiq—after which the Mahdi will appear and take over, making al-Baghdadi his loyal lieutenant. Until then, the beheadings, atrocities and Islamic cleansing of all IS domains will continue apace.

2. *Plastering the Ka`bah, Islam's most sacred space located in Mecca, on the cover of the magazine in tandem with the attention lavished herein on notable opponents of the Saudis over the years is a clear means of shouting "we're coming for you, Saudi royal family."* Maybe when the IS Toyotas turn south, Robo-Obama will change his tune on inserting "Crusader" troops into the fray.

November 15, 2014: Lecturing (on ISIS) Like It's the End of the World.

My October 23, 2014 lecture at Concordia Seminary (St. Louis)–whence I obtained my M.A.R. in 1989–on how Islamic eschatology is motivating ISIS and some other Muslim terrorist groups, was covered yesterday by the Lutheran Church-Missouri Synod's *Reporter*: "ISIS, other radical Islamists driven by Muslim eschatology."

Alas, even journalists in my own conservative (both theologically and, generally, politically) denomination have been infected by political correctness; I made a point of saying that ISIS and its ilk are, in fact, *not* "radical" but literalist when it comes to Qur'an and hadiths–but that pesky and inaccurate adjective "radical" was still inserted, robotically.

October 30, 2014: Eschatology and the Islamic State.

My public lecture at Concordia Seminary, St. Louis, last week on ISIS and Islamic eschatology was ably reviewed and summarized by Dr. Joel Okamoto, professor of Systematic Theology: "The Quad," October 28, 2014. (Just for those of you who don't have the time to watch the actual lecture....) Unlike many in the secular realm, Reverend Dr. Okamoto clearly grasped my thesis: "Hardly anyone doubts the brutality of the Islamic State, least of all the group itself. But is it really 'not Islamic?' Not if one considers its own theological claims."

October 21, 2014: Illinois Obama and the Last Crusade–Against ISIS.

The Islamic State's latest *Dabiq* magazine (#4) was issued several weeks ago, entitled "The Failed Crusade."

Where to now, St. Peter? To take over your square, obviously!

As with the previous three issues, *Dabiq*–which, again, refers to a major apocalyptic battle in Syria between Muslims and "Romans" predicted in hadiths–opens with the same quote from IS's founder, the late Abu Mus`ab al-Zarqawi: that the spark lit in Iraq will eventually "burn...the crusader armies in Dabiq." Overall, this magazine cites the Qur'an 20 times, adduces 36 different hadiths, and quotes historical Islamic scholars (such as the 14th century Ibn Taymiyah) as well as modern ideologues (al-Awlaki, Bin Ladin and al-Zarqawi)–thus making the claim that ISIS is " not Islamic" fatuous at best. Its main topics are the alleged "Crusade" and its relationship to the looming apocalyptic struggle between "Romans/Crusaders" and Muslims, and the rationalization for (re)imposing Muslim slavery of non-Muslims.

The "failing crusade" and its connection to Islamic eschatological prognostication takes up over one third of this 56-page document. Modern U.S. forays into the Middle East, particularly Iraq (and now Syria) are linked–of course!–to the Crusades of 900 years ago. American soldiers, who are shown loading coffins containing their dead comrades into C-5s, are equated with "cross-worshipping Romans" (Byzantines, that is) and not the 11th century Crusaders. This is almost certainly because the relevant hadiths refer to events from the 7th and 8th centuries, when the Eastern Roman, or Byzantine, Christian Empire was fighting off hordes of belligerent Muslims–and not to the actual Crusades, some four centuries later. The pertinent hadiths (too long to reproduce here) are explicated thusly: "Muslims will be at war with the Roman Christians….the Christians of Europe and their colonies….There will be a pause in this war due to a truce….During this time the Muslims and Romans will fight a common enemy [presumably the "Safawis," or Twelver Shi`is of Iran and Iraq]….These events all lead up to the final, greatest, and bloodiest battle–al-Malhamah al-Kubra–between the Muslims and the Romans prior to the appearance of the Dajjal and the descent of al-Masih [Jesus]. This battle ends the era of the Roman Christians, as the Muslims will then advance upon Constantinople and thereafter Rome, to conquer the two cities and raise the flag of the Khilafah over them." But according to IS exegesis, they won't stop there. The new caliphate, either before the Mahdi comes or, perhaps, after his arrival, also will conquer Jerusalem and eventually "destroy the filthy house called the White House." Along the way the armies of jihad will "break your crosses and enslave your women."

Dabiq issue 4 also expends several pages asking why the U.S. is allying in Syria with its mortal enemies Russia and Iran and their proxies, such as "the anti-Christ Nasrullat" (Hizbullah's leader Hassan Nasrallah). The "Jewish Crusader" Henry Kissinger, Michael Scheuer and Ralph Peters are quoted (selectively) on the greater dangers of Iran than IS to the U.S. (However, one might note that the ayatollahs, for all their geopolitical intransigence, have never threatened to march on the White House and enslave our wives and daughters.) This section would seem to be an attempt to corroborate the hadith which mentions a short-lived truce between the "true" Muslims and the Romans while they fight their common enemy: the Twelver Shi`is. The "cowardly crusaders" are mocked for relying on proxies like the PKK, Pershmerga and Free Syrian Army and for futile airstrikes which succeed only in killing Muslim women and children. President Obama is also ridiculed for being double-minded about fighting, "unlike Bush whose administration at least understood 'what war is and how it should be won.'" Bush is damned with faint praise: "[a]s the liar Bush truthfully said: 'Either you are with us or you are with the terrorists.'" Of course, the IS spin is that Bush's and Obama's "crusade against the Islamic State is the greatest testimony from Allah for the proper manhaj [agenda, plan] of this Khilafah."

While the IS, herein, purports to be brimming with confidence about winning the upcoming Armageddon-like battle, it nonetheless encourages Western Muslims to strike individually and pre-emptively against its enemies. "At this point in the crusade…it is very important that attacks take place in every country that has entered into alliance against the Islamic State, especially the U.S., UK, France, Australia and Germany….the citizens of crusader nations should be targeted wherever they can be found. Let the muwahhid [believers in tawhid, "unity" of Allah especially over against Christian Trinitarian theology] not be affected by 'analysis paralysis'" stemming from undertaking only operations that cannot fail. "He should be pleased to meet his Lord even if with just one dead kafir's name written in his scroll of deeds." IS even doubles down on this incitement to jihad: "Every Muslim should get out of his house, find a crusader, and kill him. It is important that the killing becomes attributed to...the Islamic State.... Otherwise, crusader media makes such attacks appear to be random killings." Exhortation to *jihad* in the West *fi sabil Allah* goes on: "If you can kill a disbelieving American or European–especially the spiteful and <u>filthy French</u>–or an Australian or a Canadian or any other disbeliever...waging war...then rely upon Allah, and kill him in any manner or way...." [including, one might well surmise, jihad-by-automobile]. "Kill the disbeliever whether he is civilian, or military...."

The other major theme in this latest IS publication is "the revival of slavery before the [Last] hour." In particular *Dabiq* takes pains to explain why the non-dhimmi Yazidis are enslavable–unlike Jews or Christians. "Their creed is so deviant from the truth that even cross-worshipping Christians for ages considered them devil worshippers and Satanists." IS claims that its scholar "research[ed] the Yazidis to determine if they should be treated as an originally mushrik ["polytheistic"] group or one that originated as Muslims and then apostasized." Obviously IS came down in favor of the former–deeming Yazidis modern descendants of ancient Persian Zoroastrians–and so ruling that "unlike Jews and Christians, there was no room for jizyah payment. Also, their women could be enslaved.... After capture, the Yazidi women and children were...divided according to the Shari`ah amongst the fighters of the Islamic State...after one-fifth of the slaves were transferred to the Islamic State's authority...." This literal application of 7th century Islamic law and history has been meted out quite methodically: "the enslaved Yazidi families are now sold by the Islamic State soldiers [just] as the mushrikin were sold by the Companions..." *Dabiq* also justifies the resurrection of such brutality as "one of the signs of the [Last] Hour, as well as one of the causes behind al-Malhamah al-Kubra." In fact, there are two entire pages of Qur'an citations and Hadith quotations explaining how slavery must exist in Islamic lands before the eschatological denouement can come.

Other topics covered in this magazine, albeit in less detail, include: the permissibility of *ghanimah* (war booty) in terms of seized weapons; gloating about successful military operations against the "nusayris" (Alawis, or Syrian government forces) and the PKK/YPG *murtaddin* ("apostates," because they are Marxists); administrative creation of two new *wilayat* from conquered regions around al-Bukamal (in southeast Syria) and Fallujah (west of Baghdad)—in order to "eliminate any remaining traces of the kufri, nationalistic borders;" scenes of putative state-building in the IS (bridges rebuilt, elderly being fed, electricity lines under repair); Defense Secretary Hagel's testimony about IS before the Senate Armed Services Committee; and, finally, five pages about the beheading of Steven Sotloff (blaming it largely on his being a "Jew and citizen of the Jewish state") and four on British hostage John Cantlie, whose IS apologia appears likely forced. The last page of this fourth issue of *Dabiq* repeats, at length, the hadith about the Muslims vanquishing the "Roman Christians" in al-Malhamah al-Kubra.

Observations:

1. Islamic State is honing its eschatological-apocalyptic message to a fine point, by making its jihad against the "Crusade," as well as the reimposing of slavery over non-dhimmis, Signs of the Last Hour.

2. The numerous Qur'anic verses and hadith citations employed in this issue of *Dabiq*—as well as the legions of such in its first three editions—prove once and for all that IS is profoundly and legitimately Islamic. Quotations from the Qur'an are neither taken out of context, nor "misinterpreted;" they are simply rendered, and applied, literally. Certain hadiths, however, are glossed as needed; for example, the prediction that the "Romans " (Byzantines) would land a major force in Syria to fight the Muslims is reinterpreted to mean the medieval Crusaders from Western Europe, because that better fits IS's message.

3. A keen awareness and indeed understanding of Western commentary on IS shows in the references to the statements of Obama, Bush, Hagel, Kissinger, Scheuer and Peters–lending further support to suspicions that the writer is an educated American.

4. IS's ongoing efforts to degrade the territorial integrity of both Syria and Iraq, as well as to engage in nation-building, proceed apace.

5. References to "Constantinople"–the old Greek Christian name for Istanbul–being conquered by Muslims would seem to indicate that IS does not consider the Turks true Muslims, and that the city requires (re) conquest.

6. IS clearly has now decided it will no longer simply focus on its near enemies in the region but will encourage its supporters to strike citizens of its various far enemies in their own homelands. This will very likely mean an increase in what the media calls attacks by "lone wolves"– better known as "roaming hyenas" whose ultimate pack loyalty is to Qur'anic literalists such as those of IS.

September 23, 2014: Br'er Mahdi? Luring the U.S. into Eschatological Quicksand in Syria.

Last night the United States and several allied Arab nations began airstrikes on the Islamic State [IS], as well as on the putative *al-Qa`ida/Jabhat al-Nusrah* offshoot Khurasan (or Khorasan), in Syria. I wonder if the American political and military leadership realizes that in so doing we are waging war to stave off the end of the world–at least, that's the opinion of many of our targeted enemies. I have previously explicated the extant and evident End Times beliefs of the major Sunni players in Syria–notably ISIS/ISIL/IS and Jabhat al-Nusrah. Now comes a new twist: according to, of all sources, an Iranian one, IS is disseminating photos of a one-eyed infant which the group claims is the Dajjal–the "Deceiver," or anti-Christ, of Islamic tradition. The story quotes Joint Chiefs of Staff Chair General Dempsey from a few weeks ago to the effect that IS has "an apocalyptic, end-of-days strategic vision." It also, interestingly, quotes me: "once the caliphate is firmly established, then the likelihood of a Mahdiyah being proclaimed increases." (Does this constitute damning with faint praise? Although nice on my trip to Tehran in 2008, official Iranian outlets have written negatively about me since.) It is curious, as well, that the *Ahlul Bay* [Ahl al-Bayt, "Family of the House (of the Prophet)"] *News Agency* would mock IS adducing the one-eyed Dajjal–since the idea is clearly found in both Sunni and Twelver Shi`i hadiths.

This goes hand-in-fist with the many eschatological references in IS's first three issues of *Dabiq* magazine–the very name of which refers to the major apocalyptic battle between Muslim and "Roman/Crusader" forces at that location in northwest Syria. But Levantine eschatological fervor is almost certainly being further inflamed by this newly-revealed Khurasan organization–which, according to U.S. intelligence and military sources, was planning "imminent" attacks on Americans, probably airliners. The region of Khurasan is, however, much more than merely "part of the old Islamic caliphate that included Afghanistan [as well as eastern Iran and parts of Central Asia]." That eastern Islamic territory was considered to be the eschatological font, as it were. There are a number of (Sunni) hadiths which predict that the Mahdi will ride in, with his jihadist entourage, from Khurasan to deliver the Islamic world and subjugate its enemies. Furthermore, the Mahdi's forces will bear the (in)famous black flags so beloved of groups like IS and Boko Haram right now. Knowing the eschatological penchant of Jabhat al-Nusrah, I thus doubt that its splinter group's name is only a geographical reference.

Finally, I sat through all 55:14 of the new IS video "Flames of War: Fighting Has Just Begun." Frankly, this bloody and boring film is simply a live-action version of *Dabiq* magazine–albeit, in the latter, one at least is not subjected to interminable, grating Arabic Islamic chants

46

and mind-numbing repetitions of "allah[u] akbar." The usual IS suspects are everywhere: jihad is a duty; the caliphate is back, and this time it's personal Bush/Obama; watch us kill "Nusayris" (Syrian Alawis), "Safawis" (Iraqi soldiers–"Safavids," referring to the Twelver Shi`i Persian Empire of early modern times), and "murtaddin" ("apostate") Kurds, usually en masse. (IS even makes some of them dig their own graves before shooting them all in the backs of their heads.)

One aspect of the IS propaganda was new, however; speaking directly to the United States, the self-styled Caliph Ibrahim says "O defender of the cross…a proxy war won't help you in Sham [Syria] just as it didn't help you in Iraq….**you will be forced into a direct confrontation…despite your reluctance**…" [emphasis added].

Observations:

1. IS is not the only belligerent in the Middle East with an apocalyptic, end-of-days strategic vision; Jabhat al-Nusrah has one, as well–as does, most likely, Khurasan.

2. Said eschatological paradigms are not "extremist" but very much in the Islamic mainstream (both Sunni and Shi`i)–and it would behoove analysts to consider them.

3. Last month, in my break-down of the second issue of *Dabiq*, I wrote the following: *IS atrocities like the beheading of James Foley and the mass murders of Shi`is and Yazidis are, in effect, "bizarre rituals intended to bring about the end of the world"* [as per *Ghostbusters*]–*or at least to spark the Mahdi's coming. I truly think that IS has passed into the realm of trying to hotwire the apocalypse.* "Caliph Ibrahim's" latest warning to us–that the U.S. is destined for direct conflict (meaning ground forces) with IS–clearly supports my contention. IS leadership is firmly convinced, based on its literal reading of relevant hadiths, that a great force of "Romans/Crusaders" (Americans) will invade Syria and that a pious group of Muslims, the Islamic State, will defeat it. Thus, I maintain that Ibrahim and his ansar

WANT massed American boots in Syria, the sooner the better—and are trying to goad us into providing them.

4. **Finally, a very important point which no one in the analytical or journalistic community notices—or cares to admit: the new Caliph refers to the United States of America as "defender of the cross."** Not "proponent of Ayn Rand," "guardian of the Enlightenment" or "warden of Jeffersonian democracy." <u>**The Islamic State's leader forthrightly and inconveniently spells out exactly why they hate us: because, in the eyes of him and his Muslim followers, we are a Christian nation**</u>. There are those who will dismiss this as a mere progagandistic trope. But they would be wrong to do so. IS, along with Boko Haram and al-Qaʿida and Jabhat al-Nusra and the Taliban (to name only a few), as well as the non-terrorist but Muslim fundamentalist strains such as Wahhabism and Deobandism and Salafism—all view the world through a simplistic but legitimately Islamic lens of *Dar al-Islam* v. *Dar al-harb*: the "house of Islam" v. the "house of war." And for 14 centuries the vanguard of the latter has been Christendom. Some decry pointing this out as crass "Crusaderism." But as that combat veteran J.R.R. Tolkien pointed out, "it needs but one foe to breed a war"—and when that enemy declares its war on us in religious terms, should we pretend otherwise?

September 11, 2014: Obama on ISIS: Oft In Lies Truth Is Hidden (on ISIS' *Dabiq* #3).

Today is September 11, 2014, thirteen years exactly since the attack by *al-Qaʿidah*-affiliated Muslims that killed almost 3,000 Americans. In a speech last night President Obama explained his belated articulation of a strategy to defeat (the) Islamic State, or IS—which he calls ISIL, the "Islamic State of Iraq and the Levant" (also known as ISIS, "the Islamic State of Iraq and al-Sham/[Greater] Syria"). POTUS made two assertions in particular that relate to the beliefs and activities of IS: 1)

"ISIL is not Islamic. No religion condones the killing of innocents…;" and 2) "ISIL is certainly not a state" since it "is recognized by no government nor by the people it subjugates. ISIL is a terrorist organization, pure and simple" with "no vision other than the slaughter of all who stand in its way."

Are these statements accurate? Regarding the first: besides its very name, Islamic State has now published three issues of its *Dabiq* magazine–two of which I have closely analyzed previously. To summarize my takes on the first two: the name "Dabiq" is taken from a Hadith (saying of Muhammad's) referring to a future apocalyptic battle between Muslims and "Romans"–understood as Western, Christian forces; both cite the Qur'an and the Hadiths numerous times (far more than the two Qur'anic citations mustered by the much-ballyhooed anti-IS fatwa put out by British imams); pan-Islamic ideas are trumpeted as far more legitimate than the "colonial" nation-state boundaries extant in the Middle East; historical examples of Islamic empires (Umayyads and Abbasids, in particular) are adduced as precedent for IS's caliphate; and the ancient Muhammadan pattern of hijrah to a safe zone–in this case, the IS–is recommended to Muslims everywhere.

In this latest issue, subtitled "A Call to Hijrah," Islamic State doubles down on dissemination of Islamic doctrines. The Qur'an is quoted 8 times; 35 Hadiths are presented; 17 different Islamic scholars are put forward (most notably Ibn Taymiyyah and Ibn Kathir). The progenitor of Islamic State, Abu Mus`ab al-Zarqawi, is quoted 6 times and given the status of "martyr." The liquidation of the treacherous Syrian *Shu`aytat* tribe–killing all the men and taking the women and children as *ghanimah*, or "war booty"–is justified on the basis of the example of Muhammad, who ordered that two men who stole his camels were punished by having "their hands and feet cut off, their eyes…pulled out with hot iron, and they be thrown out on …an area covered with black stones near Madinah…so they would ask for water to drink, but not be given any…until they died" (p. 14).

Islamic eschatology is once again given top priority, after its prominent explication in issue one but its side-lining in the second issue. "Sham," or Greater Syria, is called the "Land of Malahim," or "epic battles"–most notably *al-Malhamah al-Kubra*, the "Great Battle" which will take place at Dabiq, the town in northern Syria which the Islamic State recently "liberated." Syria is "linked…with many of the events related to al-Masih ["the Messiah," Jesus], al-Mahdi, and the Dajjal." The restored caliphate will be leading the charge against the evil Western forces, of course. But to get up to strength to do so, IS needs not just more jihadists but more educated Muslims, with their families, to build the infrastructure of the Islamic State–hence the many pages herein devoted to convincing Western Muslims of the need for *hijrah*, or "emigration" to its domains. Thus, refuting Obama's second assertion, that IS is not a state, *Dabiq* extolls the Islamic education of youth, the many abandoned homes available for occupancy, the social services which the new caliphate can provide. "Do not be a slave to work, but come on hijrah for jihad and your needs will be met." Indeed, "the life of jihad is not possible until you pack and move to the khilafah."

The final pages of this issue are devoted to the decapitation of James Foley: Obama, supporter of "Yazidi Satanism and Peshmergan Zionism," is blamed primarily, although Foley himself is also impugned for "glorifying crusaders" (his journalistic work in war zones) and for espionage. Foley is shown with a knife at his throat–but not actually beheaded. So don't take the word of the Vatican, conservatives or atheists that ISLAMIC State is, well, Islamic–just read the ISLAMIC State's publications. It also clearly has a vision–a profoundly Islamic, albeit Sunni fundamentalist, one. Whether Western politicians–notably, but not only, Obama–deny the clear causal link between Islam and global terrorism out of ignorance, rejection of reality or shrewd Machiavellian *realpolitik* is debatable. But whatever the reason, it's become not just tiresome and annoying but injurious both to the American people (who are becoming increasingly bitter toward both Democrats' and Republicans' political correctness on this issue) and to our transnational efforts to stem such terrorism (failing to address root causes is a recipe for continuing disasters, not solutions). Mr. Foley and Mr. Sotloff lost their heads, in large part because our leaders have lost not only their minds, but their spines. But even their lies cannot hide the truth.

The second part of my title quotation comes from Tolkien (spoken by the Elf Glorfindel at the Council of Elrond, referring to Saruman)–specifically, a scene from *Return of the King* in which the Orcs besieging Minas Tirith launch the severed heads of Gondorian soldiers back into the city–much as the Muslim Ottomans did in real-life sieges of Christian cities. Perhaps Victor Davis Hanson is right to ask whether the Orcs are winning. But I still hold out hope that Western civilization will produce, if not an Aragorn, at least some Boromirs to save us.

August 30, 2014: ISIS Has A Syria Strategy–An Apocalyptic One.

The newest issue of *Dabiq*, the marketing magazine for the Islamic State of Iraq and Syria/the Levant (ISIS or ISIL), is out.

Some preliminary thoughts on it:

- The focus, as per the title, is on getting Muslims to emigrate to the "Islamic State"/new caliphate–a process in which they have already had some success.

- However, Islamic eschatology is also front-and-center: the title; the al-Zarqawi quote about burning "crusader" armies at Dabiq; **the first explicit mention by IS[IS] of the Mahdi**; the "liberation" of the Syrian town of Dabiq paving the way for the apocalyptic battle there with the "Romans" (Americans, in other words).

- President Obama is singled out as a "crusader apostate" who supports "Yazidi Satanism" and "Peshmergan Zionism." It is unclear whether the labelling of this POTUS an "apostate" means that IS[IS] leadership considers him a fallen Muslim, or simply refers to his (heretical) Christian faith.

- There are several pages of text and photos dealing with the late James Foley. In fact, *Dabiq* prints two complete pages alleging to be the text of Foley's final statement, which mostly consists of condemnations of U.S. policy, blaming those for his death, and regrets that he is an American. Of course, it is impossible to ascertain whether such was coerced. But since Foley makes absolutely no mention of his Christian (Catholic) faith, it's hard to see how anyone can deem him a Christian martyr.

August 27, 2014: ISIS: Apocalypse...How?

Last week the senior leadership of the U.S. Defense Department publicly acknowledged that Islamic apocalyptic thought is playing a prominent role in modern Middle Eastern conflicts. The Chairman of the U.S. Joint Chiefs of Staff, General Martin Dempsey, in a press conference with his boss, Defense Secretary Chuck Hagel, said the following:

- *"This is an organization that has an apocalyptic, end-of-days strategic vision which will eventually have to be defeated."*

How extraordinary! The top-ranking American military commander adduced Islamic eschatology as an important issue. Perhaps my eight years of warning about Mahdism on this site has finally been heeded by certain folks.

Defense Secretary Hagel and General Dempsey also said several other things worthy of note and examination:

- POTUS has asked for $500 million "to assist the moderate [Syrian] opposition.

- "Strategically, there are limits to how much you can accomplish with airstrikes. Tactically, you can accomplish a significant amount."

- IS[IS] "will have to be addressed on both sides of what is essentially...a nonexistent border"

- "ISIS will only truly be defeated when it's rejected by the 20 million disenfranchised Sunni that...reside between Damascus and Baghdad."

- "[I]n the aftermath of the Arab Spring [sic]...we actually have groups that now kind of are loosely connected, in some cases affiliated, that run from Afghanistan across the Arabian peninsula into Yemen to the Horn of Africa and into North and West Africa. So in general the conflict against these groups...that's going to be a very long contest. It's ideological. It's not political. It's religious, in many cases."

- IS[IS] is "beyond just a terrorist group. They marry ideology, a sophistication of strategic and tactical military prowess." And "they are tremendously well-funded."

- "ISIL's vision...includes...Lebanon, the current state of Israel, Jordan, Iraq, Syria and Kuwait."

Observations:

1. Overall, it's quite positive that the DoD (belatedly) recognizes that Islamic apocalyptic/eschatological beliefs should be factored into the geopolitical equation.

2. Those of us who tend to think that Bashar al-Asad, for all his cruelty, is the least bad option in Syria are never going to be persuaded otherwise as long as DoD leaders (or State or U.S. Senators) are unable to identify, specifically, members of the chimerical "moderate opposition" in Syria.

3. References to the U.S. needing a strategic vision that encompasses both Iraq and Syria and their "20 million disenfranchised Sunni[s]" are necessary but not sufficient–because the inconvenient truth is that IS[IS]'s harsh but literalist brand of Islam is proving popular not just among Arab "psychopaths" themselves but in France, Britain and even East Asia. As I've said in previous blogs and radio interviews, until official fatwas de-legitimizing IS[IS] are put out by reputable Sunni authorities (such as al-Azhar and Yusuf al-Qaradawi), the organization will maintain at least a patina of Islamic doctrinal credibility.

4. Is the Pentagon really only now realizing that Islamic groups across the Eurasian and African landmasses are linked by a common religious ideology? That's depressing.

5. Defense Secretary Hagel: IS[IS] is not just an ultra-terrorist group with an ideology and strategic and tactical experience. It happens to be, whether we like or admit it, a territorial state.

6. General Dempsey, sir: you need to get re-briefed on what *al-Sham* constituted in Middle Eastern history, and what it thus means for the Islamic State of Iraq and al-Sham. Yes, historic al-Sham encompassed what are now Lebanon, Israel, most of Jordan and Syria. But it never included Iraq or Kuwait. Such inaccuracies make you look bad (or they would if the press knew much about the topic).

One final, albeit major, observation: the last thing the U.S. military or intelligence community needs is to have the genuine war against apocalypse-fired Islamic militants conflated with a narrowly Evangelical Christian view of matters. The U.S. government is a secular, not a religious, one–and although I have repeatedly criticized the refusal of the leader of the world's largest Christian-populated nation to do anything about global persecution of Christians, I do NOT want our forces engaged in an Evangelical Protestant "Crusade." Furthermore, and just as (if not more) importantly, opposing and defeating the Islamic "apocalyptic strategic vision"–which is shared by groups besides IS[IS]–

an only be done by analyzing said vision on its own Muslim terms, using Muslim (Arabic, Turkish and Persian) sources. Frankly, in this fight, I don't give a damn in this context what Revelation or Ezekiel or Daniel say–it matters more what's in the Qur'an, the hadiths, and Islamic commentators thereupon. I say this to my Evangelical brethren: it's not always about you and your interpretation of Christian Scripture. The rest of us (Catholic, Orthodox, Lutherans, etc.) in the fold might have something worthwhile to say on the topic, too–but this fight against IS[IS] is neither the time nor the place.

August 21, 2014: IS[IS]: Still Beheading Like It's The End Of The World.

The "Islamic State" [IS], formerly the "Islamic State of Iraq and al-Sham" [ISIS or ISIL–the latter if one prefers "Levant"], ended Ramadan 1435/2014 with another issue of its propagandistic *Dabiq* magazine.

This second issue is book-ended with apocalyptic references: p. 2 repeats the Abu Mus`ab al-Zarqawi (who went to meet the huris, 2006) quote–adduced several times in issue #1–about the spark that had been lit in Iraq eventually burning the "crusader armies in Dabiq;" while the final page excerpts a hadith foretelling the Muslim conquest of Arabia, Persia, Rome and the defeat of the *Dajjal* (the "Deceiver," the Islamic antichrist figure). IS's flagship publication also brags that the group is coming for Palestine and, as per another hadith, that it will "fight the barbaric Jews and kill those of them hiding behind the gharqad trees…" But the second installment of *Dabiq*, unlike the first, does not obsess about the End Times breaking into today's Middle East; rather, it focuses like a Bond supervillain laser beam on two related topics: the Biblical/Qur'anic flood, and the Islamic practice of *mubahalah*.

The Flood, which is the title of the entire issue, is adduced because the Islamic State posits the state of the world to be just as it was in the time of prophet Nuh (Noah)—with even the Muslims so ignorant of true religion (Islam, of course) that they are in need of saving. And the Ark today is none other than the Islamic State, where true *shari`ah* is enforced and where no one is "free to choose"—because the witless masses are incapable of choosing religious truth, and so must have it imposed upon them. Moderate Muslims who believe in choice and "peaceful means of change" are fools spouting "twisted methodology." Just as in prophet Nuh's time, "it's either me or the flood."

Dabiq #2 goes on at length about "the widespread ignorance amongst the people"—meaning Muslims, who "are like a hundred camels amongst which you can't find any that are fit for riding." Only by fleeing to the Ark of the Islamic State can Muslims be saved from "baathism, secularism, liberalism, democracy or anything else that would contradict the essence of tawhid [Islamic teaching of strict "oneness" of Allah]." IS also devotes almost one-forth of this entire publication to explicating mubahlah and invoking it over against their opponents— mainly Jabhat al-Nusrah. Mubahalah comes from the verb *bahala*, which can mean either "to curse" or "to supplicate/implore Allah." It is, in essence, a religious ordeal in which two disputing religious parties summon Allah as witness to curse the incorrect/dishonest one. It is referenced in Sura `Ali 'Imran [III]:39ff, and explicated by later Muslim commentators as referring to a dispute between Muhammad and some Christians from Najran over the position of Jesus. IS, perhaps feeling the sting of criticism from its erstwhile allies, challenges JN (as well as Syria's Islamic Front) to trial-by-mubahalah—confident that it is entirely within Allah's will. The only other major theme which IS pushes in this issue of *Dabiq* is the demand for (Sunni) Muslims to migrate to the domains of the new caliphate, or if that is not possible at least to "organize bay`at (pledges of allegiance) to the Khalifah Ibrahim" among family, friends and neighbors and post them on the Internet. Much of the rest of this magazine–some 18 pp. out of the total of 44–consists of photographs of the usual jihadist favorite subjects: dead Kurds and Shi`is, dynamited Shi`i shrines and mosques, triumphant bearded and heavily armed caliphal warriors "liberating" areas of Syria and Iraq. It ends with the aforementioned hadith predicting that the Muslims would go from conquest to conquest, ultimately prevailing over even the Dajjal.

Urban renewal, courtesy of IS: the dynamited tomb/shrine of Ahmad al-Rifa`i, founder of the Rifa`i Sufi order (picture from this issue of *Dabiq*).

Observations:

1. This second *Dabiq* appears more defensive, indeed apologetic, than the first one. The invoking of mubahalah clearly indicates that criticism from other Muslims (not from Obama or David Cameron) might have had some effect. Perhaps the rector of al-Azhar or the Grand Mufti of Saudi Arabia should take IS up on the mubahalah challenge, since the group clearly takes the issue very seriously and would have its legitimacy degraded by Allah failing to curse the Egyptians or Saudis (although IS spokes-jihadists might try to claim that any negative events in those countries amounted to evidence of divine retribution for failing the test).

2. Once again, creating such a glossy and lengthy publication in English demonstrates that the newly-minted caliphate is trying to manipulate Western, or at least Western Muslim, public opinion. Considering how many British (and perhaps also, now, American) volunteers it has attracted, continuing such a strategy makes sense.

3. Although, as already noted, this second magazine installment is less eschatological than the first one, it does nonetheless continue to invoke Islamic apocalyptic themes—showing either that the IS leadership is enamored of the End Times, it knows the resonance of such a theme for many (Western/Westernized) Muslims; perhaps both.

4. I would maintain that IS atrocities like the beheading of James Foley and the mass murders of Shi`is and Yazidis are, in effect, "bizarre rituals intended to bring about the end of the world" à la *Ghostbusters* —or at least to spark the Mahdi's coming. I truly think that IS has passed into the realm of trying to hotwire the apocalypse. God willing no one is stupid enough to try and find "moderate ISIS" with whom to negotiate.

Monday, July 14, 2014:   New Islamic State Magazine *Dabiq*: Western Forces On the Eve of Destruction.

Since the Islamic State of Iraq and al-Sham [Greater Syria] declared the resurrection of the caliphate a few weeks ago, analysts and journalists have focused on the ramifications of that putative political office the Islamic world.   However, at the start of Ramadan the new "Islamic State" and its caliph attempted to move the propaganda needle from the merely *realpolitik*-ally ridiculous to the apocalyptically awe-inspiring–by invoking Muslim eschatological traditions.

The venue for this is an online English magazine entitled *Dabiq: The Return of Khilafah*," the 50 pages of which skillfully blend Qur'anic citations (10 in total), *hadith*s (12 of these), Salafi-jihadist exegesis and imagery to legitimize the new caliphate, motivate the faithful, and reach out to (primarily) Western Muslims. The main proof text of this entire document is a lengthy hadith (saying attributed to Islam's founder, Muhammad) about a major Last Hour battle. Since IS's magazine quotes the entire hadith twice, and refers to it several other times, the tradition is worth quoting in full:

"Abu Huraira reported Allah's Messenger (may peace be upon him) as saying: The Last Hour would not come until the Romans would land at al-A'maq or in Dabiq. An army consisting of the best (soldiers) of the people of the earth at that time will come from Medina (to counteract them). When they will arrange themselves in ranks, the Romans would say: Do not stand between us and those (Muslims) who took prisoners from amongst us. Let us fight with them; and the Muslims would say: Nay, by Allah, we would never get aside from you and from our brethren that you may fight them. They will then fight and a third (part) of the army would run away, whom Allah will never forgive. A third (part of the army) which would be constituted of excellent martyrs in Allah's eye, would be killed and the third who would never be put to trial would win and they would be conquerors of Constantinople. And as they would be busy in distributing the spoils of war (amongst themselves) after hanging their swords by the olive trees, the Satan would cry: The Dajjal has taken your place among your family. They would then come out, but it would be of no avail. And when they would come to Syria, he would come out while they would be still preparing themselves for battle drawing up the ranks. Certainly, the time of prayer shall come and then Jesus (peace be upon him) son of Mary would descend and would lead them in prayer. When the enemy of Allah would see him, it would (disappear) just as the salt dissolves itself in water and if he (Jesus) were not to confront them at all, even then it would dissolve completely, but Allah would kill them by his hand and he would show them their blood on his lance (the lance of Jesus Christ)" [Sahih Muslim, "Kitab al-Fitan wa Ashrat al-Sa`ah," #6924].

Dabiq is just north of Aleppo, near the Turkish border, and al-`Amaq/al-`Amq is in the same vicinity. (Both are near Hatay, of Indiana Jones *The Last Crusade* fame.) A type of the eschatological battle described in this collection of Muslim b. al-Hajjaj (d. 875 AD) was fought at or near that location in 1516 between the Ottoman Turks and the Egyptian Mamluks. The heirs of the Eastern Romans won that battle decisively, thanks to their effective use of artillery—thus leading to the four centuries of Ottoman dominance over the Arab Middle East. To sum up this hadith: the Romans land an expeditionary force in northwest Syria; after heavy losses the Muslims defeat them and conquer "Constantinople;" the Dajjal—the "Deceiver," or Muslim Antichrist—appears and then the returned Jesus dispatches him via melting or lance.

The writers credit the late Abu Mus`ab al-Zarqawi, decapitator extraordinaire of the IS[IS] predecessor organization the Islamic State in Iraq, with first linking the jihad there to the End Time battle at Dabiq. Also, this magazine has several pages extolling al-Zarqawi's virtues and strategic vision for rec-creating the caliphate via these stages: 1) *hijrah*; 2) *jama`ah*; 3) destabilizing the *taghut*; 4) *tamkin*; 5) *khilafah*. The original hijrah was the "flight" of Muhammad and the small Muslim community from Mecca to Yathrib/Medina in 622 AD. Ever since, this exploit has served as an example for groups of Muslims who deem their society and/or rulers insufficiently pious and who thus repeat the paradigm of flee, consolidate power and return to conquer. Jama`ah is "community," the expected group solidarity that hardens during hijrah. Such a community then must act to undermine the tyrannical regime(s), the taghut (literally "despots" or "gorillas"). As the oppressive rulers are rendered illegitimate via jihad and *tuwwahhush* (literally "savagery" or "brutality"), controlling less and less territory, the true Muslims will be able to consolidate power (tamkin), ultimately leading to the caliphate–as IS[IS] has now proclaimed. This rising new Muslim power "will trample the idol of nationalism, destroy the idol of democracy" and trigger the "demolition of Sykes-Picot" (the World War I British-French agreement which laid out plans for those two nations to rule over the Arab sections of the post-war Ottoman Empire). This five-step program for attaining power can be repeated elsewhere–notably Yemen, Mali, Somalia, Sinai Peninsula, Waziristan, Libya, Chechnya, and Nigeria, as well as in certain areas of Tunisia, Algeria, Indonesia, and the Philippines.

Dabiq also takes a number of pages to lay out an Islamic theological basis for the political power being claimed by "Caliph" Ibrahim. The central argument is that "the concept of Imamah [political power] is from the millah [religious confession] of Ibrahim." Ibrahim, the Qur'anic version of the Biblical Abraham, was a "leader for mankind" because he followed Allah. If al-Baghdadi's true name is Ibrahim Awwad Ibrahim Ali al-Badri, this is likely a case of IS[IS] attempting to theologically leverage the "Caliph's" birth and regnal name. Those who oppose him are "weak-hearted" who "makes fools of themselves" and thus "renegades" whose necks it it legitimate to strike–to behead, that is. The Islamic State has "gained control over territory larger than many states…lands formerly under the control of the historical Umawi khulafa' [caliphs] of Sham and the `Abbasi khulafa' of Iraq." [The Umayyad ruled the nascent Islamic empire from Damascus, 661-750 AD; they were supplaned by the Abbasids, who ruled from Baghdad, 750-1258 AD.] Furthermore, "this new condition opens the path for the complete unification of all Muslim peoples and lands under the single authority of the Khalifah. May Allah protect this Khilafah state and continue guiding it until its legions fight the crusader armies who will gather near Dabiq."

There are several other topical sections herein: one about the "liberated" areas, with pictures of allegedly welcoming throngs; another deploying gruesome pictures of dead and maimed or severely injured children, alleged targets of the Iraqi and Syrian government forces; yet another boasting of the thousands of repentant Rafidis ("refusers"), murtaddin ("apostates) or Safawis (the Safavid Empire was the one that ruled Iran from 1501-1722 and fought, tooth-and-nail, against the Sunni Ottomans) being captured and brought to the true Islamic faith. (There are also plenty of photos of dead Shi`is, as well as some about to be executed by IS[IS].)

This magazine even hijacks Tolkien: the massed Rohirrirm cavalry about to ride down upon the legions of Orcs besieging Minas Tirith (from *The Return of the King*) are shown on the bottom of a page exalting the coming unification of all Muslims under the caliphate. One can only surmise that such an image is aimed at portraying the IS[IS] as outnumbered battalions fighting heroically against seemingly insurmountable odds–and, of course, winning, much as do the Muslims at the battle of Dabiq, vanquishing the Romans/crusaders with only the remaining one-third of their forces. But, again, on the last page, *Dabiq* comes back around to eschatology–reprinting *in toto* the aforementioned hadith from Muslim b. al-Hajjaj.

Observations:

1. _The first English-language publication by the first caliphal state to be proclaimed since the demise of the Ottoman one 90 years ago is focused on apocalyptic themes_–specifically an End Times' Armageddonesque battle and the entry into history two of the three major Muslim eschatological figures: the Dajjal and Jesus. "Caliph Ibrahim" and his staff would not have sanctioned such an endeavor without good reason. The Muslims must have one man to lead them all against the evil Westerners in the great battle soon to come in Syria. Resistance to him is futile–and treasonous. Join the inevitable winning side.

2. The IS leadership no doubt knows anecdotally what Pew data told us empirically in 2012: that eschatological beliefs in the Islamic world are not "fringe" or "extreme" but, in point of fact, are quite mainstream, even in Sunni Islam: 42% of Muslims expect the Mahdi–Islam's primary End Time actor–to come in their lifetimes, while 35% look for Jesus' imminent return. In Iraq, the figures are 72% and 64%, respectively. Syria was not included in the polling, but considering the raging bloody civil war there, it's quite likely that similar apocalyptic expectations exist–and the new caliphate aims to exploit such in Iraq, Syria and beyond. And while *Dabiq* appears aimed at a Western (Muslim?) audience, and at Muslims living in diaspora here, it's also quite accessible to anyone in the Middle East proper with a computer, Internet access and rudimentary English skills.

3. *Dabiq* adduces, and advertises, a hadith which speaks of the Antichrist and Jesus–but not the Mahdi. Traditional exegesis of this (and similar) hadith(s) holds that the leader of Muslims at the Battle of Dabiq/al-`Amaq will be the Mahdi himself. Does this mean that the IS leadership (and rank-and-file) considers Ibrahim to be not just caliph but Mahdi–but is simply loathe to say so in its first publication? Or is the head of the "new caliphate" a ruler who prepares the way, and the realm, for the actual eschatological leader?

4. Either way, the clearly-stated doctrine of *tawwahhush* gives this new, self-styled caliph a license not just to kill but to brutalize and sow panic as a means of undermining any target regime. This is working in Syria and Iraq. Is Jordan or Saudi Arabia next? As my friend Dr. Ted Karasik wrote yesterday (at *al-Arabiya*), tawwahhush might mean biological, chemical or nuclear/radiological warfare. A caliph might decide to deploy such weapons, either on his own recognizance or as a means of hotwiring the apocalypse/arrival of the Mahdi. And if Ibrahim/al-Baghdadi thinks himself the Mahdi, then any and all

weapons are acceptable to wage *jihad fi sabil Allah*: "in the path of Allah."

5. As I noted previously, a number of Sunni factions are speaking out against the caliphal claims of the IS: Lebanese shaykhs; professors at al-Azhar in Cairo; Yusuf al-Qaradawi; even pro-caliphate Hizb al-Tahrir. To this list we can now add current Turkish politician and former head of the Organization of Islamic Cooperation, Ekmeleddin Ihsanoğlu, as well as a coterie of British imams. These condemnations are good, but more, and more official ones, are needed. Where are the fatwas from the world's most influential Muslim, Dr. Ahmad Muhammad al-Tayyib, rector of al-Azhar; or Dr. Ali Guma, former Grand Mufti of Egypt? Kinetic–military–operations against the IS are of course necessary, and are allegedly being carried out by the likes of Ansar al-Islam and, most doggedly, Jaysh Rijal al-Tariqah al-Naqshbandiyah ("Army of the Men of the Naqshandi [Sufi] Order"). Although composed primarily of former Saddam Hussein government and military members, many of his Ba`ath (Arab Socialist) party, it seems that many in JRTN are also practicing Sufis–Islamic mystics. The Naqshbandi order is one of the oldest and perhaps the largest of the dozens (at least) of extant Sufi networks, and it has historically been the one most prone to waging violent jihad; for example, Naqshbandis fought many insurrections against the Ottoman Empire. If the newly-minted caliph indeed has Mahdist aspirations, there is perhaps no group better suited to beat it out of him and his followers. Still, it's possible for opponents of the IS to win the shooting war but lose the ideological one.

The Caliphate has returned, whether we like it or not. The IS, as evidenced by Dabiq, clearly thinks the eschatological clock is ticking. Let's hope it won't be necessary to raise the Mahdist alarm.

ISIS and Beyond: Mahdism across the Middle East

April 27, 2014: The Blood-Spangled Banner of the Mahdi, *Jabhat al-Nusra* and Syria.

My friend Charles Cameron, who blogs regularly on strategy and other high-brow issues at *zenpundit.com*, just recently pointed out that the major jihadist group in Syria, *Jabhat al-Nusra*, has yet again (on April 23, 2014) trumpeted its Islamic eschatological beliefs. As per the Middle East Media Research Institute [MEMRI]: Jabhat al-Nusra cleric: "We are fighting the Safavid-Shiite alliance…and we are fighting the Zionist-Crusader alliance…." Sami al-`Uraydi, senior JaN religious authority: "Thanks to Allah, the banner has been raised. The first to raise the banner in this century was Sheikh Osama, may Allah accept him in Paradise. The banner passes from one lion to another, from one man to another, until it will reach Muhammad bin Abdullah, the Mahdi. Allah willing, the banner will not be lost, until it has reached Muhammad bin Abdullah, the Mahdi. The age of great wars began with the 9/11 attacks." MEMRI entitles this video clip translation "Al-Qaeda's Jabhat al-Nusra Conquers Military Post in the Syrian Golan, Commemmorates Bin Laden." A far more accurate appraisal would be "Major Sunni Jihadist Group Adduces the Mahdi."

I have been warning of the dangers of Mahdism for years (even before the publication of my book *Holiest Wars* in 2005), on my website and in other publications, lectures and media appearances. Once again, let me point out that according to no less an authority on public opinion than Pew, belief in the imminent coming of the Mahdi is widespread in the Islamic world–among Sunnis as much, if not more so, than among Twelver Shi`is. All told, almost 700 million of the world's 1.6 billion Muslims expect the Mahdi to come in their lifetimes. Yet most analysts and commentators still consider this primary Muslim eschatological belief to be "extremist" and thus not worth studying. Wake up, CIA and State. Call me. More specifically, I warned about the eschatological elements active in the Syrian conflict–on all sides–in a piece last September [2014], entitled "Intervening (in Syria) Like It's the End of the World?" Thus, I was only **seven months ahead** of *Reuters'* "Apocalyptic Prophecies Drive Both Sides to Syrian Battle for End of Time."

What does this latest JaN communique tell us?

1. History matters. JaN clerics employ half-a-millennium old Islamic discourse, which nonetheless still resonates with many in the *ummah*: the Safavids were the militant Twelver Shi`i rulers of Persia/Iran from 1501-1736 (they were also mystical Sufis–albeit violent ones) and the inveterate enemies of the Sunni Ottomans. Of course, JaN also trots out the clichéd Crusader trope, as well as the Zionist one. But note that pride of antagonistic place is given to the other Muslim enemy this time.

2. Usama bin Ladin is not just lionized and prayed to be in Paradise, but held up as a forerunner to the Mahdi.

3. The Bin Ladin-orchestrated 9/11 attacks (sorry, "Truthers") were not just terrorism but, according to JaN, of an entirely higher register: they commenced the "age of great wars" which will lead to the coming of the Mahdi, who will conquer the entire world for Islam.

4. That JaN "banner" is the flag with the *shahadah*–the Muslim profession of faith–emblazoned on it. Eschatology thus intrudes on the present, as the standard by which the many members of the world's second-largest religion live is conflated (quite reasonably and legitimately, according to hadiths) with the Mahdist moment and movement.

5. At the risk of sounding like a broken record–when will Mahdism, which is being shouted from not just rooftops but battlefields, be taken

seriously in the IC, military ranks and diplomatic corps? Mahdism has been the most potent form of jihad waged across at least a millennium of Islamic history, from North Africa to Southeast Asia. It's not going away because of the Internet or Barack Husayn Obama or John Kerry (in fact, all of those are probably exacerbating it). And now militant and revolutionary Islamic messianism is being openly proclaimed among a major al-Qa`ida affiliate–among violent men who revere Usama bin Ladin and Ayman al-Zawahiri. To paraphrase a particular movie favorite of mine: "Militant Mahdism is out there. It can't be bargained with. It can't be reasoned with. It doesn't feel pity, or remorse, or fear. And it absolutely will not stop, ever, until all non-Muslims are converted–or dead."

December 15, 2013: Domes of the Rock, Chain and Iron.

Over Thanksgiving I spent eight days in Israel, having been invited there by my friend Dr. Moshe Terdiman, founder of the think-tank "Research on Islam and Muslims in Africa." I lectured at the Truman Center of Hebrew University on "Iran's Global Da`wah–Focus on Africa" and at the Ezri Center for Iran and Persian Gulf Studies, Haifa University, on "Does Fiver Plus Sevener Equal Twelver? The Shi`a of Yemen and Arabia and their Relationship to Iran." Also, on Thanksgiving Day (November 28) I delivered the keynote address, "Sufis v. Salafis in Islamic Africa," at the first (hopefully hereafter annual) "Islam in Africa" conference held in Israel and attended by several Israeli ambassadors to various African countries, as well as the ambassadors of Nigeria, Ethiopia, Kenya, South Africa and Ghana to Israel. When not working, I had four days to investigate the Old City of Jerusalem. Although I had been there twice before (2003 and 2007), this trip was uniquely interesting in a number of way. First, compared to my first two trips, there were many, many more African Christians (Nigerians and Ghanaians, in particular) on pilgrimage. Possible reasons might include: the growing wealth of Africans; greater awareness of transnational Christianity on their part; easier access (both from home and by the Israelis) to Jerusalem; increasing piety among African Christians; or some combination thereof. A countervailing trend was the presence of many more Muslim women wearing the *niqab* (face-covering) and *burqa`* (body-covering), not simply the *hijab* (head and chest covering)–proving that even in Israel the idea that *Islam al-hall*, "Islam is the solution," continues to gain in popularlity. Most importantly, I was finally able, at last, to gain access to *al-Haram al-Sharif*, known to Jews and Christians as the Temple Mount; and although I could not access *Qubbat al-Sakhrah*, the "Dome of the Rock," I was at least able to get close and take pictures as well as explore the area around it (in the meagre hour allotted for "infidels"). One of the most fascinating edifices which are accessible to Christians and Jews is *Qubbat al-Silsilah*, the "Dome of the Chain" immediately to the east of the Dome of the Rock:

Dome of the Chain, in front of the famous Dome of the Rock (from my trip there 11.13).

Timothy R. Furnish, Ph.D.

Yours truly inside the Dome of the Chain, 11.13. Not ready for Judgement!

When I got back home, I researched this strange structure, mainly via a superb, scholarly article by Gülru Necipoğlu, entitled "The Dome of the Rock as Palimpset: `Abd al-Malik's Grand Narrative and Sultan Süyleman's Glosses" from *Muqarnas*, Vol. 25 (2008), pp. 16-105. According to Necipoğlu, even before the building of the Dome of the Rock the 7[th] c. AD Umayyad caliph Mu`awiya "propagated the use of the term 'land of the Gathering and Resurrection [on the Day of Judgment]' (ard al-mahshar wa 'l-manshar) with regard to Jerusalem" and he "furthermore attempted to extend Jerusalem's sanctity to the entire province of Syria-Palestine (al-sham), the locus of his capital, Damascus." Mu`awiya "thus established a precedent for identifying the holiness of the sanctuary in Jersualem with cosmology, eschatology, and the legitimization of dynastic caliphal authoriity...." (Necipoğlu, p. 19). The later Umayyad caliph `Abd al-Malik had the Dome of the Rock built before he died in 705 AD as well as, most probably, the Dome of

73

the Chain, constructed "on the site where David [was said to have] judged the Children of Israel by means of a chain of light suspended between heaven and earth....which could distinguish those who were speaking the truth in legal disputes from those where were lying [and which was] withdrawn to heaven when a disputant attempted to trick it. The same tradition identifies the Dome of the Chain as the place where the Prophet encountered the maidens of Paradise at the time he was miraculously transported to Jerusalem on his Night Journey."

Also, Necipoğlu mined Islamic pilgrimage guides–Arab, Ottoman Turkish and even Persian–from the ninth through the 16th centuries AD for how they viewed the structural layout of the Temple Mount. Many of them play up the eschatological meaning of the various edifices on the area around the Dome of the Rock and al-Aqsa Mosque, as well as the surrounding topography; for example, the "Straight Bridge" (*sirat al-mustaqim*) which "is visualized...as leading from the Mount of Olives to the Haram al-Sharif" simultaneously "evokes the 'straight path' repeatedly mentioned in the Qur'an...." (p. 77). In sum, the Dome of the Rock and Chain, and "the signs of the Hour mapped onto the surrounding complex are only reminders and precursors of their real versions, a preview of things to come." (p. 79). Overall, says Necipoğlu, the Dome of the Rock in Islamic thought "salutes the end of time...." (p. 81).

How the 1.3 million Muslims in Israel feel about the eschatological heritage of al-Haram al-Sharif–or even whether they are aware of it–is beyond my ken; but it is noteworthy that in the bookstores of the Old City I found five books on the Mahdi and the Muslim End of Time, four of which I purchased and plan to read (the other one was too thick and expensive to buy and cart back home): 1) *Ahdath al-Kafiyah wa-Fitan Akhar al-Zaman* ("Traditions of Secrecy and the Conflicts of the End of Time"), Cairo, 2012; 2) *Nihaya al-`Alam: Ashrat al-Sa`ah al-Sughra wa-al-*

Kubra ("The End of the World: Minor and Major Signs of the Hour," Riyadh, 2010; 3) *al-Qawl al-Sunni fi Fitnah al-Dajjal wa-Zuhur al-Mahdi* ("The Sunni Doctrines on the Conflict of the the Dajjal and the Appearance of the Mahdi," Cairo, 2011); and *Ashrat al-Sa`ah wa-al-Fitan al-Malahim* ("Signs of the Hour and the Conflicts and the Epic Battles," Gaza, 2012). Cairo, along with Beirut, is one of the major Arabic-language publishing venues, so I assign no great import to Islamic eschatological works published there. However, the publication of any work on this topic in the Kingdom of Saudi Arabia is striking, considering how much the Saudis fear a repeat of the regime-threatening attempted Mahdist coup of 1979; and a publisher in Palestinian Gaza putting out a book stirring the Islamic eschatological pot may well indicate that the Palestinian Muslims are ready for apocalyptic battle with the Israelis–or, conversely, that they are ready to throw in the kaffiyeh on their own human efforts and, rather, just wait for the Mahdi to come smite their oppressors.

Muslim eschatological fervor is boiling over in nearby Syria, as I analyzed in September, 2013. The extent to which Muslims in Israel are aware of, and inflamed by, this is unknown; what is known is that Damascus and Jerusalem are much more prominent in Islamic traditions (both Sunni and Shi`i) about the coming of the Mahdi and the subsequent eschatological events than are Mecca and Medina. Therefore, it would behoove Western geopolitical and intelligence analysts–both in and out of government–to put some effort into studying this topic, rather than relegating it to the theater of the absurd or myopically obsessing over what Evangelical Christians think about the end of the world. I would also add that *the historical eschatological significance of Jerusalem to Muslims is a major argument* **against** *the thesis that the Iranian regime wants nuclear weapons in order to destroy Israel* (I have already argued at length elsewhere that this charge little accords with Twelver Shi`i doctrines): Islam's third-holiest site is that religion's most important eschatological locale, and no one is more respectful of such traditions than the ayatollahs in Qom and Tehran. Thus, *if al-Quds is nuked or even contaminated with fall-out from a bomb on Tel Aviv, the Mahdi and Allah will not only be displeased but unable to stage the eschatological denouement.* The presence of the Domes of the Rock and Chain in Jerusalem is thus, in my studied opinion, and even greater deterrent to Islamic nuclear attack on that city than is Israel's more prosaic Iron Dome anti-missile system.

November 11, 2013: Days of Future Mahdism Have Not Passed.

Some time back I was asked by a friend/follower on Twitter about scenarios that could lead to a Mahdist movement taking power somewhere in the modern Muslim world. I will now attempt to construct a plausible set of circumstances that would encompass a Mahdi claim being taken seriously by a sufficient number of Muslims such that it would become a political and military movement.

First, for the scoffers, let me adduce (again) the 2012 empirical polling data from Pew, "The World's Muslims: Unity and Diversity." The data on Mahdism in particular I broke down last year, pointing out, *inter alia*, the following crucial data: some 42% of Muslims (surveyed in 23 countries) expect the "imminent" appearance–meaning in their lifetimes–of the Mahdi. In actual numbers, that amounts to about 670 million Muslims. Belief in the Mahdi's coming is highest in: Afghanistan, 83%; Iraq, 72%; Turkey, 68%; Tunisia, 67%; Malaysia, 62%; Pakistan, 60%; Lebanon, 56%; Morocco, 51%; Palestinian territories, 46%; and Egypt, 40%. So much for the academic theory that Mahdism is just a medieval holdover in Islam, held by only the uneducated and marginal; on the contrary, Mahdism is quite strong in the Islamic world, across sectarian lines–for of the 10 countries listed above, only two (Iraq and Lebanon) are majority Shi`i; the rest are predominantly Sunni.

Mahdism , then, is as potent a belief in the Muslim world today as it ever has been–although in the past it tended to take reified form (both Sunni and Shi`i) more often and, if not always more successfully–certainly often violently.  For example, Ibn Tumart (d. 1130 AD) claimed to be the Mahdi and created a movement that conquered much of what is now Morocco, Algeria, Tunisian and Spain.  The Isma'ili Shi`is took over Egypt in the 10th century AD and their Imam-Caliphs ruled it, as well as much of the Maghrib and even the Hijaz, until Salah al-Din ended that dynasty in 1171. Muhammad Ahmad (d. 1885) of Sudan is perhaps the most well-known Mahdi in history, thanks to Winston Churchill's *The River War* and the movie *Khartoum*. The Ottoman Empire was bedeviled, over the centuries, by dozens of chaps (usually Sufi mystics) who believed themselves to be the Mahdi and led rebellions (as, for that matter, was true of the Sudanese Mahdi–legally an Ottoman subject and a Sufi, too). One self-styled Mahdi even cropped up in Republican Turkey in 1930. Twelver Shi`i Mahdism was a major impetus for Ayatollah Khomeini's revolution in Iran in 1979–but it was also, the same year, the motivation for the Mahdist revolution manqué of Juhayman al-`Utaybi (d. 1980) and his messianic brother-in-law Muhammad al-Qahtani (d. 1979) in Saudi Arabia. But since 1979, Mahdist movements have seemed rather puny by comparison. The Islamic Republic of Iran remains the only state purveyor of the belief system. On the non-state side, Iraq (post-U.S. occupation) has seen the rise of not just Muqtada al-Sadr's *Jaysh al-Mahdi* [Army of the Mahdi] and it's even more violent offshoot *Asa'ib Ahl al-Haqq* [Battalions of the Family of Truth] but also, albeit less known: *Ansar al-Mahdi* [Helpers of the Mahdi], the extremely jihadist *Jund al-Sama'* [Army of Heaven] and the more benevolent *Jaysh Husayn* [Army of Husayn]. JaM has become a political force in Iraq, and JaS engaged in combat with U.S. and Iraqi government forces–but neither came close to taking power, either via the ballot box or the gun. Non-state Mahdist movements exist, as well, in Morocco (also called *Ansar al-Mahdi*) and in Kyrgyzstan (another *Jaysh al-Mahdi*). Solo, free-lance Islamic messiahs have also proliferated in Saudi Arabia in the last few years–much to the chagrin of the establishment, quite paranoid (with good reason) about Mahdism since al-`Utaybi and his men occupied the Great Mosque of Meccas for three weeks in 1979. Nigeria saw a Mahdist movement known as *Yan Tatsine* between WWII and the late 1970s. Several Mahdist Muslims have arisen and developed followings in India and Pakistan since 1947 (as Yoginder Sikand details in *Pseudo-Messianic Movements in Contemporary South Asia*, Global Media Publications, 2008). Even Turkey is home to a non-jihadist strain of Mahdism, developed by Adnan Oktar, a.k.a. "Harun Yahya," whose followers claim that his esposual and re-working of Said Nursi's (d. 1960) Sufi Lite metaphysic makes him the true Mahdi.

Mahdism's path to power has three stages (according to Jan-Olaf Blichfeldt, *Early Mahdism: Politics and Religion in the Formative Period of Islam*, Brill, 1985): 1) disseminating revivalist propaganda aimed at undermining an extant (Islamic) regime; 2) forming a renegade "military theocracy" and attempting to seize power; and 3) conquering, or forming separately, a territorial state based on Mahdist beliefs–one that eventually wanes in ideological fervor and is supplanted or conquered in turn (albeit sometimes after a number of years). Many pre-modern movements made it to levels one or two, and some–Ibn Tumart, the Sudanese Mahdi, others on a smaller scale–even reached level three. Since 1979, however, no Mahdist movement has made it past the second level (al-`Utaybi's), and most have been stymied at the first (the aforementioned groups in Iraq, Morocco and Kyrgyzstan; and the authors of reams of pro-Mahdist books, articles and websites). For a modern Mahdist movement to gain ground among Muslims as not just an abstract belief system but a concrete political and/or military movement, reaching Blichfeldt's third stage, it would seem that it would need to win support in one (or more) of the following: 1) a state; 2) a transnational organization; and/or 3) a terrorist organization.

Other than the Islamic Republic of Iran, where Twelver Shi`ism is the regnant ideology but which—because of Sunni antipathy—is limited in the reach of its Mahdist *da`wah* ("summons, propaganda") to Yemen, Azerbaijan, Lebanon and a few pockets elsewhere, state Mahdism faces at best slim prospects. (And even in Iran, no one dares claim to be the Mahdi, because to do so would shatter the future hope of the Twelfth Imam's return which is the regime's raison d'être.) Although a man claiming to be the Mahdi ran for the Egyptian Presidency last year, and a number of self-styled Mahdis have announced themselves in Saudi mosques in the last several years, it's hard to envision a scenario in which a Mahdi claimant could first win an election, or seize control, in a major Sunni Muslim nation-state. His path to power would probably start in a non-state venue.

What about the transnational organizations with an Islamic bent? I would submit that the four major ones are the Organization of Islamic Cooperation, the Muslim Brotherhood, Hizb al-Tahrir and the obscure, but quite influential, Tablighi Jama`at. The OIC is the Islamic "UN," if you will (and, indeed, is the world's second-largest transnational organization, behind only the UN itself)—and that organization's potential as the springboard to a new caliphate has been examined before. The Muslim Brotherhood is the Sunni Muslim world's foremost Islamist political movement, primarily—but not solely—Arab. Hizb al-Tahrir, or "Party of Liberation," is a transnational movement to resurrect the caliphate (Sunni Muslim rule under one man) which is banned in many countries (but not the U.S.) as a terrorist group. And Tablighi Jama`at is an ostensibly non-political Islamic re-pietization movement which began in India but has spread to many countries of the

world and is said to have as many as 80 million members. The OIC is
dominated by men who strive for (greater) Islamic unity, and long for
the days when "Islamdom" was the only global counterweight to the
West's "Christendom"–but they are decidedly non-mystical and non-
messianic, and so any attempt by a self-styled Mahdi to have himself
elected Secretary-General of this organization would likely falter as the
elector Foreign Ministers either fell out of their chairs laughing or ran to
reach for their decorative daggers and scimitars.   The MB, unlike the
OIC, is a popular, conservative grass-roots Sunni (mainly Arab)
movement that aims for Islamic unity and polity via re-Islamizing society
from the ground up; as such, and following its founder Hassan al-Banna
(d. 1949) and his "apostle" Sayyid Qutb (d. 1966), the MB has little
tolerance for Sufi mysticism–the usual provenance of Mahdism.   One
can hardly imagine an Islamist technocrat like Muhammad Morsi
adopting Mahdist beliefs. Whereas the OIC works at the rarefied
Foreign Ministry level between Islamic states and the MB does so via the
more mundane local political processes within Islamic countries, HT
strives to do a bit of both, albeit sans any official state blessing (and,
indeed, often outright state opposition and repression).   HT has tried
declaring a caliphate–as in, for example, Zanzibar–then hoping that
Muslims would jump on the bandwagon and lobby for it to replace the
extant government; alas for them, such has not yet come to pass. Still,
the group is active in many countries (including the U.S.) and continues
to churn out theoretical tracts, and hold conferences, on how a caliphate
might be (re)constructed.   And a caliphate would be a very plausible
platform for a self-proclaimed Mahdi to appropriate. TJ is the most far-
reaching and arguably influential transnational Islamic organization,
rather akin to the Catholic Church's Opus Dei program for revitalizing
the laity's faith and putting it into action. It has been deemed by some a
"conveyor belt" to terrorism–but this is true only insofar as TJ is a path

to stricter adherence to more conservative, indeed fundamentalist, Islamic norms (see my entry on this group in the *World Almanac of Islamism*). Unlike the MB, however, TJ is not totally opposed to Islamic mysticism, and even incorporates some Sufi practices (such as *dhikr*, "remembrance" of Allah via repetitive prayers) into its program. A charismatic, mystically-oriented Muslim leader with Mahdist aspirations is probably more likely to emerge from TJ's ranks than from any of these other organizations. *If such a man were to bridge the gap between TJ and HT, wedding the former's piety, Muhammadan emulation and transnational reach to the latter's political program, zeal and activism–then a non-state caliphate with a Mahdi in charge is possible.* Both are Sunni, too, so neither could accuse the other of heretical Shi`ism. The biggest obstacle to a TJ-HT Mahdiyah would be HT's technocratic bent (akin to that of the MB), which could conceivably be overcome by its zeal for one-man Islamic rule; possible since a Mahdi would be a super-caliph, and thus perhaps acceptable.

What of the legions of Muslim terrorist groups? Would any of them be amenable to Mahdism? Many are Salafi/Wahhabi or MB, and most Muslims of that bent are ardently opposed to mystical Islam and thus, presumably, to Mahdism. But the gap between Salafis and Sufis can be overstated–it is not always absolute. In the past Sufis waged some of the most violent jihads in history, and many Sunni Mahdis came from Sufi contexts (because of the orders' penchant for charismatic leadership and extant quasi-military organization). Even today some Sufi orders, such as the Qadiris, often agree with the Salafis on the importance of *shari`ah* and Islamic government. Others, like the Naqshbandis, have historically been fond of waging jihad against Islam's enemies. And a fusion of Sufism with Salafism or MB ideas has been attempted before, as by Sa'id Hawwa (d. 1989), a Syrian Naqshbandi Sufi who also belonged to the MB and envisioned the Naqshbandi order as the spiritual guide for the politically–active MB and, more relevantly for the issue at hand, that jihad should be off-limits until the caliphate's reestablishment. At least one Sufi terrorist group exists (Iraq's *Jaysh Rijal al-Tariqah al-Naqshbandiyah* [Army of the Men of the Naqshbandi Order]) and many more of them have strong eschatological doctrines—such as the Haqqani offshoot of the Naqshbandiyah. On the Salafi side, at least some of those groups have been infused with eschatological and Mahdist fervor—as, for example, *Jabhat al-Nusra* [Support Front] in Syria, whose members already view that country's civil war as the precursor to the End Time events of the Islamic hadiths. And at least 10 of the groups on the State Department terrorist organization list claim to be fighting to reestablish a caliphate: all the al-Qa`idah [AQ] affiliates; *Abu Sayyaf* (Philippines); *Lashkar-e Taiba* (South Asia); *Jemaah Islamiyah* (Southeast Asia); *Harakat ul-Jihad-i-Islami* (Bangladesh); *al-Shabab* (East Africa); Indian Mujahidin; and most likely the Abdullah Azzam Brigades (transnational). This is not Mahdism per se, but as aforementioned with HT any desires for one-man Islamic rule are *ipso facto* complementary to Mahdism, which, essentially, constitutes an eschatological one-man polity. AQ members reportedly held mystical, if not Mahdist, veneration for Usama bin Ladin (see my book *Holiest Wars*, pp. 156ff). A future AQ leader, who manages to plan and execute an even more "successful" attack on the U.S. or Israel than 9/11—say, via a nuclear weapon—might gain caliphal or even Mahdist cachet sufficient to bring together not only a number of terrorist groups but perhaps even the like of HT and TJ. It might be a "virtual Mahdiyah" with no geographic center and a peripatetic leader— but a sort of transnational, messianic entity nonetheless, commanding the political and religious loyalty of tens (or hundreds) of millions of Muslims and having a ready-made military wing in several Islamic terrorist organizations. Such a leader might even be able to draw support, if not allegiance, from Twelver Shi`i groups like Lebanon's Hizbullah or the various ones in Iraq, if he were to adduce a genealogy that included any of the Twelver Shi`i Imams (such as was done by the 15th century AD Indian Mahdi, Sayyid Jawnpuri, who although Sunni claimed descent from Musa al-Kazim, the seventh Imam).

Mahdism is, historically, closely tied to belief in the *mujaddid*, the "renewer" of Islam predicted in several hadith to come every 100 years; thus, eschatological expectations in Islam have tended to skyrocket as the turn of each Muslim century approaches, as was the case in 1979 (al-`Utaybi), 1881 (the Sudanese Mahdi), etc. The year 1500 AH (After Hijrah) will occur in 2076 AD. Couple that with the empirical data from Pew indicating strong eschatological beliefs among many Muslims, the global Islamic community's growing sense of victimization at the hands of the Christian West (and Russia), the burgeoning influence of transnational Islamic movements like the pious TJ and political HT, as well as the continued (indeed, flourishing) popularity and power of jihad-waging terrorist groups—and the emergence of a political and/or military Mahdist movement in the coming decades appears to be a good bet.

Bottom line: An alliance of non-state groups like TJ and/or HT with AQ Central (and very possibly the South Asian terrorist organizations) naming one man as caliph, who then reveals that he also considers himself the Mahdi, is the most likely path to modern Mahdism. Such a hypothetical movement would be powerful and dangerous enough if it merely stalled at the renegade military theocracy stage. Should this new Mahdi and his followers gain the support of (or take over) an extant Muslim-majority state (Egypt? Turkey? Post-Saudi Arabia?), moving into stage three of political Mahdism, the world would have its hands full—especially were he to do so where he would gain a nuclear arsenal, such as in Pakistan. I won't be around in 2076, but my boys' (and grandchildrens'?) celebration of the American Tricentennial might well be tempered by the threat of an Islamic Mahdi.

September 6, 2013:   Intervening (in Syria) Like It's The End of the World?

Syria no doubt appears to many Americans as simply yet another foreign, Islamic land which the POTUS (this time Democrat, for a change) wants to bomb and/or invade despite, or even perhaps because of, the natives' penchant for scimitar-wielding, jihad-waging and mass killing–like Afghanistan, Libya or Iraq.   While perhaps necessary, this view is woefully insufficient to do justice to the importance of Syria in Islamic history and eschatology.   And any understanding of apocalyptic Islam in the modern Syrian *fitnah*, or "civil strife," is impossible without, first, a basic grasp of the historical and eschatological background to that crucial region. So put away your video poker games and pay attention!

Afghanistan, with apologies to our (shrinking list of) Muslim allies there, has always been a backwards periphery of the Islamic world vis-à-vis the Arab Middle Eastern heartland.   It did have some eschatological resonance, however, stemming from the ancient traditions–enshrined in hadiths, alleged sayings of Islam's founder, Muhammad–that "black banners from the East" would come to Syria and Iraq and (re)establish true Islamic rule after a period of Islamic devolution. This trope was, indeed, exploited early on in Islamic history when the fomenters of the Abbasid revolution (and eventual caliphate) invaded from Khurasan (eastern Iran/western Afghanistan) and overthrew the extant Umayyad Caliphate, centered in Damascus. But Afghanistan has never been a major locus of Islamic learning or power since then, and its eschatological utility has been as a mere staging area, not a center of action.

As for **Libya**, after the Islamic conquest it was little more than a barely-Islamized Berber frontier between Egypt and the more powerful and sophisticated polities to its west, and even after the Ottomans came "Cyrenaica" was of little import in any Islamic equations before the

Sanusi Sufi jihad against the occupying Italians in the early 20th century. In terms of eschatological significance, Libya had and has none. Iraq has always been more critical to Islamic history than far-eastern Afghanistan or thinly-populated North African Libya—albeit less so than Syria. **Iraq** was on the fault-line between Western and "Eastern" civilizations, going back to Roman and Byzantine times, when it was a contested buffer zone between those empires and the various Persian ones. The region of Iraq itself was divided, after the coming of Islam, into Sunni and Shi`i sections—the former often under Ottoman Turkish rule, the latter in the orbit of (or at least doctrinally sympathetic to) the Safavid, and subsequent other Shi`i, Iranian states. To this day, especially post-American occupation (which empowered the Twelver Shi`i Iraqi majority to take power), Iraq is religiously and even eschatologically important for the Twelvers of the world primarily because six of the twelve Imams' tombs are there and, after his reappearance, the returned 12th Imam al-Mahdi will rule from Kufa, Iraq.

However, despite Baghdad's undeniable importance as a political and intellectual center from its founding in 750 AD to its demise at the hands of the Mongols in 1258, Iraq pales in importance next to **Syria** for the majority Sunni Muslims, particularly Arab ones. Syria was the first area outside the Arabian Peninsula to be conquered, and not only was it wrenched away from the superpower al-Rum (the Byzantine Christian Empire), but al-Sham, "Greater Syria" centered on Damascus yet included Jerusalem, the capture of which "proved" Islamic superiority to the other, corrupted monotheistic religions: Judaism and Christianity. This fervent triumphalism only intensified after the hated Crusaders were expelled from their 88-year occupation by the Syrian Kurd Salah al-Din in 1187, and the "Zionist occupation" of al-Quds ("The Holy" [city], Jerusalem) since 1948 is seen by many Arab (and other) Muslims are merely a temporary setback, which the Mahdi and

Jesus will rectify–perhaps soon. Thus many hadiths predict eschatological events transpiring in what the French and Brits used to call "the Levant," the most important among them including: *al-Sufyani*, (a "type" of the Muslim antichrist, *al-Dajjal*, "the Deceiver") will emerge from Syria; Christians will (re)conquer Syria; the Mahdi will reveal himself; the Dajjal himself appear; Jesus will return by descending into Damascus; the armies of the Mahdi and the Sufyani will battle; and Jesus will kill the Dajjal in or near Jerusalem. After all this the Mahdi and Jesus will jointly rule over a Muslim planet, and eventually both will pass away.

The true end of history, and the Final Judgement, will not come for some years after that. Interestingly, the Sunni Mahdi and the Twelver Shi`i one perform virtually the same role, the major differences being 1) the former will step onto the stage of history for the first time, whereas the latter will return from a millennium-old mystical *ghaybah*, or "occultation;" and 2) Sunni eschatologists prognosticate that the person whom Shi`is believe to be their 12th Imam will actually be the Dajjal– and Shi`is say the same about the Sunni Mahdi! Thus, <u>Syria is **the** most important eschatological venue of Islam</u>, bar none. Quoting sayings of some of their twelve Imams, at least one Iranian government official has superimposed eschatological themes on the Syrian conflict–Hujjat al-Islam (or "Hujjatollah," a cleric ranking below Ayatollah) Ruhollah Husayniyan, who claims that the strife in Syria is the prelude to the Imam al-Mahdi's coming and revolution. (This sort of "newspaper exegesis" has been going on for years in Tehran and Qom, actually.) And Twelver Shi`is in neighboring Iraq and Lebanon are not only enthused about this idea, but have been motivated by Mahdism to go join the fight for Bashar al-Asad and the Alawi regime over against its Sunni opponents!  As I pointed out in a recent article on Syria, the Twelver Shi`i Islamic Republic of Iran has supported the Syrian Alawi-

Ba`athist rulers for decades, despite the latters' heterodox, at best, quasi-Muslim (Alawi) beliefs and official Arab secular-socialist (Ba`athist) political affiliation. Why? Because the ayatollahs have geopolitical and economic concerns that override mere doctrinal differences between Twelver Shi`ism and its offshoot sect Alawism: access to their non-state proxy Hizbullah in Lebanon, giving them a salient against Israel; an Arab state ally in Damascus; and potential access to the Mediterranean for any oil and gas pipelines, via Iraq. Sunnis, particularly Salafi-jihadist ones, find it far harder to dismiss Alawi religious aberrations, considering that the intellectual "godfather" of modern Sunni fundamentalism, Ibn Taymiyah (d. 1328) issued *fatwa*s against the Alawis some 700 years ago, and those condemnations–which make Alawis legally killable for Sunnis–have recently been reiterated by Salafi clerics.

There are credible reports that both the leadership and many members of *Jabhat al-Nusra li-Ahl al-Sham min Mujahidin al-Sham fi Sahat al-Jihad* ("The Front of Support to the People of Syria from the the Holy Warriors of Syria in the Battlefields of Jihad"), the most formidable opposition fighting force, and one of the most vociferous Salafi-jihadist ones–as its name clearly indicates–"believe that the Syrian revolution provides a golden opportunity for them to work towards the realisation of this prophecy, and they work in the hope that they may become the people mentioned in these hadiths." JaN also advocates re-establishment of the caliphate, imposition of *shari`ah* to include relegation of Christians to second-class dhimmi status, and killing of Alawis. All of these views are also present, to varying degrees, in the other major Islam-based opposition groups, which *in toto* comprise about half of the Syrian regime's opponents (and a majority in the north and east of the country): *Ahrar al-Sham*, "Free Men of Syria;" *Kata'ib al-Faruq*, "Battalions of Faruq" (a name for the second caliph of Islam); *Liwa' al-Tawhid*, "Banner of Unity" (meaning strict monotheism–an implicit critique of Christian Trinitarianism;) *Suqur al-Sham* ("Falcons of

Syria"); *Ansar al-Islam,* "Protectors of Islam;" *Ahfad al-Rasul,*
"Descendants of the Messenger [Muhammad]; and *Ghuraba,* "Strangers"
or "Expatriates."

The Faruq Battalions were initially part of the Free Syrian Army,
originally the largest opposition group, composed mainly of Syrians and
military units that had deserted the Syrian Alawi-dominated military.
The FSA has been trying to downplay connection to the KaF, since one
of the latter's members was filmed eating the heart of a dead regime
soldier. Even "moderate Islamists" like those in Suqur al-Sham [SaS]
favor imposing the jizyah tax on Syria's millions of Christian, should
they overthrow al-Asad. No doubt the eschatological fervor varies
across groups, as well–but is almost certainly extant, to some extent, in
all of them, not just the ones deemed "extremist." As evidence thereof,
I shall adduce Syrian Sunni Shaykh Muhammad al-Yaqubi, a highly- and
Western-educated Islamic scholar and preacher who supports the
opposition–and also believes that the eschatological end game of Islam
is playing out in Syria, with the Mahdi and the Sufyani soon to appear.
Al-Yaqubi, it should be noted, is also a Sufi, an Islamic mystic of the
Shadhili order. Islamic apocalyptic thought and praxis have often been
connected to Sufism, and I have warned in numerous talks and articles
about the threat posed by a confluence of mystical and Salafi-jihadist
thought. Now, this appears to be happening in Syria–as well as, it
should be noted, in neighboring Iraq, where the Naqshbandi Sufis have
waged jihad against not just the former American occupiers but Baghdad
government forces.

Eschatology is making both sides in the Levant–Sunni and Shi`i–
more violent and zealous. The quasi-Shi`i Alawi regime (backed by its
Twelver Shi`i patron) may have used chemical weapons; but some of the
Sunni groups it is fighting are increasingly employing the equally-
horrific practice of decapitation–which may have now passed from the

mundane Qur'anic-based register of just deserts for infidels into a macabre realm of sacrifices to Allah intended to "hotwire the apocalypse." While certain (usually Leftist) writers in the U.S. obsess about Evangelical Christians trying to fit the Syrian Islamic civil war into a Christian eschatological blueprint, the truth is that such Evangelicals have no significant political power (and the ones I know are adamantly against President Obama's proposed strikes on the al-Asad military)– they just like to opine, talk, and sell books. The true believers in the Mahdi, the Sufyani and the return of the Islamic Jesus–who comprise hundred of millions of Muslims, according to polling data–should be the real focus of concern, most especially those of their ranks putting their beliefs into practice in Aleppo, Dayr al-Zur and Idlib. The Obama Administration would do well to consider the apocalyptic aspects of the Syrian civil war before committing our forces to helping those of the Mahdi (if we back the Sunni jihadist "opposition" via air strikes) or the 12th Imam (if we do nothing, and tacitly assist al-Asad and his Twelver Shi`i allies).

Comparing Christian and Muslim Eschatologies

May 13, 2013: Lojacking the Apocalypse

Yesterday, during the obligatory but decidedly non-liturgical (and, let's be frank, non-Biblical) Mother's Day sermon, I tuned out (please don't tell my pastor!) and was re-reading the Petrine epistles–which I'll be teaching, along with Jude and both letters to the Thessalonians, during June at my church. Although I'm a Lutheran, I often use the Orthodox Study Bible, where I found this very interesting and relevant commentary note on II Peter 3:10-12 (which talks about the "day of the Lord" coming as a "thief in the night" and the passing away of this world): "Christians can actually **hasten the coming of that day**. How? Through evangelism…prayer…holy living…and repentance and obedience." [Ellipses are where I removed the Biblical citations, lest any of my secular readers start feeling queasy, oppressed or, God forbid, targeted for conversion.]

"'Maranatha!' after we nuke our enemies!" No, wait, that's not right... (Christ from the upper level of Hagia Sophia, Istanbul–from my visit there in 2008.)

What a striking contrast with, on one hand, the much-publicized (and–derided) view of some Evangelical Christians about how to advance Jesus' return (usually by rebuilding the Jewish Temple); and, on the other, that of some Muslims (mainly Sunni jihadists), who similarly believe that the coming of the Mahdi can be "hotwired."

This Orthodox Christian view of gently and piously coaxing Christ to return is a far cry from the "if you build it, He will–nay, must!–come!" importuning of a John Hagee or Hal Lindsey. And it is thus light-years away from the (thankfully minority–so far) Islamic position that nuking Tel Aviv or New York will force Allah to send the Mahdi and his tag-team partner `Isa. Actually, despite mainstream media hyperventilation, the Orthodox Christian stance is the majority Christian one, shared by

Catholics, Lutherans and Anglicans/Episcopalians. (Evangelicals, although numerous and particularly galling to liberals in the U.S., comprise a minority of the world's Christians–although you would be hard-pressed to get them to admit that fact.) Most interesting (at least to me) is that, based on my research, the Twelver Shi`i view is very similar to this pious pleading one advocated by Orthodox Christianity, and not at all like the Sunni jihadist one–contra alarmist, and frankly ignorant, screeds about Iran's apocalyptic aims.

December 4, 2012: When the Man Comes Around: Christian and Muslim Post-Apocalyptic History.

Back in October 2012 I presented "After the End of the World: Modern Christian and Muslim Views of Post-Apocalyptic History" for the Southeast World History Association conference "The Ends of the World" at Georgia State University in Atlanta. Herewith is a summary of that presentation.

ἀποκάλυψις ("apocalypse") originally meant "uncovering"–hence the "revelation" of St. John–not "total destruction." So, lexically, "post-apocalyptic history" is not entirely an oxymoron. Furthermore, even assuming *arguendo* the "Doomsday Prepper" meaning of apocalypse, it's not accurate to posit that after said event the planet is necessarily a "wasteland, terrorized by roving bands of irradiated mutants" (and/or zombies–as per Skipper of *Penguins of Madagascar* fame. History can go on after the apocalypse–especially in the Islamic view.

It's not an oversimplification to observe that in Christian thought humans largely cease being historical actors with the Last Judgement, becoming (mere) objects in the divine plan. But even for those Christians (often Evangelical Protestants) who separate the Second Coming from the Judgement, usually by making His return and 1,000 year (millennial) reign precede the latter, history also largely comes to a screeching halt thereby–again, because in the millennium humans are not masters of their own destiny but pawns (or, if you prefer, sheep) in the God v. Satan conflict. Thus, for two millennia Christians have been oriented much more toward pre-apocalyptic prognostication than envisioning what the Millennial and/or New Jerusalem polity would look like: for example, the First Crusaders (1096-1099) hoped to spark Jesus' return by retaking Jerusalem; and now, over nine centuries later, some Evangelicals want Israel to rebuild the Temple because they believe that will hotwire His descent.

There are a few exceptions to this pre-apocalyptic focus: most notably, the 16th c. "Kingdom of Münster" wherein theocratic and nihilistic Anabaptists established what they claimed was the first outpost of the "New Jerusalem" (of Revelation 21), albeit with polygamy, decapitations and communism; and, on a far larger level, the "Taiping Rebellion" in Qing China (1850-64) in which Hong Xiuquan claimed to be Jesus' "younger brother" and led a pseudo-Christian, apocalyptic movement that may have caused the deaths of as many as 30 million Chinese. (It is also worthy of note that the Qing government was assisted in putting down this rebellion by a British officer, Charles Gordon—who, two decades later, would be hired by the Ottoman Empire to put down a similar, but Islamic, messianic movement in Sudan! In that latter case, however, Gordon would be killed.)

Despite these two glaring examples of pre-apocalyptic violence, they are indeed the exceptions and not the rule in Christian history. Islamic history is another matter entirely, for it is rife with movements led by men who considered themselves *al-Mahdi*, the "divinely-guided" one predicted in a number of hadiths (alleged sayings of Muhammad), albeit absent not the Qur'an. The job of the Mahdi—or, for the largest branch of Shi`is, the returned Twelfth Imam (the last male descendant of Muhammad, believed to have gone into occultation over a millennium ago)—is to usher in the global rule of Islam and he operates entirely within the normal run of space-time. Thus, Morocco's Ibn Tumart (d.

1130 AD), Sudan's Muhammad Ahmad (d. 1885) and Saudi Arabia's Muhammad al-Qahtani (d. 1979) on the Sunni side; and all the Egyptian Fatimid caliphs (969-1171 AD), as well as the Safavid Shahs of Iran (1501-1722) on the Shi`i one considered themselves Allah-directed architects of the burgeoning, eventually global, Islamic state. And this state would exist (so they all thought) for some considerable period of time before the actual End, the Last Trumpet and the queuing up for judgement. The modern rulers of Iran likewise see themselves as creating the "Mahdist state in microcosm" which will serve as a "vanguard" for the emergence and coming rule of the Imam al-Mahdi. Thus, in Islamic messianic thought human efforts within history—primarily jihad in all its range of meaning and activity, from (mere) da`wah, or "propagation," to holy war—are capable of influencing the eschatological timetable and helping erect the foundation of al-malakut Allah, "the kingdom of Allah." In a very real sense the Mahdi is apocalyptic, then, because Allah is revealing to him how he should proceed with Islamizing the planet. This is a major difference from the historical Christian view of apocalypse and history in which, as aforementioned, the post-apocalyptic Kingdom can only be established by Christ Himself once He returns and not by any of his followers (or at least any of the sane ones).

In one very important respect, however, there appears to be convergence between Islam and Christianity regarding apocalyptic and eschatology: the Evangelical subset of "Christian Zionism" which predicates that rebuilding the Temple will allow (force?) Jesus to return is similar to the Muslim view—held primarily by some jihadist Sunnis and not, as many commentators allege, by the Twelver Shi`is—of "hotwiring the apocalypse:" using a nuclear weapon against Israel (or the United States) in order to spark the Mahdi's emergence. This attribution to the ayatollahs of such a belief flies in the face of Twelver Shi`i teachings and modern Iranian history. In fact, while the Sunni apocalyptic jihadist view most closely resembles modern Evangelical "Christian Zionism" (although the latter is far less violent), the Twelver Shi`i position most closely tracks the historical Roman Catholic/Orthodox/Lutheran Christian one–that there is little to nothing humans can do to advance the messianic timetable, except "prepare and wait."

One major reason for the historical difference between mainstream, historical Christianity and Islam on this issue had not occurred to me until I heard the presentation (at the same SEWHA panel) by Professor Matthew Myers of Shorter University, entitled "Surviving the End of Your World: Coping and Crisis in Early Christian Communities." Professor Myers elucidated the integral role of suffering in the pre-Constantinian church, which led me to consider two matters: 1) the unimportance–and, indeed, despising–of suffering in the early (and modern) Sunni Muslim world, where such is seen as evidence of God's disfavor; and 2) perhaps more importantly, the Sunni and Shi`i view that salvation is primarily communal–that of the *ummah* or "community"–whereas in Christianity there is much more focus on individual soteriology. One might reasonably conclude that Islam's emphasis on the Borg-like success of Islam *in toto* lends itself to a more developed historical consciousness regarding the post-apocalyptic world. Also, the Christian concept of martyrdom is one of suffering and dying for Jesus' sake in the face of persecution, whereas a "martyr" (*shahid*) in Islam is most decidedly **not** one who suffers placidly and passively, but who dies fighting *fi sabil Allah* ("in the path of Allah")–acting to change history, one (body) piece at a time. That is quite a significant contrast.

Finally, it's also worthy of note that the Islamic view of post-apocalyptic history is reminiscent of that held by a near-Church Father, Origen (d. 254 AD), who believed that eschatological time in some sense was coterminous with mundane history, and that God and His creatures would cooperate in healing the creation. Origen also believed, as the

Qur'an implies (Surah al-A`raf [VII]:12ff) that Satan might be forgiven. Of course, Origen also castrated himself, so his judgment is suspect.

Johnny Cash's man who comes around (as per his 2002 song) will be Jesus Christ; for Sunnis and Shi`is it will be the Mahdi (coming for the first time or returning matters little). While there are many similarities between the Christian and Muslim views, the even larger differences between Jesus and the Mahdi have ensured that the world's two largest religions will continue to have quite divergent approaches to the apocalypse—both what triggers it and what comes in its wake.

April 26, 2012: Goatskins and Torahs and Arks—Oh My!

Previously I have commented on political Mahdism in North Africa and "al-Andalus" (once-Islamic Spain), leading with an observation that Muslim messianism is an integral substratum of all Islamic (Sunni as well as Shi`i) civilization and not reducible to (or dismissible as) a belief that is merely episodic and ephemeral.

Today I wish to adduce two further examples of the very deep roots which Mahdism has in Islamdom. One new case, from Twelver Shi`i Iran, consists of an unidentified ayatollah on one of the state-run TV channels there babbling on breathlessly at some length about how the **real** Torah (Hebrew Scriptures) and "Injil" ("Gospel," what Muslims call the New Testament) are currently in the possession of the 12th Imam al-Mahdi, probably somewhere in Kufa or Najaf, Iraq—and he has these divine books wrapped up in a goatskin for safe-keeping, until such time as he finally reveals himself (whereupon said holy books will serve as literal proof texts of his divine legitimacy for Jews, Christians and Muslims—or so the theory goes).

A somewhat different take on the Mahdi proffering his bona fides exists in the Sunni tradition, as articulated most recently (and more cogently) by Adnan Oktar, a.k.a. "Harun Yahya" ("Aaron John"), the famous Turkish sect leader whose followers fancy him the Mahdi. The Sunni Mahdi has a bit more class about stowing recorded divine revelations than the Shi`i one, however–rather than rank animal skins, he will use the Ark of the Covenant, which he will (re)discover near Lake Tiberias (the Sea of Galilee) upon his return, according to several Sunni hadiths (alleged extra-Qur'anic sayings of Muhammad). Oktar glosses these hadiths to mean that the Mahdi could find the Ark in Antioch, Mecca, Jerusalem or even Istanbul (although only the first of those is "near" the relevant body of water).

Observations:

1. This trope that the Mahdi will reveal the true teachings of Judaism and Christianity–which will no doubt look remarkably like those of Islam–stems from the core Islamic doctrine that both the other major monotheistic faiths are "corrupted," in need of purifying and, indeed, supplanting.

2. Asserting the 12th Imam al-Mahdi of Iranian and Iraqi Shi`ism is already present on Earth is a major development in that branch of Islam; heretofore, for the previous eleven centuries since he went missing, Twelver Shi`is have been limited merely to looking forward to his advent and only on rare and remarkable occasions (such as with the claimed eschatological inception of the Safavid Dynasty in the early 16th century) has this orthodoxy been challenged with allegations that the waiting is over. Other examples of the claim to realized Mahdism in Iran/Iraq, as with the Bah`ai faith starting in the 19th century, have resulted in marginalization and persecution. The eschatological escape hatch (from heresy) for this ayatollah would seem to be that he never claims any particular person in Kufa or Najaf is the Mahdi–but only makes vague allusions to an unspecified Mahdi being there (in a David Nivenish sense, one suspects).

3. Note that the Twelver Imam al-Mahdi lurks about Kufa or Najaf, Iraq. Certain Shi`i traditions hold that the once-and-future Mahdiyah (Mahdist state) will be headquartered in one of those two cities–another

reason for Iran to have as its eventual goal the incorporation of at least those parts of Iraq into its ambit.

4. I would wager that Adnan Oktar adds the possibility of Istanbul being a resting place of that particular ancient "radio for talking to God" just in case he ever decides to openly claim the Mahdiship, and/or to keep the air of Mahdist legitimacy hovering about the old Ottoman imperial capital. (Who knows, maybe President Erdoğan will beat Oktar to it–although I'd expect a caliphal claim from him first.)

5. On a more archaeological note: perhaps it is not out of the realm of possibility that some shred of historical memory survived in the Sunni hadiths regarding the Ark, and that rather than being buried under the Temple Mount, sequestered in the Chapel of the Ark in Axum (Ethiopia), or lost in a huge government warehouse, the Lost Ark of the Covenant is hidden somewhere in northern Israel?

December 28, 2011: Tebowing the Mahdi.

There is a discussion group on Yahoo in which Muslims (and a few Christians) are debating, seriously, the question "Is Tim Tebow the Mahdi?"

It began two weeks ago, after Tebow's sixth consecutive, and seemingly miraculous, NFL victory. But after two consecutive Bronco losses, including his four interceptions against the Bills, Tebow might have to be downgraded from Mahdi to, say, mere *mujaddid*–"renewer" of the Denver franchise. Of course, the final say on that remains with the Caliph of Comebacks, and Sultan of Super Bowls XXXII and XXXIII, John Elway.

While Tebow is not the Mahdi, it may be that the Mahdi will Tebow.

September 15, 2011: Between the Devil and Imam al-Mahdi: Islamic and Christian Eschatology since 9/11.

On Sunday, September 11, 2011, I lectured on "Eschatology since 9/11" at the Concordia University-Irvine (CA) memorial "9/11: Ten Years Later." Herewith are some of my major points from that talk:

- Sometimes momentous events spur eschatological aspirations in the Islamic world, as happened when Ottoman Sultan Süleyman besieged Vienna twice in the 16th century and was thought to be the Mahdi. Conversely, the cusp of almost every Islamic century has seen Mahdi claimants who took it upon themselves to fight for the end time caliphate—such as Muhammad Ahmad in 1300 AH/1883 and the Saudi Mahdists of 1400/1979. The 9/11 attacks are examples of events leading to Mahdist expectations and claims, while as the important date 1500 (2076 AD, by the way) approaches, the world will increasingly see self-styled Mahdis striding onto the historical stage and influencing events.

- There are several different varieties of Mahdism extant in the modern world: Sunni v. Shi`i (Twelver, Sevener/Isma'ili, and Fiver/Zaydi) ; State (Iran) v. Non-state (Jaysh al-Mahdi, Ansar al-Mahdi, Jund al-Sama'—all of Iraq); violent (JAM, JAS, al-Qa`idah splinters) v. non-violent (Turkish Gülenists, followers of Adnan Oktar); programmatic (most of the aforementioned) v. "Sudden Mahdi Syndrome"—a chap who seems to suddenly decide he's the Mahdi, and take action accordingly.

- Mahdism and expectations of a global Islamic state are increasingly Pan-Islamic, with cross-pollination between heretofore distinct Sunni and Shi`i world-views—and this line is more and more promoted by Iran's leaders as a means of achieving titular, if not real, leadership of the entire *ummah* over against their arch-enemy, Saudi Arabia.

- An eschatological "blowback" in the Christian–particularly evangelical Protestant–world has developed, and the idea of the Mahdi/12th Imam of Islam as the Antichrist of Revelation has taken hold (via authors such as Perry Stone, Joel Richardson, and Jack Smith); caveats, however are: no Rapture of believers occurs in Islam; and Jesus returns as a Muslim prophet, having been neither crucified nor resurrected according to the Qur'an.

In Islamic eschatology, unlike Christian, the "savior" returns within the normal space-time continuum and reconfigures the world as a powerful, divinely-guided (but not really mystical) historical actor (an Islamic Napoleon, in effect)–whereas in Revelation much of the action takes place post-history (*Left Behind* books notwithstanding).

Messianism as a revolutionary political and military movement has been the norm in Islamic history, whereas in Christian history such has been the exception (16th c. German "Kingdom of Münster," 19th c. messianic Taiping rebellion in Qing China) rather than the rule.

Bottom line here is that Muslims and (certain Protestant) Christians are locked in a dialectic in which each sees the GWOT/"war on Islam" as not just military but spiritual and, indeed, eschatological–very similar to what happened in the times before and after the year 1000 AD, which saw Islamic conquests leading to Crusades, and Crusades in turn sparking more jihads.

- Watch the Sufis! These mystics of Islam could either turn out to be the soporific antidote to frenetic, jihadist Mahdism–or its most willing recruits (both are roles which Sufis have played in the past vis-a-vis Mahdist movements). The aforementioned Gülen and Oktar movements are the former; the Naqshbandis in modern Iraq have assumed the guise of the latter.

- Muslim eschatologists are now practicing "newspaper exegesis," borrowed from the likes of Hal Lindsey (author of *The Late Great Planet Earth*) and LaHaye and Jenkins (*Left Behind* authors). Before 9/11 this was mainly the province of Sunni writers; but since then the Iranians have adopted this paradigm, most notably in their government-sponsored video "The Coming Is Upon Us" (which I wrote about earlier this year, in "Letting Slip the Jinns of Jihad?").

- Anti-Semitism (more properly, since Arabs are Semites too, anti-Judaism) is not an ideology that just developed in the Islamic world courtesy of Nazi influence. Not only did the early Islamic community, at Muhammad's order, wipe out the Jewish tribe of Banu Qurayzah in Medina, but there are Islamic hadiths, "sayings" allegedly going back to the religion's founder himself, that the Islamic antichrist—al-Dajjal (literally "the Deceiver")— and his followers would be Jewish. Thus, ramped-up Islamic eschatology goes hand-in-fist with rising anti-Jewish rhetoric and actions among too many Muslims, and both feed into Egyptian, Turkish and Iranian disgust with Israel, over and above the mundane issue of Palestinian rights.

Iran and Twelver Shi`i Mahdism

March 4, 2015: Bibi and Tea Partiers and Iran–Oh My!

I was on *NewsmaxTV* earlier today–specifically, Ed Berliner's "Midpoint" show–discussing Israeli PM Netanyahu's address to Congress, the reception thereof, and its connection to the reality of the Iranian nuclear weapons program.

Two major points:

1. I am off the (conservative) reservation in that I do **not** believe–based on my years of studying Mahdism, Iranian history, Twelver Shi`i theology and modern Islamic Republic politics–the IRI wants to nuke Israel (for my reasoning, refer to "Apocalypse Row," 3.2.15).

2. I'm a conservative, but not a member of the Tea Party. My interlocutor during the second clip, (failed) Tea Party Congressional candidate from Texas, one Katrina Pierson, reminded me why: an emphasis on original intention of the Constitution's writers does not automatically translate into expertise, much less wisdom, on any other issue–such as, let us say, March Madness picks, macroeconomics, or Mahdism. Ms. Pierson seemed hell bent on painting me as some sort of clueless liberal, just because I dared to say that Bibi Netanyahu was wrong, at least partially, in his assessment of Iran. But gross ignorance about Iran and, in fact, the entire Middle Eastern political situation (at one point she actually said that Iran was supporting ISIS, which I called her on) remains the hobgoblin of such little minds, Tea party and otherwise. I wish that it were only the Left that puts political posturing ahead of objective analysis–but, alas, that is not always the case.

March 2, 2015: Apocalypse Row: Netanyahu, Nukes, and Iranian Eschatology.

Israeli Prime Minister Benjamin Netanyahu will speak to a joint session of the U.S. Congress on Tuesday, March 3, 2015. If his speech earlier today at the American-Israeli Public Affairs Committee (AIPAC) was any indication, the Islamic Republic of Iran and its pursuit of nuclear weapons will be the major topic. Partisan bickering (about whether the Republican majority in the House and Senate wished to insult President Obama) aside, the central issue boils down to whether Bibi is correct in his long-held belief that the IRI leadership amounts to a "messianic, apocalyptic, radical cult" which must be stopped at all costs from going nuclear (as he first said six years ago).

He is not.

Now as my usual friends and colleague sharpen their knives, allow me to explain. First off, I am a staunch supporter of Israel, as both a Christian and an American, and have been there three times in the last decade. Also, now that Turkey, under Sultan Erdoğan, has slipped back into Neo-Ottomanism, Israel is the only truly democratic nation in the Middle East. Along with the Kurds, the Israelis are our closest allies in that region.

But that does **not** mean that everything Israeli is automatically correct. And this claim that Iran wants nuclear weapons in order to use them on Tel Aviv and thus spark the coming of the 12th Imam al-Mahdi is a gross misreading of Twelver Shi`i doctrines as well as of Iranian politics.

I examined this issue in depth for the Institute for Near East & Gulf Military Analysis back in 2011, in a paper entitled "A Western View on Iran's WMD Goal: Nuclearing the Eschaton, or Pre-Stocking the Mahdi's Arsenal?" The major points therein:

- Belief in the return of the 12th Imam from *ghaybah*, "occultation," is not "fringe" or "extremist" but a mainstay of this brand of Islam (just as is the doctrine of Jesus' return for all orthodox Christians).

- The 12th Imam's reappearance is totally up to Allah's discretion; nothing humans can do will advance his timetable. "Hotwiring the apocalypse" depends not on WMD usage or any other violent activity but, rather, hinges on creating the Mahdist state in microcosm (i.e., the IRI) and then waiting on Allah to send the Mahdi to rule it.

- The *anjuman-i hujjatiyeh* ("Hujjatiyeh Society") is not some insane group dedicated to destroying Israel but an organization dedicated to re-converting Baha'is to Twelver Shi`ism—and, furthermore, was banned in the early 1980s for being insufficiently supportive of Ayatollah Khomeini's clerical rule.

- As per the excellent article by Ze'ev Maghen, "Occultation *in Perpetuum*: Shi`ite Messianism and the Policies of the Islamic Republic," *Middle East Journal* (Spring 2008), the ruling ayatollahs are probably the most vociferous opponents of a true Mahdist claim on the planet—because acknowledging anyone as such would end their rule of Iran, and with it their wealth, power and privilege.

- Twelver Shi`i views of jihad mandate that *jihad-i ghalaba*, "victorious holy war," be prohibited until the return of the 12th Imam—NOT employed to importune him to appear. Usage of nuclear weapons is thus really **not** allowable for the apocalypse-hotwiring which many pundits impute to Iran.

- Yes, some Iranian leaders have spoken, repeatedly, of Israel being "erased from the pages of history." But I believe that this means they believe in a gradual demographic disintegration of the "Zionist entity," and not a mushroom cloud over Israel.

- It is possible for men to have long beards, wear turbans, express eschatological beliefs and yet still be rational political actors. The Supreme Leader and his cronies all know that were Iran to use a nuclear weapon against Israel, their nation would be a radioactive ruin about 15 minutes later. The Mahdi has no desire to rule over such a wasteland. Plus, it would deprive the clerics of their wives and Rolls Royces.

- All of the above by no means makes the IRI a peaceful or trustworthy state. The ruling ayatollahs want nuclear weapons not only to hold onto their power (as per the ruling clique in Pyongyang) but to provide immunity against possible American military strikes and to increase Tehran's regional clout–just not to summon the Mahdi via a nuclear conflagration.

President Jarrett, er, Obama and Secretary of State John Kerry are fools to think that **any** written agreement will disabuse Khameini and his ilk of their lust for nuclear weapons. But attempting to counter the administration's naiveté with inane bluster that misrepresents our enemy's beliefs and intentions amounts to falling off the horse on the opposite side. Instead, let's try sitting upright on a strong horse and avoiding partisan extremes of misapprehension.

March 17, 2014: Don't Lose Your Head Over Mahdi Beheading Threats.

While in Iran in the summer of 2008 to present a paper at the annual Mahdism conference in Tehran, I sat in on a number of panels that discussed various aspects of the future rule of the returned Twelfth Imam. (My own presentation compared self-proclaimed Sunni Mahdis to the Twelver Shi`i prognostications about this expected utopian rule by their "true" Mahdi.) As I reported in my post-trip article "The Importance of Being Mahdist" (in *The Weekly Standard*), one Iranian presenter discussed whether the Mahdi would allow non-Muslims to convert–or simply kill us all.   Opinion was divided as to which was more likely, although as I recall the latter option was deemed well within the Rightly-Guided One's purview. As a Christian, and American, I decided then was not the time to offer my own two riyal's worth.

No detail was provided as to the Mahdi's preferred execution method–until now. According to a "Mehr" news agency story, explicated by Reza Kahlili in *"The Daily Caller,"* last week the interim Friday prayer leader in Iran's capital, Ayatollah Muhammad Emani Kashani, warned that "when Imam Zaman ["Imam of Time," or the Mahdi] comes, **he will behead the Western leaders**" although he will "not harm the oppressed nations."

Analysis:

1. Khalili's hyperventilating aside, the idea of the Mahdi as a violent Islamic warlord is neither new nor–for any of my readers from the CIA or mainstream media–a "hijacking" of the concept. Also, it is not particularly Shi`i. Both Sunnis and Shi`is believe in this eschatological figure who will create a global caliphate, mainly via force. (As I've explained many times in other writings, interviews and lectures, the biggest difference in the Muslim view of the Mahdi is that Sunnis think he has not been here yet, while Twelver Shi`is think he is a blood descendant of Muhammad who disappeared in the 8th c. AD and will return.) The Mahdi simply emulates and recapitulates the mission and career of Muhammad–and thus is not, contra Khalili, a "prophet" because he brings no new message from Allah but simply continues and expands Islamic conquest.

2. Decapitation is a favorite method of Islamic execution of "infidels," and has been practiced by Muslims–both leader and lay–for

millennia. Again, it is not "extremist" in Islamic terms. Please see my heavily-sourced article "Beheading in the Name of Islam" (*Middle East Quarterly*, Spring 2005) if you have any doubts as to the Islamic legitimacy of the practice.

3. Khalili's article also adduces a 2011 eschatological video sponsored by the Iranian government. I broke down this video, in terms of Mahdist tropes and images, in an article entitled "Iran's New Mahdism *Da`wah* Video: Letting Slip the Jinns of Jihad?" At the risk of hubris, I think my analysis is more comprehensive than his, especially as regards the clear influence of Evangelical Christian eschatological writings on the Islamic world.

4. Ayatollah Kashani's reference to the Mahdi not harming "oppressed nations" (nor, presumably, their leaders) is part-and-parcel of the Islamic Republic's Muslim liberation theology rhetoric, which crudely divides the world into *mostazafan*, "oppressed," and *mostakhbaran*, "oppressors." The sources for such a worldview are two: Twelver Shi`ism's victimization mentality, and modern Iranian thinkers' and clerics' neo-Marxist influences. Since 1979 Iran has been using this ideology as part of its global *da`wah* in both creating an anti-Western/Christian bloc, and in spreading (Twelver Shi`i) Islam to the Sunni masses in Africa and Southeast Asia, and even to the Christians of Latin America (as seems to have worked with Hugo Chavez).

5. Yes, Christianity also has its violent eschatological figure—the Second Coming Christ, particularly as described in Revelation 19:11ff: eyes of flame, riding a white horse, robe dipped in blood, wielding a sword and a rod of iron which he uses to kill His enemies. However, there is a major difference between Christianity and Islam in terms of each's violent messiah. In Christendom, it's difficult bordering on impossible for an earthly leader to assume or claim to be the returned Christ and lead such a crusade (the few exceptions, such as Hong

Xiuquan, leader of the 19th c. Taiping Rebellion in China, prove the rule). In the Islamic world, on the other hand, self-styled Mahdis leading jihads have been a staple of history in both Sunni and Shi`i realms—although predominantly in the former. (I fully explored this topic in a paper I wrote for an eschatology conference at Georgia State University, the condensed version of which is available herein, earlier.)

This essay's title comes from one of Queen's lesser-known songs, "Don't Lose Your Head"—which was the unofficial soundtrack to the movie *Highlander*.

June 16, 2013: Rouhani May Not Go to Extremes, But He's Hardly "Moderate".

The journalistic mob has spoken: the newly-elected President of the Islamic Republic of Iran, Hasan Rouhani, is a "moderate" (so says CNN, *WaPo*, Globalpost, MSNBC, *alArabiya*, *The Guardian*, and virtually every other news outlet in this quadrant of the galaxy; in fact I think Walter Cronkite has chimed in agreement from his post-mortal coil state). But precious little corroboration of this adjective is adduced in any of these fawning articles, besides Rouhani's vague talk of "reforms" and "greater personal liberty." So great is the media's hatred for outgoing President Mahmud Ahmadinejad that journalistic groupthink has coalesced, almost instantaneously, around the trope that Rouhani must be an improvement.

But is he? First off, Dr. Hasan Rouhani (who may or may not have a doctorate from Glasgow Caledonian University), is a Twelver Shi`i cleric—a *mujtahid*, a "reinterpreter" of Islamic law—albeit of lesser rank than an ayatollah). Ahmadinejad, on the contrary, was a layman. Furthermore, Rouhani's biography clearly shows that he was one of Khoneini's first supporters and, to this day, has never disputed the *vilayet-i faqih* ("rule of the [Islamic] jurisprudents") set up in 1979—in fact, of course, no man could be elected to any post above, say, prison torturer in Iran without manifesting unwavering support for that system.

Rouhani's former role as chief nuclear obfuscator, er, negotiator vis-a-vis the Europeans is also adduced as evidence of his "moderation" when, in fact, it simply proves his canniness in pulling the *suf* (wool) over diplomacy-needy European eyes. His ability to speak English, which of course also sets him apart from that eschatological rube Ahmadinejad, is taken as evidence of cosmopolitanism and flexibility–by gullible foreign ministry and U.S. State Department apparatchiks. Rouhani's (allegedly) published works include multivolume sets on Islamic political thought and monographs on *fiqh* (Islamic jurisprudence), *shari`ah*, Khomeini's political thought and the Shi`a Imams–not exactly grist for reformist mills.

So what gauge, exactly, are media and analysts using to ascertain Rouhani's "moderation?" Belief in the imminent coming of the Mahdi, it would seem. Whereas Ahmadinejad often spoke of the 12th Imam al-Mahdi returning in short order to fix the world (by humbling "Arrogant Powers" led by the U.S. and Israel and establishing global Islamic rule), Rouhani is on record as having criticized this position–and to journalists almost totally ignorant about Islam in general and Twelver Shi`i eschatology in particular, the enemy of Ahmadinejad and his apocalyptic arrogance must be our friend. Actually, however, belief in the return of the 12th Imam is no more an outlier in Twelver Shi`ism than belief in the Second Coming of Jesus is to Christians; it is, rather, a staple of the faith. Rouhani and Ahmadinejad are both totally in sync on this issue–they just disagree, it seems, on the timetable. (As for those who claim that Ahmadinejad believes in "hotwiring the apocalypse"–using nukes against, say, Israel to hasten the Mahdi's coming–they need to read my 2011 study refuting that proposition). And Ahmadinejad differed, sometimes publicly, with Ayatollah Khameini–trying to assert his rural-based lay populism over against urban clerical rule. Finally, in more prosaic terms, Ahmadinejad ran afoul of the senior clerics and the

Supreme Leader for contravening the ayatollahs' Islamic fundamentalist views of male-female relations–kissing his former teacher's hand, for instance; and daring to hold hands with late Hugo Chavez's mother at his funeral. Who's the real moderate, then?

April 26, 2013: You Can't Always Get Who You Want–for the Mahdi.

Recently I wrote a lengthy article for *History News Network* dealing with the possible eschatological influence on the Brothers Tsarnaev (the Boston jihadists) of the "black banners from Khurasan"(eastern Iran/western Afghanistan/Central Asia)–whence will come the Mahdi and his army, according to a number of Sunni hadiths. Now it appears that, as Dr. Egon Spengler said in *Ghostbusters*: "it looks like it may actually happen" (although he was referring to the coming of Gozer the Gozerian, "moldy" Sumerian deity–not the Islamic Mahdi). *The Economist*, in its latest (April 27, 2013) edition, is reporting that the Islamic Republic of Iran suffers from a plague of Mahdis, in "You're a fake: Iran's multiplicity of messiahs." A "score" of "fake messiahs were picked up by security men in the courtyard to the mosque in Jamkaran, a village near Qom, whose reputation as the place of the awaited Mahdi's advent has been popularized nationwide by President Mahmoud Ahmadinejad." The article also states that according to an Iranian "seminary expert," Mehdi Ghafari, "more than 3,000 fake Mahdis were in prison" and that an unnamed Tehran psychiatrist says "Mahdi-complexes" are common in Iran; in addition, the correspondent alleges that Ayatollah Hossein Kazemeyni Boroujerdi was incarcerated in 2007 for claiming to be the Mahdi, not merely the Mahdi's representative (as most accounts describe). The article closes by imputing the blame for Mahdist fervor in Iran to Ahmadinejad, with his speeches about the topic and his telling Iranian ambassadors that they were "envoys of the Mahdi."

Yours truly, Jamkaran, Iran, 2008. No fake Mahdis were harmed in the taking of this picture.

Observations:

1. At the risk of redundancy (but being for the benefit of media and government types): both the Sunni and Twelver Shi`i brands of Islam contain traditions about the coming of al-Mahdi, the "rightly-guided one" who will make the entire world Muslim (either through conquest, suasion, or a combination thereof); for Sunnis he has not yet truly appeared (despite the many claimants over the centuries) but will, eventually, emerge onto the historical stage via political and military exploits—while for Twelver Shi`is he has already been here as the 12th male descendant of Muhammad who went into *ghaybah*, divine

"concealment," some 11 centuries ago but who will return and Islamize the planet.

2. Heretofore the vast majority of self-styled mahdis–technically speaking, *mutamahdi*s, or "false" ones–in modern Islamic history have been Sunni. Twelver Shi`ism has tended to manifest not full-blown mahdis but rather clerics who claim to be somehow in contact with him–such as two Iraqis, Ahmad al-Hasan al-Yamani, leader of the sect *Ansar al-Mahdi*, and Mahmud al-Sarkhi, head of *Jaysh al-Husayn* (Husayn was one of Muhammad's grandsons and the second Twelver Imam, "martyred" at Karbala in 680 AD). There are exceptions to this, however, going further back in history: for example, the man responsible for Iran's conversion to Twelver Shi`ism was the Safavid Shah Isma'il I (d. 1524), who allowed his followers to cast him as the Mahdi in order to conquer Iran. (See Colin P. Mitchell, *The Practice of Politics in Safavid Iran: Power, Religion and Rhetoric*, 2009, particularly pp. 30ff.) Interestingly, the founder of the modern Islamic Republic, Ayatollah Khomeini (d. 1989), also did not discourage imputations of Mahdism to himself. But for the most part, men claiming to actually BE the Mahdi in Iran have been the exception, not the rule, for one major reason: such a claim is politically risky, as it challenges not just the religious establishment–which for a millennium has had a vested interest in the occulted (i.e., alive but conveniently not present) Imam al-Mahdi–but the political one, implicitly delegitimizing any and all rulers. This is particularly the case under the Islamic Republic post-Khomeini, whose very *raison d'être* depends on preparing the way/state/armaments for the Mahdi, but not actually handing power over to someone claiming to be him. Wanna-be Mahdis cropping up in the world's primary Twelver Shi`i country are a novel, fascinating and potentially hazardous phenomenon.

3. The correspondent who filed this story speculates that the Mahdist multitude might be a result of Iran's "economic doldrums." Of

course, those of us who read *The Economist* know that that fine magazine tends to reduce most conflicts to economic motives (many of its writers even seem wedded to the now-discredited thesis that poverty causes terrorism). Deprivation, whether real or relative, does play a part; but of equal or greater importance is probably "the shift of the Mahdi paradigm from the [historical] expression of anti-establishment yearnings to an ideological tool sponsored and advocated by the state...." (Abbas Amanat, *Apocalyptic Islam and Iranian Shi`ism*, 2009, pp. 244-45). The clerical regime seems to have been attempting to tame the rural Iranian populist tradition of the "thirteenth Imam" (Farhad Kazemi, "Ethnicity and the Iranian Peasantry," in Esman and Rabinovich, eds., *Ethnicity, Pluralism and the State in the Middle East*, 1988, pp. 201ff)–whom the masses think will come and humble arrogant rulers (and clerics) and empower them instead. But instead they may have simply proved the truth of the prediction that "[s]ooner rather than later there will be an unpredictable turn from merely expecting the Mahdi to the actual manifestation of the Mahdi that does not necessarily bend to their [the ayatollahs'] authority" (Amanat, p. 250).

4. I seriously doubt that Iranian jails are full of thousands of self-styled Mahdis; I suspect many of them are guilty of nothing more eschatological than complaining too publicly about the price of gas or having too large a satellite TV antenna on their homes. But even if reduced by a factor of ten, the Islamic Republic does nonetheless appear to have a serious problem with apocalyptic antipathy toward the government. And a regime predicated, in no small part, on Mahdist ideology finds itself being hoist by its own philosophical petard. As Dr. Peter Venkman observed in that jail cell in *Ghostbusters*: "Somebody's comin'...whoa oah!" The ayatollahs in charge just may not like who shows up

5. How might Mahdist claimants in Iran be "hazardous?" Well, on one hand, they could be a danger to the regime itself, if not clearly and presently but perhaps chronically, in that their constant manifestation could prove corrosive to Tehran's legitimacy, both religiously and politically. On the other hand, I have been warning for years about a possible convergence between Sunni and Twelver Shi'i Mahdism (as does Amanat, p. 70), particularly of the non-state, populist variety. Heretofore such Mahdist zeal seemed to be coming mostly from the Sunni world—but now the other side of Islam has its free-lance eschatology, too. Should both trends somehow unite under one apocalyptic banner, pressure cooker IEDs will be the least of our worries.

March 26, 2013: Between a Stone and a Hard Case: Old School v. New School Mahdism.

The President of the Islamic Republic of Iran [IRI] has elevated the recently-deceased El Jefe of Venezuela, Hugo Chavez, to eschatological status—claiming that he would return along with Jesus and the Mahdi to establish peace and justice by, presumably, providing cheap oil to the planet's masses and humbling various political Satans, both Great (the U.S.) and Small (Israel). As a result, Mahmud Ahmadinejad's hyperbolic encomium has incurred the wrath of Iran's more orthodox ayatollahs, whose spokesman Ahmad Janati went beyond the lukewarm criticism first offered by Ahmad Khatami and openly accused Ahmadinejad of *irtidad*, "apostasy" (literally "retrogression" or "desertion" in Arabic). According to a story in *alArabiya.net* (March 15, 2013), Janati "said Iran's clergy had been 'upset' by the remarks" and that he wished the President "had spent a few days in seminary before discussing such issues. Chavez was a populist and anti-American. His political agenda was completely acceptable. But he was not a Muslim." The Saudi site seems to have taken the story from AFP (Agence France-Presse), which may help explain the strange statements in the article imputing to

Ahmadinejad the language that Chavez would be "resurrected" along with Jesus and the "Perfect Man"–the Mahdi. Neither in Sunni nor in Twelver Shi`i Islam is Jesus "resurrected"–because, according to the Quran (Sura al-Nisa' [IV]:157-8), Jesus was not crucified at all and according to hadiths (in Bukhari, among others), he was taken to heaven and will return again. And as for the Mahdi: neither the not-yet-appeared Sunni Mahdi, nor the returning 12th Imam of the largest branch of Shi`ism, has to be "resurrected" (unlike Chavez)–since the Sunni one has not come yet, and the Twelver one never died; whether this inanity reflects AFP's secular ignorance of Islamic eschatology, or was inserted by the Sunni Saudi editors of *alArabiya* as a slam on Shi`i belief, is unknown. In any event, Iran's President should probably be thankful that his term expires in a few months, or else the ayatollah-ate would probably be finding ways to impeach him–despite his long-standing Shi`i orthodoxy.

Meanwhile, a newly-minted American Twelver Shi`i Muslim has been claiming that the Mahdi is already on Earth. I just discovered that Sean "Ali" Stone, son of famous movie director Oliver Stone, spoke at the Universal Muslim Association of America–a Shi`i group–in Reston, VA, last year about his conversion, the Mahdi, and current events. Despite having a Jewish mother and being raised Christian, Stone averred that he "did not change religions" but simply "accepted Muhammad (pbuh) as a prophet" and that he "loves Imam Ali and Imam Husayn." The (Twelver) Shi`a, he maintained, are "for the oppressed," over against the "Satanic empire that rules the world." Stone also went on to excoriate the popular culture for holding up the likes of Rihanna as worthy of emulation, not least because she is a "product of the Illuminati." Rather, people should, like him and all Shi`a, "have faith in the Mehdi" [as he pronounced it], who is "already choosing his sides, his army." (Also, Stone reminded the enthusiastic audience that "it's not the Shi`a way to murder people–that's Wahhabi, Salafi [practice.].'") Shi`a Islam's most famous recent convert then explained that he "was told in Iran by one of the top jinnmasters that the Mehdi showed himself in 2006 in the invasion of Lebanon–the 33-day war–because no one expected Israel to lose that war." Stone claimed [still quoting the Iranian "jinnmaster," presumably] that "there were fireballs from heaven" which "destroyed whole Israeli tanks" and that "there were many reports of Israelis with their arms severed–clean–by swords" and that "when analyzed, the wounds indicated swords thousands of years old. Are these signs of the return of the Mehdi? The jinnmaster thinks so. I think so." Stone then moved into literary-cultural criticism, opining that "the reason The Wizard of Oz is an old man is that Frank Baum is telling you truth"–about the aforementioned "Satanic empire." Stone more than once mentioned the recent economic recession as proof that "the system is collapsing–indeed, that the U.S. government wants the system to collapse for some unspecified, nefarious reason. Against that, "the great sword of Ali is our ability to speak, to educate," and Stone concluded by calling upon all Shi`a Muslims to "take responsibility for all of mankind as did Christ, Muhammad, and all the prophets."

Observations (on both stories):

1. The Iranian regime's penchant for assimilating ideologically-aligned non-Muslims into its anti-Western, socialist front does know some limits–such as elevating Citgo's oil daddy to prophetic status.

2. Mainline news outlets remain woefully uniformed about basic Islamic doctrines (the idea that the Mahdi/12th Imam, or Jesus, will be "resurrected").

3. Sean Stone may be sincere, but he's also sincerely stupid. He reminds me of a friend I had in graduate school at Ohio State: she was doing a doctorate in Arabic, and announced to me one day "I am a Catholic Muslim" (or perhaps it was "Muslim Catholic"). "No," I told

her, "you're simply confused–because Christianity proclaims Christ crucified and resurrected, while Islam denies both. Ergo, you cannot logically adhere to both belief systems." Despite your claims to the contrary, Mr. Stone–you DID change religions, because Muhammad's teachings directly contradict the New Testament.

4. Stone's conspiratorial ramblings about systemic collapse and Satanic powers constitute exactly the sort of mush-headed liberal (and perhaps libertarian) world-view that the IRI is trying to exploit vis-à-vis the West. And despite Stone's logical, historical and theological ignorance, he will influence at least some in our society because his concern for the poor is so obviously "Other" than Christian and so sticks it to The Man/Ruling Class/1%/GOP.

5. Stone's gullibility is stupefying. If there had been fireballs from heaven that obliterated Merkava tanks, wouldn't CNN have caught them on tape? If mysterious sword wounds had decimated IDF soldiers, might *al-Jazeera* or the BBC have noted such? Does he really believe this tripe? Alas, it seems he does.

6. Neither I, nor any of my academic Iranian friends, have ever heard of "jinnmasters" in modern Iran. Such existed in the past in Islamic areas, but were generally Sufis–as the famous mystic and poet Jalal al-Din Rumi (d. 1273) was said to have been. But Sufism was forced underground in Iran, first with the Safavid conquest of the 16th century, then more forcefully after the 1979 Revolution (for a host of reasons, most notably the Twelver establishment's distrust of Sufi shaykhs' charisma). So just who is this "jinnmaster" to whom Stone claimed to have spoken?

7. It is somewhat hopeful that Stone refers to Ali's sword as being one of truth and learning–but that only came after the account of the Mahdi lopping off Israeli arms and dusting Israeli armor, remember.

8. These two accounts of Shi`a Mahdism—by and life-long Shi`i, Ahmadinejad and a new convert, Stone—really encapsulate the old and new(er) schools of thought on the topic: the former focuses on the Mahdi wielding a sword and slaying Islam's enemies, while the latter is more open to ecumenically incorporating Islamic messianism into its older brother, the Christian brand. Ironically, however, here we see that it is the new Muslim, Stone, who more forcefully adduces the ancient type of Mahdi; while the old Muslim, Iran's President, appears more willing to engage in a bit of syncretism in the name of politics.

March 9, 2013: Hugo Just Left Caracas—But Is He Bound for Jamkaran?

As everyone except the low-information voters should know by now, former Venezuelan jefe, er, "President" Hugo Chavez went to that great Comintern in the sky a few days ago. If there's a Socialist heaven, Hugo is even now comparing notes on how well he liberated the masses, duped the useful idiots and thwarted the capitalist Yanquis with the likes of Che Guevara, Vladimir Lenin and Saul Alinsky. But according to the President of the Islamic Republic of Iran, Mahmud Ahmadinejad, St. Hugo is breaking bread in the afterlife with two rather less secular figures: Jesus and Muhammad al-Mahdi. Well, technically, Hugo can only be hanging out with Jesus, since the Mahdi is—according to Twelver Shi`i doctrine going back over a millennium—in a state of *ghaybah*, "occultation," and thus not (yet) in heaven with Allah. (The more populist, albeit crass, Iranian view is that he is literally accessible via a well behind Jamkaran mosque.)

Ahmadinejad, whose zeal for the return of Imam al-Mahdi exceeds even mainstream Twelver Shi`i expectations, said that "I have no doubt that he [Chavez] will return alongside Jesus Christ and the Mahdi...to establish peace and justice in the world." In addition, Iran's President "supported allegations made by Venezuelan Vice President [now President] Nicolas Maduro, who said shortly before Chavez's death that he had 'no doubt' the country's enemies [we perfidious Yanquis, of course] had somehow given the leftist leader the cancer from which he eventually died." Ahmadinejad "said Chavez was a 'martyr' who fell to a 'suspect illness.'" Remember: Chavez had visited Iran 13 times, and Ahmadinejad had reciprocated with half-a-dozen trips to Venezuela in the last eight years. Ahmadinejad's rather heretical statements did not go uncriticized. Ayatollah Ahmad Khatami (no relation to the former President), an influential member of the *Majlis-i Khobregan-i Rahbari*–the "Assembly of Experts of Leadership" which chooses and oversees the Supreme Leader–rebuked Ahmadinejad for claims that were "not appropriate" and for "exaggeration." Khatami was even understated in his criticism, considering that there are no eschatological hadiths (Sunni or Shi`i) which mention a Venezuelan Catholic coming on the clouds of heaven with the Muslim dynamic duo.

What prompts Ahmadinejad to make such extravagant claims about a non-Muslim political leader? The conjunction of ancient Twelver Shi`i beliefs and modern IRI political interests, clearly. The Mahdi, in both Sunni and Shi`i traditions, will "fill the world with justice and equity as it had been filled with injustice and inequalities"–he will serve as something of a global Robin Hood, in effect. Such Islamic belief has been institutionalized in the modern IRI, held up since Ayatollah Khomeini's time as the "vanguard" of the future Mahdist state. Added to this in the last several decades has been Western neo-Marxist thought, in which global geopolitics is a zero-sum game pitting the planet's *mostazafan*, "oppressed," against the *mostakhbaran*, "oppressors" (or "arrogant powers," as Ahmadinejad is fond of fulminating against in speeches–led of course by the United States). Article 154 of the IRI's Constitution makes clear that Tehran's ayatollah-ate sees itself as leading the Earth's 99% against the 1%: Iran "supports the just struggles of the oppressed against the oppressors in every corner of the globe." This

Islamic liberation theology plays well in certain corners of the globe, especially when backed up by Iranian petrodollars. The IRI, and Ahmadinejad in particular, had seen Chavez as its nonaligned brother in arms, waging rhetorical (and, when possible, guerrilla/asymmetric) warfare against the Great Satan/El Diablo Grande. While Islam is at best a marginal religion in America Del Sur, Tehran had been hoping to leverage its advancement into the Latin parts of the Western Hemisphere via a Venezuelan salient. The IRI could realistically entertain such aspirations because of the close similarities between Latin American populism and Iran's Shi`i *da`wah*; both are:

- Lower/Middle-class based
- Indignant and conspiratorial about external meddling, particularly American
- More fond of Leftist rhetoric than concrete socio-economic development
- Politically schizophrenic: revolutionary when out of power, conservative when in control
- Heavily dependent on European political philosophy, especially Marxism
- Obsessed with charisma-based leadership.

In particular, Ahmadinejad and Chavez both are, er, were characterized by:

- Having been democratically-elected (at least once)
- Authoritarianism once in power
- Populism and socialism
- Anti-Americanism
- Resource nationalism (both via oil, primarily)
- Judicious repression of opponents.

In September 2009 Hugo was in Mashhad, Iran and said the following: "The Messiah [Jesus] and the Mahdi are not dead, they are alive and well and will soon return to spread justice over all the world. This afternoon Imam Khameini told us that as long as we two Presidents are united in our hearts and minds, as long as we pursue the same humanistic deeds together, and as long as we continue seeking justice, the Mahdi and the Messiah will emerge very soon. Therefore, we must struggle so that his holiness the Mahdi and the Messiah emerge to spread justice all over the world." Chavez was too modest to include himself in that august, holy company—but Ahmadinejad has done so for him, posthumously.

Observations:

1.   Twelver Shi`ism is the brand of Islam most compatible with Western political and theological (Christian) liberalism, particularly Catholic liberation theology—since all three promote the "preferential option for the poor"

2. Iran's incessant efforts to win friends and influence people in the Christian community via "ecumenical messianism"—which I saw firsthand during my trip to Iran in 2008—certainly bore fruit with Hugo

3.   Thus, Iran's Islamic salient into Latin America has suffered a setback with Chavez's shuffling off his mortal coil.   But there are a number of organizations which might be very amenable to IRI blandishments, such as: the Sunni Islamic *da`wah* group *Murabitun* active in Mexico; the Twelver Shi`i offshoot Hizbullah America Latina active in Argentina and Venezuela, which espouses an "Islamo-Christian liberation theology" combining the thought of Khomeini and Fr. Gustavo Gutierrez, liberation theologian; and Aztlan, the Chicano/Hispanic irredentist movement which aims to detach the southwestern U.S. from "Anglo" control—a cause which Tehran would certainly consider supporting, especially should the U.S. threaten Iran's territorial integrity via backing, for example, the Baluch separatist group *Jundullah* in southeastern Iran

4. These first three points notwithstanding, Mahmud seems to have allowed his personal affection for Hugo to outrace his political instincts. Elevating even a close personal and political ally to the status of the two greatest eschatological figures in Islam is an encomium too far. Perhaps Ahmadinejad figured that since he will be out of office in a few months, he had nothing to lose. Or maybe he really has lost his Muslim mind.

By the way: this post title is a riff on ZZ Top's "Jesus Just Left Chicago."

February 27, 2012: The Vanished Imam Paper–Out of Occultation!

Summer 2008 I went to Iran and presented a paper at the Fourth Annual "International Conference of Mahdism Doctrine" in Tehran. Just a bit ago I stumbled upon the online posting of this unpublished (at least outside Iran) paper, entitled "Through A Glass Darkly: A Comparison of Self-Proclaimed 'Mahdist' States Throughout History to the Theory of the (True) Mahdist State Yet to Come."

Logo of the 2008 Mahdism Conference, Tehran, Iran.

The paper is heavily freighted with historical theology, comparing Islamic Mahdist movements to documented occurrences of political messianism in Christian contexts. If such is your interest, check it out! Unlike some (ok, many) of the ideologues and sycophants presenting in that venue, I tried to be scholarly and analytical. I think I succeeded fairly well. At least the Pasdaran let me return home.

December 28, 2012: You Say You Want a (Mahdist) Revolution? Occupy Wall Street and the Islamic Republic of Iran.

Over the past month a number of Western (liberal) media commentators have tried to draw parallels, and even connections, between the "Arab Spring" and "Occupy Wall Street" protests—even as some of the Arabs themselves have disavowed any such correlation. But now, as a recent excellent (and firmly tongue-in-cheek) piece by Charles Dameron at Radio Free Europe/Radio Liberty points out, at least one prominent Iranian ayatollah believes (or at least says) that all those unwashed, economically-illiterate reprobates using police cars and American flags as Persian-style toilets are portents of the return of the 12th Imam! According to Ayatollah Mohsen Haydar, speaking in a mosque in Ahvaz on November 7th: "The Occupy Wall Street movement [OWS] is the big step to prepare the ground for the appearance of the 12th Imam."

As I've explained before (and elaborated on in an unpublished paper for the government, "Iranian Da`wah in Latin America and Africa"), one of the major beliefs about the Mahdi—shared by both Twelver Shi`is and Sunnis—is that he will not only take over the world for Islam, but that he will serve as something of a global, Muslim Robin Hood, redistributing wealth from the 1% to the 99% (if I may use OWS terminology). Also, since its inception, the Islamic Republic of Iran has been a vocal and active (via diplomacy and terrorism) opponent of the extant economic and political world system, trying to put itself forward (with some success) as the leader not just of the world's disenchanted Muslims but of the entirety of what used to be known as the "Third World" and/or the "Non-Aligned Movement" (the latter during the Cold War)—usually described by Marxist and neo-Marxist commentators as "exploited" by the First/Developed World. So, it's easy to see why a Twelver Shi`i cleric would try to co-opt anti-capitalism rallies in the world's vanguard of the "Arrogant Powers" (otherwise known as the "Great Satan") and enlist them as signs and rumors of the return of the 12th Imam al-Mahdi.

In the spirit of proletarian solidarity, here is "Revolution," by the Beatles, with lyrics revised for Ayatollah Haydari and the OWS crowd:

You say you want a revolution
Well you know
We all want to change the world
You tell me to end the occultation
Well you know
We all want to change the world
But when you talk about destruction
Don't you know that you can count me out—IN!
Don't you know it's gonna be alright

You say you got a real solution
Well you know
We all want to see the plan
You ask me for a contribution
Well you know
We're all doing what we can
But if you want money for people with minds that hate
All I can tell you is you no longer have to wait
Don't you know it's gonna be alright

You say you'll change the Constitution
Well you know
We'd all love to see it dead

You tell me it's the institution
Well you know
You're better off green than red
But if you go carrying pictures of Imam Mahdi
You won't have any more ATM fees
Don't you know it's gonna be alright....

October 22, 2011: Pay Lots of Attention to That Mahdi behind the Curtain!

Some Americans may be familiar with the plight of Iranian Christian Pastor Yousef Nadarkhani, who is facing a death penalty for alleged "apostasy." Far fewer, if any, are likely to know that the Islamic Republic is also hounding expatriate Iranian Christians—and in the name of the Occulted Mahdi! According to "Christian Solidarity Worldwide:"

Eleven Iranian Christians who fled Iran in the wake of a government campaign against evangelical Christianity have received threats via email from 'the unknown soldiers of the Hidden Imam' calling on them to either repent or face extra-judicial execution. The 'unknown soldiers' are alleged to have links with Iranian security services.

The email, which was sent to each individual on 14 September, warned the recipients that although they may have managed to flee Iran, they are not hidden from the 'acute eyes of the unknown soldiers', who claim they have been advancing to the heart of the 'Zionist regime' over a number of years. The email concludes by offering the eleven Christians 'the opportunity to repent and ask forgiveness from the presence of the Hidden Imam.... Otherwise, according to the Fatwa given by Mehdi the Hidden Imam, they must be killed.'

Reverend Samuel Yeghnazar of Elam Ministries, who has been closely involved in the house church movement in Iran, has indicated that he and his network of churches are taking the threat very seriously.

Observations:

1. Are these "Iranian security services" from the Iranian Republic Guards Corps–Quds Force [IRGC-QG] (the same group alleged to have been involved in the botched plan to hire Mexican drug dealers to assassinate the Saudi ambassador to the U.S.), or perhaps from the more shadowy *Ansar al-Mahdi*, an Iranian "Praetorian Guard" group tasked with protecting top IRI leaders as well as covert ops? The phrase "unknown soldiers of the Hidden Imam" would tend toward the latter explanation, since Ansar al-Mahdi means "Helpers of the Mahdi." Or it could simply be a more *ad hoc* faction: President Ahmadinejad's executive assistant? zealous members of the Bright Future Institute? an ayatollah with a macabre sense of humor and excellent online skills?

2. "Asking forgiveness" of the 12th Imam al-Mahdi is an interesting novel twist, since he is traditionally not a figure who proffers atonement (like Christ), but rather one that guides the Shi`i community while in *ghaybah*, "occultation" (hiddenness) and leads it directly once returned to earth. Does this represent a novel understanding of Twelver Shi`i theology, and/or a convergence with Christian beliefs?

3. Should these "apostates" spurn the (alleged) merciful Mahdi, they are threatened with death–and that according to a putative fatwa rendered by the Hidden Imam! This is fascinating. Either the Mahdi's minions sending these emails are lying through their teeth, or they really believe that the 12th Imam is back in communication with his flock and actively issuing guidance in the form of Islamic jurisprudential rulings. Both Ahmadinejad and Musa al-Sadr of Iraq have in recent years claimed to be in contact with the Mahdi–but neither has ever asserted something as sophisticated as a fatwa had been forthcoming from him. While it's quite tempting to scoff at such allegations, there are possible serious

ramifications thereof—such as, for example, the remote but real possibility that if the Hidden Imam can issue rulings against Christian converts from beyond the spectral veil, he might also be able to do likewise regarding utilization of nuclear weapons.

4. In 873/4 AD Muhammad al-Mahdi, according to Twelver Shi`i propaganda, disappeared but remained in communication with his followers via "deputies"; this was the so-called "Minor Ghaybah [Occultation]." In 941 he went silent, and this "Greater Occultation" was supposed to last until his physical reappearance. However, with this account of a Mahdist fatwa and the aforementioned other claims of commo links with the 12th Imam being re-established, it seems that the Greater Occultation has devolved back into a Minor one—something not predicted by Twelver Shi`i doctrines and hadiths. Is this just a case of geopolitical considerations trumping more mundane theological ones, or is a more profound re-ordering of Twelver doctrines occurring? In either event, it seems that the 12th Imam al-Mahdi is, while not fully revealed, also no longer fully hidden behind his curtain.

October 3, 2011: Will the Real Mahdi Please Grab the Kindjal?

On September 22, 2011 Iranian President Ahmadinejad delivered his by-now traditional U.N. address invoking the Mahdi and excoriating the West in general and the U.S. in particular for the sins of slavery, colonialism, racism, wars and rumors of war against Islam and Muslims, indebtedness, forcing dogs and cats to live together and going off the gold standard. (Okay, I made that penultimate one up.) This litany of grievances against the "arrogant powers" will not be redressed, according to Ahmadinejad, until the return of the 12th Imam as the Mahdi, who will come to rule the world in accordance with "universal human values such as monotheism, justice, freedom, love and the quest for happiness" and usher in a period of "shared and collective management of the world" in order to build a "bright future." Sounding increasingly like an out-of-touch liberal describing Barack Obama, Ahmadinejad also gushed that this "perfect human being" will be a "true and sincere lover of all human beings" who "will come alongside Jesus Christ to lead the freedom and justice lovers to eradicate tyranny and discrimination, and promote knowledge, peace, justice, freedom and love across the world." This...is...Imam al-Mahdi, the once and future 12th Imam, the "Ultimate Savior of mankind!" (One suspects that the European and American diplomats who walked out during his address might have done so not for political reasons but because they desperately needed insulin, courtesy of this massive Mahdist sugar rush.)

However, even as a somewhat astute analyst of Iranian Shi`ism and Mahdism, I am confused—because the month before, *Ahlul Bayt News Agency* (an official Iranian media organ), published quite a different view of the returned 12th Imam in a piece entitled "Imam al-Mahdi's Code of Conduct with Enemies," by Najmuddin Tabasi.

Tabasi's Mahdi is nothing like the one described by Ahmadinejad, who seems to return from *ghaybah* somewhere in Candyland. For Tabasi, the Mahdi's enemies "will deserve nothing but annihilation"—these enemies will include those with bloodstained hands, the "indifferent," those who fight against the Imam Mahdi, and the "crooked-minded." Tabasi bases his analysis on the exegesis of a number of Twelver Shi`i hadiths (sayings allegedly going back to Islam's founder, Muhammad, as well as to—at least for the Shi`a—the line of Imams descended from him). For example, one from Imam al-Sadiq says that while the "Prophet" [Muhammad] "used to deal with enemies leniently, gently and kindly...Hadrat al-Qa'im [His Honor the Arising One—the Mahdi], however, will adopt the policy of killing...and accept no one's repentance." (This claim of Muhammad's gentleness would come as a surprise to the Jews of the Banu Qurayzah, some 700 men of which were slaughtered by beheading at Muhammad's order.) Imam al-Sadiq also is said to have related that the Mahdi will be empowered and allowed to "kill deserters and the wounded." According to Imam al-Baqir the Mahdi will "not take anything but the sword or give...anything but the sword," starting with the tribe of Quraysh—meaning those recalcitrant Arab Sunnis. In another hadith al-Sadiq describes the future deliverer of Shi`ism as one who "wil behead anyone who would not accept the faith, or [at least] ask him to accept the jizyah" (the poll tax on *dhimmis*, or non-Muslim Jews and Christians). Imam al-Rida later added that the Mahdi either will order, or personally practice, amputating the hands of certain Arab tribes who oppose him "and hang them in the Ka`bah" (whether the hands or the mutilated persons is not explained clearly).  The Mahdi, according to yet another of the 12 Shi`i Imams, al-Kazim, will "rise up against the Jews, Christians…and the infidels of the east and west" and "behead anyone who refuses to become Muslim…." (And to think that, in the article I published a few years back on the Qur'anic and hadith roots of decapitation, I posited the issue as almost exclusively a Sunni one!) On the infamous Sunni hadith that on the Day of Resurrection the rocks will betray the Jews hiding behind them, the loquacious Imam al-Baqir glossed that said Jews will be followers of al-Dajjal [the "Deceiver," or Muslim Antichrist], who will of course be defeated by al-Mahdi and Jesus working together—whereupon the Mahdi will proceed to Kufa (Iraq), "unsheathe his sword and kill" more opponents, then make that city his capital. In addition, the returned 12th Imam will make a sortie over to Najaf and "from the noon of Monday until the night…draw his sword…and put them all to death"—such that "the flowing blood will be as high as the foreleg" [of a horse, presumably]." According to Imam al-Sadiq, most of these the Mahdi kills will be "infidels and hypocrites;" "so many," in fact, "that God would be pleased."

The Mahdi of the Shi`i hadiths sounds more like a pre-modern Terminator than the syrupy saint of sweetness and light adduced by Ahmadinejad at the U.N. Why is that? Either view can be correct, but both cannot be. It's hard to believe that Ahmadinejad simply misunderstands the clear words of the traditions of his branch of Islam; so either 1) he's re-interpreting, which may be allowed in Twelver Shi`ism by *mujtahid*s–but certainly is not permitted to a politician with a PhD in Traffic Control; 2) he's practicing *taqiyah*–allowable lying, in effect, for Shi`is. If it's the former, then Khameini has bigger problems than we had thought and Ahmadinejad is a true moderate on the order of a Persian Gorbachev. But if it's the latter–as is more likely for a pious Muslim like Iran's President–then that's yet another reason not to trust him as a geopolitical interlocutor.

What difference does it make, you may well ask–my good secular or Christian (or "other") reader–how Muslims like Ahmadinejad view their messianic figure? In one sense, perhaps very little–since I've argued in other publications the chance that someone might stake a valid claim to be the returned 12th Imam al-Mahdi is slim to nonexistent in modern Iran (unlike the situation in Sunni contexts, the history of which indicates "freelance" Mahdis have many times proclaimed themselves and, not occasionally, even gained power). But in another sense, this is an important issue, indicating as it does that the second-largest branch of Islam (Twelver Shi`ism) shares with the largest (Sunnism) a fervent belief in, not a victimized and suffering Christ-like Redeemer but, a global warlord who will not only humble his enemies but decapitate, dismember and destroy them–and this figure is venerated as worthy of emulation by millions!

May 10, 2011: Usama bin Ladin: The New Vanished Imam?

The original vanished Imam is, of course, Muhammad al-Mahdi, the 12th descendant of Islam's founder through the line of Ali, Muhammad's son-in-law—who will, according to Twelver Shi`is, sooner or later return to usher in a global Imamate. Heretofore the most famous *modern* vanished imam had been Musa al-Sadr, the influential Lebanese Shi`i cleric who "disappeared" on a trip to Libya in 1978–and who, according to some sources, was still alive, albeit imprisoned, well into al-Qadhafi's reign. (This fascinating story is detailed in Fouad Ajami's 1986 book *The Vanished Imam: Musa al-Sadr and the Shia of Lebanon.*) But now the world's most famous Sunni jihadist may himself be achieving vanished imam status. While normally a Twelver Shi`i doctrine, there **is** historical precedent for an occulted (Arabic *ghayb[i]*, "absent, hidden, concealed, invisible") leader in Sunnism: in 1821 an Indian Sunni *mujahid*, Sayyid Ahmad Barelwi, "disappeared" fighting against infidels (British Christians and Indian Sikhs) and his followers never admitted he was dead; rather, they chose to cling to the belief that Barelwi was about to return and lead their jihad against the unbelievers. This belief in a vanished, but undead, Sunni imam played no small part in inspiring a jihad that lasted for many years.

Now another event has reinforced my view that Ibn Ladin is being invested with the mantle of a vanished imam. During last Friday's prayers at al-Nur mosque in Cairo, Salafis and their ilk, led by Shaykh Hafiz Salamah, held a funeral service for Usama bin Ladin in which he was confirmed as a *shahid* ("Martyr") and wherein *salat al-gha'ib* were performed–literally "prayers for the absent"–but *gha'ib* also means "hidden, concealed, invisible, unseen" and is in fact a word derived from the same Arabic root as the aforementioned *ghayb*. Furthermore, this prayer service transmogrified into a pro-UBL-as-the-"Emir of

Jihad" pep rally, replete with cries of "Death to America" and, as the mob marched to the U.S. embassy to protest his "assassination," ones of "Bush [is a] terrorist." Well, at least the Egyptians are willing to give our former President some credit for taking out Ibn Ladin (unlike the American media or the Obama Administration).

Bottom-line: for eschatologically-minded Muslims–in this case, Sunni–Ibn Ladin may be merely dead, but *sans* a body there's no proof he's really, most sincerely dead. And, as such, he will continue to inspire jihadism and anti-Americanism and, very likely, attacks against Coptic Christians in Egypt and probably against Christians in other majority-Islamic nations. The angst at our killing of Ibn Ladin among too many Muslims, especially in a fairly Westernized and "moderate" Islamic nation like Egypt, demonstrates that his form of violent jihad was, and still is, far more popular in the Muslim street than most analysts are willing to admit.

April 6, 2011: Iran's New Mahdism Da'wah Video: Letting Slip the Jinns of Jihad.

Recently the Islamic Republic of Iran put out a video entitled "The Coming Is Upon Us," wherein current events and personalities are explicated in terms of their alleged relevance to the arrival of the Mahdi, the"rightly-guided one" in Islam who will make the entire world Muslim. In Sunni doctrine, the true Mahdi has not yet appeared on Earth (despite the proliferation of *mutamahdi*s, or "false mahdis," over the centuries, as I detailed in my first book *Holiest Wars*). For the Twelver Shi'i Muslims of Iran (as well as Iraq, Lebanon, Bahrain and Azerbaijan), on the other hand, the Mahdi has already been here, in the person of the twelfth male descendant of Islam's founder Muhammad. This final Imam, according to Twelver Shi'a the rightful leader of the entire ummah, is believed to have disappeared in the ninth century AD /third century AH–a belief which, from a rational historical perspective, would have developed in order to explain away his death and, with it, the extinction of the line of imams and of Twelver Shi`ism. In both Sunni and Twelver Shi`i thought the Mahdi will be assisted by the returned Islamic prophet Jesus in defeating the forces of evil led by *al-Dajjal*, the "Deceiver" (analogous, in some respects, to the Antichrist of Revelation), whereupon he will go on to establish a global caliphate or imamate. In both major sects of Islam there are views of the Mahdi as doing so peacefully; but there are also equally strong traditions that the Mahdi will usher in *malakut Allah*, the "kingdom of Allah," via bloody jihad against those who refuse to acknowledge the prophethood of Muhammad and supremacy of Allah. The jinn of Mahdism was released from its lamp after the Islamic Revolution of 1979, having been largely stoppered by the Pahlavi shahs; but it took the election of Mahmud Ahmadinejad, 2005, for the fervently Mahdist ayatollahs (and not all are) to begin a concerted effort aimed at getting Sunni Muslims (and, indeed, even Christians) to buy Mahdist lamps—or at least give them an exploratory rubbing and see what comes forth.

The 28-minute video opens with the usual suspects of Mahdist iconography: nature, fast-forwarded opening flowers, sunrises— presumably in order to emphasize the peaceful, renewing character of Islam's messiah figure. This bucolic imagery then transforms into shots of mosques, chanting crowds in Qom, the Ka`bah and the Arabic name al-Husayn in red script (Husayn, one of Muhammad's grandsons, is the chief Twelver "martyr," having been decapitated following an abortive coup against the ruling Sunni Umayyad dynasty in 680 AD). After that come ominous shots of Middle East maps, President Obama, Saddam, al-Qadhafi, Nasrallah. Following this apocalyptic stage-setting, the video segues into a pattern of citing specific Sunni and Shi`i eschatological hadith texts (which are extra-Qur'anic sayings allegedly going back to Muhammad and, for Shi`is, to the 12 Imams) then adducing events, individuals and/or situations that supposedly fulfill these utterances.

The first is the hadith about "a people [who] will rise from the East, preparing the way for the Mahdi." Brief videos of the Islamic Republic's founding fathers, ayatollahs Khomeini and Khameini, follow right after and merge seamlessly with an explication of the hadith about "the emergence of the Khurasani." Khurasan being an ancient Arabic term for eastern Iran/western Afghanistan, it's only logical in the Mahdist mindset to link this hadith with shots of Ahmadinejad (but images of Moqtada al-Sadr, head of southern Iraq's Jaysh al-Mahdi milita, are a bit perplexing). The fifth Imam, al-Baqir, is quoted to the effect that three major signs—"fear, great earthquakes and sedition"—will precede the Mahdi's arising. A Shi`i hadith that another sign presaging the Mahdi will be "the worst kind of humans becoming leaders" is adduced; this of course is followed by a most unflattering shot of George W. Bush, as well as ones of Ariel Sharon, Benjamin Netanyahu and Barack Obama. (So much, it seems, for the promise of President Obama restoring our image in the Islamic world.) Prurient pictures of bare-headed Muslimahs accompany the Alid hadith that "women will rid themselves of the hijab," while the Muhammadan one that "adultery will be common, men will dress like women, and men and women will consort each with their own sex" is illustrated with shots of gay and lesbian parades in—where else?—San Francisco.

Hammering home the theme of the "nation from the East" that will serve as John the Baptist to the Mahdi's Messiah, images of Khomeini are interspersed with ones of a man on a white horse, his head hidden inside a bright cloud of light—who will, presumably, do something about the slaughter of "1 million Muslims" by the West; the 10,000 nuclear weapons held by the Americans; the 1 billion in the world who are hungry; and the myriads of youth who "worship evil." Francis "Hokoyama" is shown, along with a quotation from his book

The End of History, stating that Islam is the only system that "threatens the modernized West." This, presumably, allowed America to rationalize its post-9/11 "war against Islam." It is suggested that the Americans invaded Iraq because they might have been "looking for certain individuals"—like the Mahdi; Iraq (Kufa), after all, will be the Mahdi's world capital.

Some Twelver Shi`i scholars believe that after the Mahdi's appearance, the first of his foot soldiers to arrive will be from Yemen; thus, the attacks by the Yemeni and Saudi governments on the Shi`is of Yemen (the Zaydis, who are Fiver Shi`is with whom the Twelvers of Iran had ancient ties) makes perfect sense in this light. As for Egypt, the fall of Mubarak and the rise of the Muslim Brotherhood there are perfectly in accord with unspecified hadith. Regarding Palestine, Imam Ali is quoted to the effect that "the Jews will come from the West while the Arabs are disunited." The video claims that "the current generation will witness the defeat of the murderous Zionist regime," the annihilation of which "is one of the most important events in the age of the Coming." The Saudis are equated to the Abbasids, the ruling dynasty in Baghdad from 750-1258 which stymied Twelver Shi`i aspirations to power. As for Iran itself, unspecified hadiths that speak of Iran "serving as preparer of the conditions for the coming of the last messiah" and of "a man from the city of Qom" being instrumental in this, are highlighted with shots of Khomeini.

The "man of Khurasan," or "Sayyid Khurasani," who will lead the people of the East before the coming of the Mahdi is said to be—of course—Ayatollah Khameini. Now while Khameini does ostensibly meet the hadiths of "disorder in his right hand" (partial paralysis thanks to a near-assassination) and an army to put at the Mahdi's service ("scores of warships, hundreds of bombers, thousands of missiles and millions of willing martyrs" under his command), his Azerbaijani origin makes it a

136

stretch to say that he is from Khurasan. The "Yamani" eschatological figure is said to be Hassan Nasrallah, head of Lebanon's Hizbullah Shi`i militia–because it is claimed that his ancestors came to Lebanon from Yemen. The Khurasani and the Yamani will" coordinate the revolt against evil"–and in case there was any doubt about the nature of this evil, a burning American flag accompanies this section.

As for the Dajjal, we are treated to a montage of Usama bin Ladin, al-Qadhafi, King Abdullah of Jordan, Israeli Prime Minister Netanyahu, President Obama and the King of Saudi Arabia–who are, it seems, "types" of the actual Iblistic (Satanic) figure who will oppose Jesus and the Mahdi. The Dajjal, of course, is linked to the Freemasons, who aspire to "a devilish government of the world centered in Jerusalem" and whose signs are the "devilish eye" (the reverse side of the Great Seal of the U.S., the famous "Novus Ordo Seclorum" with the eye on top of the pyramid) and the "six-pointed star" (of David). George Bush is shown making the sign of the devil–which Iranian propaganda film makers seem to have confused with the University of Texas "hook'em horns" hand sign. All these Freemasons and satanic Texans work for the Dajjal–who looks amazingly like the Witch King of *Lord of the Rings*.

Another positive eschatological figure who will set the geopolitical table for the returned Twelfth Imam is Shoaib bin Saleh, sourced from Shi`i hadith and rumored to be President Ahmadinejad of Iran. He will be appointed by the Khurasani, and will have as his final goal the conquest of Jerusalem just before the Mahdi returns. Many shots of Jamkaran Mosque (where it is believed by many Iranians that the Mahdi will rematerialize) and of Ahmadinejad drive home this point. The video ends with the co-narrators pleading for viewers to "come forth with the jihad of faith" because "we have the hope of seeing the beautiful face of the Last Imam in the very near future."

Very little here is new under the sun—at least to anyone who has been following Islamic Mahdism, and Iran, closely. As I wrote *in The Lutheran Witness* ("Dueling Messiahs: Jesus v. the Mahdi in Iran," February 2, 2009) following my trip to Tehran in 2008 for the annual Mahdism conference: "It was clear that the conference—and the sponsoring, government-funded Bright Future Institute—had a dual aim. On one level, it was an attempt to spread Mahdism among Sunni Muslims, to convince them it's acceptable to believe in the Mahdi....Shi`i Iran is hoping—to rival Sunni Saudi Arabia as the leading Islamic nation, and is trying—with some success—to use belief in the Mahdi as leverage to do so. But the ayatollahs who rule Iran are also trying to gain influence in the non-Muslim world by pushing Mahdism among Jews and particularly Christians, claiming that the messianic hopes of both religions will be fulfilled in the Twelfth Imam, the Mahdi." The Islamic Republic has also, since its inception in 1979, seen itself as the self-appointed leader of the planet's dispossessed over against the "arrogant powers" who exploit them—putting Iran at loggerheads with the not just the most arrogant power, the U.S., but the entire post-World War II international political, diplomatic and economic system which the U.S. vouchsafes. Since one of the Mahdi's major goals will be to institute a globally "just" economic order, it is incumbent upon the ayatollahs and their supporters to begin creating such an equitable Islamic state in microcosm in Iran—which is what Tehran and Qom believe they have been doing for a quarter-century.

While the overall tenor of this Mahdist propaganda video is unexceptional, three aspects of it do stand out. First, in its prognostication about the eschatological game plan and players, Iran's clerical regime seems to have Shi`ized the "newspaper exegesis" approach popularized in evangelical Christian circles by Hal Lindsey and Carole Carlson in their 1970 book *The Late Great Planet Earth*. (I say

"Shi`ized, not "Islamized," because there is a veritable legion of Sunni eschatological works published since 1967 that take their apocalyptic cues from evangelical Christianity–but this video is the first major effort by Iranian Twelver Shi`is to do likewise.)   Second, several major eschatological actors spelled out in the Sunni traditions–most notably al-Dabbah, "the Beast" and Yajuj wa-Majuj, "Gog and Magog"–are totally ignored, while another, al-Sufyani, is mentioned only in passing. Since the Shi`i writers and producers saw fit to adduce other Sunni hadiths when it suited their purpose, one can only surmise that they constituted rather inconvenient eschatological truths for Shi`i exegetes–presumably since convincing analogs for al-Dabbah, Yajuj and Majuj and al-Sufyani could not be found.   Finally, it is striking that this video claims"this current generation" will witness the defeat and annihilation of Israel, and that Ahmadinejad, channeling Shoaib bin Saleh, will "have as [his] final goal conquering Jerusalem and on the threshold of the Coming this holy place will be conquered by him and his forces." Again, this is nothing that has not been alleged by the Iranian leadership for some years, as I explained several months ago in "A Western View of Iran's WMD Goal: Nuclearizing the Eschaton or Pre-Stocking the Mahdi's Arsenal?" But in these allegations the Tehran-Qom axis does seem to have moved its role vis-à-vis the Mahdi from the passive to the active register. An eschatological alarm clock has even been set, one might argue, in the contention that Shoaib bin Saleh's authority starts seventy-two months before the Mahdi comes–and since Ahmadinejad was first elected President of Iran in August 2005, time should be up.

However, the fact that the timetable still runs constitutes clear evidence that Iran's apocalyptic hourglass will never totally run out of sand. While some ayatollahs would no doubt like to try and "liberate" Jerusalem, the collective clerical clique is far too intelligent and fond of its own skin to actually attack Israel directly with conventional weaponry, much less with nuclear weapons in an attempt to "hotwire the apocalypse." Israel-bashing is much more valuable to the clerical regime as a propaganda tool than as a true weapon. (Think the interrogation scene in *The Dark Knight*: the Joker tells Batman "I don't want to kill you—what would I do without you?) Most importantly, the Mahdi would not be very happy with his devotees if they were to present him, at his Coming Out party, a radioactive wasteland over which to rule—as even the most virulent anti-Israel ayatollah knows would be the inevitable outcome of any Iranian assault on al-Quds. This video, then, shows the Islamic regime certainly crying eschatological havoc—but a far cry from letting slip the jinns of war.

March 8, 2011: Ayatollah You So.

According to Iran's *Ahlul Bayt News Agency*, the Sunnis of Baluchistan are chomping at the bit just as much as Shi`is in waiting for the coming of the Mahdi [link is now dead]. In Chahbahar, Sistan-ve-Balochistan province's largest city, Sunni *alim* (cleric) Mowlavi Abdorrahman Mollazehi said that "Sunni folks believe in reappearance of Imam of the Time, like Shi`a folks, and his glorious reappearance is near at hand." Mollazehi also reportedly praised Tehran's *vilayet-i faqih* (clerical rule) system and blamed the Americans for trying to "foment discord" between Sunnis and Shi`is.

Observations:

1. At the risk of hubris, I will point out (again) that I have been warning for years of a) the strength of Mahdism within Sunnism—*contra* conventional (and scholarly) "wisdom" which maintains that only Shi`ism holds such a belief, and b) the convergence on this issue between Sunnis and Shi`is, driven in no small part by IRI propaganda.

2. Sistan and Balochistan (Baluchistan) province is in Iran's far southeast, bordering Pakistan and also Afghanistan. It's probably majority Sunni, with a large minority of Twelver Shi`i—but it also is home to significant minorities of Sevener Shi`is (Isma'ilis) and, most

interestingly, Zikris. Zikris (from the Arabic Sufi term for "prayer session," *dhikr*) are descendants of followers of Sayyid Muhammad Jawnpuri (d. 1505 AD), a Sunni Sufi (Chishtiyah order) of Gujarat who declared himself the Mahdi in 1495. His sect was at first violent, declaring jihad against the Muslim Gujarati sultans and repressed violently in return. "Then, with the failure of Jesus to appear in the Muslim year 1000 (1591 AD), the Mahdavi movement lost its conviction and fervor" (Furnish, *Holiest Wars*, p. 40) and transformed into a quietist sect–the Zikris. One might surmise that Zikri beliefs have had some influence on those of Sunnis in this region. One might also speculate that Zikri beliefs could undermine Twelver Shi`i expectations of the coming Mahdi, since according to the former he has already been here.

3. Sistan and Baluchistan contains an indigenous anti-IRI (Islamic Republic of Iran) organization, *Jundullah* ("Army of God"), which is equally Sunni and nationalist Baluch. (Tehran accuses the U.S. of supporting Jundullah.) It's possible that Mollazehi has been co-opted by Iran's clerical regime to serve as an anti-Jundullah mouthpiece–and that this accounts for much of his pro-Mahdist rhetoric.

February 17, 2011: The Mahdist Song Remains the Same.

Last Friday President Mahmud Ahmadinejad of Iran said that the anti-government uprisings in Tunisia and Egypt were being directed by the 12th Imam (whether still occulted or not, Ahmadinejad did not elaborate). "`This is a global revolution, managed by the imam of the ages,' he told the crowds gather in and around Tehran's central Azadi Square." Iran's President also "predicted the formation of a world government, ruled by the 12th Imam."

Imam Ali Mosque, Qom, Iran (from my trip there, 2008). Mahdist HQ for driving the "Arab Spring?"

For anyone who's been living in a well (other than the 12th Imam himself, that is), Iran's brand of Shi`i Islam is called "Twelver" precisely because it posits that there were 12 imams, or rightful leaders of the Islamic community, after Muhammad the Muslim prophet. The majority Sunni Muslims have always disagreed, however, and so none of those imams (except the first one, Ali) ever held real power. And in fact the 12th one, Muhammad al-Mahdi, died in the 9th century AD and so the sect developed the belief that he had, instead, gone into *ghaybah*, "occultation," whence he would return before the end of time to create a global Islamic state (imamate or caliphate), along with the help of his returned friend the "prophet Jesus." This belief is a staple of Twelver Shi`ism, and not some particularly cultish variation thereof (as Glenn

Beck and others claim). However, what is rather novel about Ahmadinejad's propaganda is his seeming belief that the 12th Imam has already returned, or is at the door. (Note, too, that WaPo's article title shows the mainstream media once again ignoring Ahmadinejad's Mahdism: "Ahmadinejad says Egypt, Tunisia were inspired by Iran's anti-Western protests." They should have written "Ahmadinejad claims long-dead Shi`i leader running the protests.")

January 13, 2011: "Nuclearizing the Eschaton, or Pre-Stocking the Mahdi's Arsenal?"

That's the title of my newly-published paper on the website of INEGMA (Institute for Near East and Gulf Military Analysis). This is the print version (somewhat revised) of the presentation I gave at the Hudson Institute in Washington, DC, last summer.

My thesis is that the Islamic Republic of Iran is NOT pursuing nuclear weapons in order to "hotwire the apocalpyse" and, via a nuclear attack on Israel, spark the return of the Twelfth Imam as the Mahdi; my research indicates that Twelver Shi`i theology does NOT support such a position (although there are Sunni apocalyptic groups that do hold to that view) and thus that Iran's WMD aspirations are more mundanely geopolitcal rather than eschatological.

September 6, 2010: Waiting is (Still) the Hardest Part– Especially If You're a Zionist.

According to Hujjatollah Mojtaba Zolnour, Ayatollah Khameinei's deputy representative to the IRGC (Iranian Revolutionary Guards Corps), "Zionists are waiting for the Hidden Imam to appear to kill him" (Radio Free Europe's "Persian Letters," September 1, 2010). Zolnour alleges that those wily, perfidious Zionists have assassins staking out the likes of Mecca and Karbala, ready to send the 12th Imam (back?) to the domain of the 72 huris. Of course, according to the fevered Mahdist imaginations of the Zolnours in Tehran and Qom,

Israelis are part of the occupying forces in Iraq—hence their ability to case Karbala.

This paranoid fear for the life of Islam's major messianic figure is strange indeed. First, we have heard this before: earlier this year President Ahmadinejad claimed that the U.S. was "hindering the Mahdi's return;" and Moqtada al-Sadr (he of southern Iraq's Shi`i *Jaysh al-Mahdi*, "Army of the Mahdi"), said the same thing in 2006 [link now dead]. Second, who is the intended audience for this claptrap—the Basij (the IRGC's domestic, paramilitary auxiliary)? the rural *hoi polloi*? Iraqi Shi`is? the non-existent Palestinian Shi`i demographic? And third, do not clerics like Zolnour who utter such unadulerated silliness realize just how impotent and vulnerable it makes their expected deliverer appear? Imagine Christian televangelist John Hagee or, much more seriously, Pope Benedict XVI claiming that the returned Jesus Christ could be hindered, much less killed, by, say, Marxist or "Zionist" hit teams. Yet for some reason influential Twelver Shi`i spokesmen (Zolnour, Ahmadinejad and al-Sadr) continue this refrain of the coming Mahdi's vulnerability to profane powers and their weaponry.

It's almost enough to make one wonder whether these men might be laying the propaganda ground for the attempted assumption of the Mahdi's title by someone, and his inevitable subsequent demise at the hands of Americans, Sunnis or "unbelieving" Shi`is—er, I mean, "Zionists!" Which would, of course, give the Islamic Republic of Iran an excuse to....well, fill in the blank. But a live-fire test of a nuclear weapon certainly comes to mind.

August 8, 2010: Working On Mahdi Time.

According to the Kurdish news outlet *Rudaw*, Mir Hossein Mousavi—the leader of Iran's opposition "Green Movement"—is accusing President Ahmadinejad's administration of "suspending government projects" pending the arrival of the 12th Imam, the Mahdi. "Some people believe Mahdi will come in the next six months or next year. That is why the government has stopped working on several industrial, as well as water and energy projects," Mousavi ridiculed. "They paralyze the economy on the pretext of Mahdi's coming." Mousavi also claimed that such "superstitious beliefs were growing within the ruling elite" and that "his supporters had increased into the military circles [sic] including high ranking officials of Iran's Revolutionary Guard Corps."

Observations:

1. It has become commonplace to accuse "hardline" elements within the Islamic Republic government of such eschatological inanity— but it would be nice to have some proof thereof. Mousavi may simply be trying to curry favor with secular allies, within and outside Iran, over against the admittedly-apocalpytic-minded Ahmadinejad.

2. Ditto for the charge that Mahdist expectations are running rampant in other sectors of the regime. How about a fatwa, article, sermon text or even purloined email to back up such a charge? Preferably something on Mesbah-Yazdi's personal stationery.

3. Which sector of the "ruling elite" is most prone to this alleged Mahdist hysteria? Ahmadinejad's populist clique? The "hardline," "reformist," or irredentist ayatollahs? The Hujjatiyeh organization? After all, remember, accusing Shi`is of belief in the Mahdi's return is like accusing Christians of belief in Jesus' return–it may alarm secularists, but it's not exactly abnormal.

4. Due to imprecision on the part of either the *Rudaw* reporter or Mousavi himself, it's unclear whether "his supporters" refers to those of Mousavi, Ahmadinejad or the Mahdi himself. It seems to refer to Mousavi, in which case Tehran is no doubt nervous that opposition to Ahmadinejad, and thus perhaps also to Supreme Leader Khameini, would be on the rise within the vilayet-i faqih's Praetorian Guard.

5. Somehow I doubt that the Iranian nuclear weapons, er, peaceful power industry has seen much of a slowdown....

Image created by yours truly using Paint.

August 1, 2010: Magical Mahdist Tour.

According to a story last week by one of the Islamic Republic of Iran's news agencies, celebrations of the 12th Imam's birthday have now spread to Liverpool, England. Such festivities honoring the occulted Muhammad al-Mahdi's birthday, and not his death, remind true believers that he's only sleeping and that it won't be long until his return, which could happen any time at all. However, since the last imam disappeared over a millennium ago, telling his follower that "you won't see me" until you come together and get back to the pure faith and community of the early Muslim umma, he's been something of a nowhere man, and queries directed at him usually get no reply at all (except perhaps when made by Ahmadinejad). When the Mahdi does come, he will lead an Islamic revolution, getting rid of the Western global taxman. Until then, Twelver Shi`is will just have to let it be. Insha'allah, he won't come in through the Jamkaran bathroom window, which while not long might constitute somewhat of a winding road to reappearance. Remember, all things must pass–including, thankfully for the reader, this post (although I could go on, and on....).

Thursday, July 29, 2010:   Blue Mahdist Cult.

This past week PBS' *Frontline* ran a dispatch by Babak Sarfaraz, "The Hidden Imam and His Cult," which while showing flashes of astute analysis also makes a number of questionable statements about Mahdism in Iran. For example, Sarfaraz claims that "the cult of Mahdi...had never become a full-fledged mass movement until the last 20 years." He also refers to the "ultra reactionary millennialist Hojjatieh [sic] Society." Twelver Shi`ism–with its core belief in the occultation of the 12th Imam who will return as the eschatological Mahdi–has been the majority religion of Iran since the early 1500s, and mass movements motivated by a perceived imminent Mahdist arrival have occurred many times in the last 500 years (most notably during the reign of the Safavids, in the early 16th century; and during the outbreak of the Babi/Baha'i movement, during the late 19th century). Working for *Frontline* (and being, presumably, Iranian) does not absolve one from knowing the history of the faith and region upon which one is reporting. As for the Hojjatiyeh: that organization, if it still even exists in Iran, is neither "ultra reactionary" (a term that should be banned from liberal outlets like PBS for overuse) nor any more millennialist than Twelver Shi`ism in general. *Anjuman-i Hujjatiyah* was founded in the 1950s to reconvert wayward Baha'is to Shi`i Islam, and was dissolved by Ayatollah Khomeini in 1983 because of insufficient support for the *vilayet-i faqih* ("rule of the jurisprudents"). The organization is, if anything, **less** millennialist than mainstream Twelver Shi`ism (as I explained in a lecture at the Hudson Institute in June 2010).

Most interesting are two allegations by Sarfaraz. The first is that "by 2008, the newspapers were replete with reports of self-procalimed "Mahdis" announcing their reappearance and offering various prophesies or end-of-the-world scenarios. Every week, someone claimed to be the Mahdi or to be in special communion with him." And the second is this: "What finally convinced Khamenei that the Mahdaviat movement had gone far enough was last year's presidential election and its aftermath. For instead of aligning closer to the Supreme Leader, the ungrateful and ambitious president has decided to become a major rival to his erstwhile benefactor." It would be nice to see some corroboration for the claims of multiple *mutamahdi*s ("false mahdis"), but I suspected, after going to Iran in 2008, that such might be the case. As for the alleged Ahmadinejad-Khamenei rivalry: Western caricatures aside, it's very likely that the President of Iran is actually more popular in his own country now than the Supreme Leader, and has been since last summer's post-election disputes. Ahmadinejad's blue-collar Islam, his own personal charisma (especially among the lower classes and in rural areas) and his Iran-Iraq War veteran status may put in in a pivotal position should the Iranian military decide to assume power from the ayatollahs.

September 2, 2008: The Importance of Being Mahdist.

My article on the political aspects of the Mahdism Conference in Iran (which I attended last month) has been published by *The Weekly Standard* in the September 8, 2008 issue, under the title "The Importance of Being Mahdist."

August 25, 2008: Persian Letters.

August 10-17 I went to Iran for the Fourth Annual International Conference on Mahdism. It was an all-expenses-paid trip courtesy of the Bright Future Institute, a quasi-governmental organization dedicated to paving the way for the reappearance of the Twelfth Imam as the Mahdi. Traveling to Iran is not something one should attempt solo. I've been to other Middle Eastern countries on my own but I would never have gone to Iran without official sanction from the IRI government. And even then I barely made it, as my visa did not arrive until just four days before my Air France flight–Atlanta to Paris, Paris to Tehran–departed.

As the pilot announced the descent into Imam Khomeini International airport, many of the Iranians on the flight downed their last Heineken or glass of wine and the women began reaching into their bags for chadors. At the end of the walkway, prior to customs, I was met by Dr. Ali Haddad of the Bright Future Institute, as well as officials from the Foreign Ministry and airport security. Along with another American, Evan Anderson (a representative of the National Cathedral in Washington, D.C., who works for the Episcopal Bishop there in interfaith dialogue), I was escorted to the VIP lounge and provided tea while the bureaucrats took off with passports and documents. Eventually Mr. Anderson and I were led off to be fingerprinted, something reserved for Americans and for which the BFI folks were most apologetic. It was explained to us that this was "just politics" and Iranian retaliation for American policy regarding Iranians entering the U.S. I refrained from asking our hosts if they had ever heard of 9/11. Rode with Ali Haddad and a driver to the Hotel Laleh in Tehran, about an hour drive (the new and impressive Imam Khomeini airport is between Tehran to its north and Qom to its south, actually closer to the former; I was told that it is reserved for international flights only, no domestic ones at all). On the drive I asked Ali if Iranians preferred Barack Husayn Obama over John McCain; he said "most Iranians who follow U.S. politics do not think it will make any difference".

Hotel Laleh is a five-star establishment in Iran, built under the Shah and finished in the early 1970s. It was nice enough, most importantly having a WESTERN-style toilet and perhaps a dozen TV channels (although air conditioning in that hotel, at least, meant air slightly cooler than that outside–and Tehran was around 90 during the day when I was there). Most channels were in Farsi, and my two years of that language in grad school didn't really prepare me for following the programs (although many of them consisted of imams and Qur'anic verses). I did watch some of the Arabic channel al-Jazeera, however. And Iran's Press TV is in English. BBC and CNN came in for perhaps an hour in the early mornings before, I presume, the government censors woke up and turned on the scrambler equipment. Regarding IRI TV: Press TV was better than I had expected but is still tendentious as hell; for example, there were a number of stories on Ethiopian Christian "atrocities" against Somali "freedom fighters" involving "gunning down busloads of old women and children" with "American support." And the lead-ins to every segment of the show consists of shots of Israeli planes, Israeli troops firing, American soldiers knocking down doors, and Arabs and Muslims being taken off in ambulances and/or weeping. If that was my only source of news, I'd be anti-American and anti-Israeli, too. Maybe Pew, Zogby and other pollsters might want to figure out a way to factor that into their next report on how much Bush has caused us to be hated in the rest of the world?! But you have to love a weatherwoman in a chador!

After recovering on Monday, I ventured out on Tuesday to the Tehran bazaar and the Gholestan Palace, formerly the seat of the Qajar Dynasty (ruled Iran late 18th-early 20th century). Americans were only allowed out of the hotel with a translator/minder; in my case it was Laleh, a wonderful woman who had graduated university with a degree in English translation and had been hired by BFI just for this conference.

The Tehran bazaar was quite disappointing, perhaps because my frame of reference was the Istanbul bazaar–but of course Tehran loses in every respect when compared to Istanbul: no water ways nearby, hotter, drabber, more repressive. And the Qajar palace complex was run-down and in woeful need of repairs (again, contrast this with the well-kept and -preserved Ottoman Topkapi Palace in Istanbul). Is it that the Iranians don't care about this site—because of ideology and/or lack of tourism—or because they don't have the funds to keep it up and run all those centrifuges as well? Interesting conversation: I asked Laleh if she'd ever been to Iraq, and she said "yes," she'd been on a pilgrimage to Najaf and Karbalah with her family a few years ago. I refrained from pointing out that if Saddam were still in power that would never have happened. Cultural note: Iran seems to be living through an extended episdoe of "That 70s Show"—and I'm not just talking about Internet connection time or President Ahmadinejad's sartorial style. Men in Iran wear designer jeans, too-tight shirts and have more hair—both head and facial—than I used to see at Boston concerts. Of course, contrast that with the women in chadors—and you can wear any color you'd like, as long as it's black—with only their faces and hands uncovered.

One of the nice BFI folks mentioned to me, Wednesday morning that he did not know Sunni Muslims also believed in the Mahdi! This was in the context of discussing my paper, "Through a Glass Darkly: A Comparison of Previous Mahdist Movements and States to the Future Eschatological Mahdiyah." This led to a conversation with another individual from the Institute about Qur'anic and Biblical exegesis, in which at one point I said "that's not what the Salafis say." I was told "I am talking about true Islam." (Contrast this with what I was told by an Egyptian Sunni whom I met on the flight from Atlanta to Paris; after informing him where I was going and why, he sniffed "Shi`is? They are not real Muslims!")

Post-lunch on Wednesday I had a taped interview with the BFI folks. The hojjatollah sitting in was quite nice (although he spoke no English) and looked amazingly like my friend Reverend Joe Perez (although I'm sure he's not as good a basketball player). At one point I thought I'd stepped in it, when asked "what do you say to those people who say Islam is a violent religion?" I mentioned that all three monotheistic religions have violent histories BUT I did point out that Jesus never led armies in battle or ruled a state, both of which Muhammad did, and that it was crucial for folks like the BFIers to disabuse those Muslims who support violence of their tendency to try to emulate the Prophet's 7th century practices in this regard. I was later interviewed by Press TV along the same lines and gave much the same answers. And yet I made it back!

Also, on Wednesday evening the same fellow who served as translator during my BFI interview was talking with me and I asked him my stock "Jaywalking" question: what do Iranians think of Barack Husayn Obama? He said "he cannot win, because America is so racist." Wondering if he'd been in contact with the DNC, I asked him how he knew this? "Because of American movies, like 'American History X.'". There you have it, folks–proof positive BHO cannot win. Guess they're not allowed to see "Glory, "The Oprah Winfrey Show" or the NBA in Iran.

Finally, on Thursday, the conference kicked off at the Hall of Leaders in north Tehran, a short-range missile distance from the Elborz Mountains.

On the way to this opening session I met Scott Peterson, *Christian Science Monitor* correspondent based in Istanbul who's been to Iran numerous times and written on Mahdism, Jamkaran, etc. The hall was quite nice, with a domed, almost conical ceiling that let in some light and housing two large TV screens–ayatollahtrons?. Two large seals flanking the screen said "Muhammad" and "Allah,"from left to right. Pix of Khomeini and Khameini (of course) are in the center of the dais area. The inside tables for attendees have microphones and set-ups for simultaneous translation, since the conference's official languages were Farsi, Arabic and English (take that, France!). After the IRI national anthem there was prayer and Qur'an recitation (just what is a Christian supposed to do during those?) and finally the parade of opening ceremony speakers began. Grand Ayatollah Makarem Shirazi praised the BFI for "paving the ground for the reappearance of the Mahdi" through nine publications in 30 languages and for having Ph.D.-granting status now. Ayatollah Khoshani–who was not on the program, but got to speak anyway (this sort of thing happened throughout the conference)– wished us all a "Happy Imam Mahdi's Birthday" (it would be on August 17, three days hence) and mentioned speaking with Cardinal Ratzinger before he became Pope Benedict XVI about the future return of Jesus. But his ecumenical side dissipated when he finished his talk with "May God grant us freedom from torture and oppression at the hands of the Zionists, the White House and the British in Lebanon, Palestine and Iraq. We hope this time next year we'll witness the return of Imam Mahdi."

President Ahmadinejad–who had been sitting perhaps 30 feet to my left–then, spoke, after being honored for the publication of his new book. His devotion to Mahdism being well-known, as one can imagine he hit all the familiar tropes in his speech. After mentioning that globalization "is not just happening, it is Allah's plan" Ahmadinejad–of course–recited a litany of Western-imposed global horrors that will not be rectified until the Mahdi reappears: Palestine, Iraq, Afghanistan, Africa, and Chinese cheating at the Olympics. Ok, I'm kidding about the last one. He really meant American cheating. The A-man wears platform shoes to get him up to that 5'7" fighting size, but he does have charisma: he was mobbed by clerics and non-clerics alike, both entering and leaving the building.

Break for coffee, tea and snacks. Iranians are fond of cake with pistachios piled on top, but their coffee is a bastard variant of Nescafe and while their tea is top-notch trying to get any drinks or snacks makes one liable to losing a digit, if not an entire arm. I thought I was back at a grad student soiree in the States.

The second half of the Mahdism Conference opening session gave me a sense of *déjà vu* all over again. Dr. Hamid Mowlana gave us a list of 10 aspects of "strategic Mahdism," which included the creation of "an axis of justice-seekers" (take that, President Bush!); rejection of all Western ideologies, in particular the "end of history" (this rejection of Fukuyama's came up over and over again in the conference—wonder if they've heard of Robert Kagan?); of course, the expectation of the Mahdi's return. And that latter belief should be disseminated outside Iran via schools and universities, the media and the diplomacy of the IRI! After a concluding speech by Ayatollah Sohrabi, which either didn't make much sense or found me wishing I'd had some Nescafe straight-up, we finally broke for lunch (back at the hotel).

Finally, at 3:30 PM Thursday, August 14, the conference panels kicked off. The schedule included two simultaneous panels in two different halls, 16 in each over two days, for a total of 32 paper presentations. As Dr. Ismail Poonawala of UCLA said to me "this conference is not academically rigorous at all, because no critical papers are allowed." Indeed. The conference was more pro-Mahdist propaganda than anything else, and in fact a number of the clerics who presented "papers" might just as well have been delivering a Friday *khutba* in the mosque. Favorites topics included globalization, messianism in other religions (mostly Christianity, but there was a bit on Jewish messianism and even one paper on Buddhist millenarianism) and preparing for the Mahdi's return. It was at times surreal, as statements of comity with Christians regarding Jesus were interspersed with erudite discussions about whether the Returned Mahdi would convert Christians and Jews, or simply kill us all. And there was the irritating tendency of the clerical panel moderators to let non-scheduled speakers filibuster, taking time away from those of us actually on the program. But while I did put a lot of effort into my paper–26 pages on previous Mahdist movements and states (the Muwahhids, the Fatimids, the Sudanese Mahdists and the failed Saudi Mahdism of al-Utaybi) and how they must be seen as "types" of the future Mahdiyah–it was really just a rationale for going to Iran.

The closing ceremony of the conference featured a speech by Ali Larijani, former IRI nuclear negotiator and current Speaker of the Majlis (Parliament). I have dealt with that speech in a piece scheduled to run in *The Weekly Standard* soon, but suffice it to say that rumors of the ideological split between Larijani and Ahmadinejad are greatly exaggerated. I was one of four foreign conference presenters "honored" by being asked to come sit on the dais behind Larijani during his address. If pictures of that should surface, please do not consider my seating location to be, in any wise, an endorsement of the statements and political positions of Ali Larijani or the IRI!

On Saturday, August 16 conference participants were taken to Qom, a several-hour bus ride south of Tehran. I was told Qom's population was 2 million (compared to Tehran's 13+ million). The first place we visited was the (in)famous Jamkaran Mosque, believed by many Shi`is to be built on the site of a brief rematerialization by the Mahdi centuries ago.

**Twelver Shi`i men praying and weeping for the return of Imam al-Mahdi.
Jamkaran mosque interior—from my trip there, 2008.**

One of the BFI chaps actually was arrested by IRI security, because he had obtained permission for us to take pictures, a privilege which one of the mosque tenders then tried to revoke. And I was given, as a gift, a prayer stone made of clay from Karbala (site of Imam Husayn's martyrdom, according to Shi`is, in 680 CE). This picture is from the right wing of the mosque, the left being for women and the center being the main prayer area where we were forbidden from taking pictures. Amazingly, I totally forgot to go to the well in the back of the mosque where one can allegedly drop prayer requests to the Mahdi.

I was asked by the Press TV team if Khomeini was popular in America. I winked broadly at them and said "Oh, yes, VERY popular." They cracked up, knowing exactly what I meant.

I departed Iran at 0200 on the Mahdi's birthday (Aug. 17), having left the U.S. on my own birthday. For some reason he got more press, although the home-made cards from my sons trump that, if you ask me. Besides a case of "ayatollah's revenge," I took away from Iran a number of important observations, which I will be writing up and, hopefully, publishing over the next few weeks.

January 2, 2007: Springtime for the Mahdi?

On Christmas Day *IRIB*, the English-language radio voice of the Islamic Republic of Iran, posted a long, rambling–but revealing–transcript of a program entitled "The World toward Illumination." There are a number of installments in this series of broadcasts aimed at predicting when the Mahdi/Hidden Imam will come: number 1, number 2, and number 4–but curiously, no number 3.

Several Western websites and blogs have been claiming that this document predicts the Mahdi will come in the spring of 2007–but this is untrue. What it actually says is the spring equinox is but one of the possible dates for his appearance, along with a Friday, or the 10th of Muharram, or the 25th of Zhu al-Qa`dah. No year is specified, however. Furthermore, the author(s) also take care to point out that "only God knows about the exact timing of the reappearance of Imam Mahdi..." Eschatologists (almost) always hedge their bets.

The rest of "The World toward Illumination" is an eclectic mix of mainstream Islamic escahtological thinking, typically Middle Eastern conspiracy theorizing and specifically Iranian pseudo-philosophical cultural critique of the West. The Mahdi needs to come because of "the unjust world order imposed by the so-called big powers." But the Mahdi will not only serve as a global Muslim Robin Hood, taking from the rich and giving to the poor; he will also usher in "astounding growth of science and technology.... The Mahdi will correct man's scientific mistakes and bring up new and astonishing methods that had never occurred to man before." He will also unite humanity—under the banner of Islam, of course—and create a "justice-spreading universal government...." And while "expansionists [neocons?] may be averse to such concepts," they will fail to stop him.

"After his uprising from Mecca all of Arabia will be submit [sic] to him and then other parts of the world as he marches upon Iraq and established [sic] his seat of global government in the city of Kufa. Then the Imam [Mahdi] will send 10 thousand of his forces to the east and the west to uproot the oppressors." This is interesting, both because it does not posit the Mahdi emerging from Iran but from Arabia—thus dovetailing with Sunni beliefs about the Mahdi—and it predicts that Kufa, in southern Iraq, will be the seat of the Mahdiyah. I wonder if [former Bush I Secretary of State] Jim Baker and [former House Foreign Affairs Chair] Lee Hamilton will have to reconvene their study group and recommend we negotiate with the Mahdi?

The Mahdi's personal appearance is described, drawing on the usual hadiths (traditions): "radiant forehead, black piercing eyes and a broad chest," as well as "exuding the fragrance of paradise." He "will appear all of a sudden on the world scene with a voice from the skies announcing his reappearance at the holy Ka`ba in Mecca. The cloak and other special belongings of Prophet Muhammad...will be with him." (No explanation given as to how Muhammad's cloak, currently under lock and key in the old Ottoman sultan's palace in Istanbul, will make its way to Sa`udi Arabia.) The Mahdi will shortly thereafter move to Medina, where he will gather an army and defeat "Sofyani" (al-Sufyani), the traditional opponent of the Mahdi (likely modeled on an enemy of Muhammad in the 7th c. CE), who will have invaded from Syria and besieged Kufa. Sofyani will "commit great crimes against humanity in

Iraq, slaughtering people who bear the names of the infallible Imams [that is, Shi`is]. But a "venerable, God-fearing individual from Iran...fights oppression and corruption and enters Iraq to lift the siege of Kufa and holy Najaf and to defeat...Sofyani.... He then pledges allegiance to Imam Mahdi." Then Jesus descends from heaven [remember, in Islam he never died on the cross but was taken to heaven] and serves as the Mahdi's "lieutenant." "The seat of the Mahdi's global government will be the city of Kufa, where his headquarters will be the Sahla Mosque....From here he will dominate the east and the west to fill the earth with justice."

If the Mahdi has not yet come "it is not because the world is not full of oppression, but because the time must come for the people to be wise enough....Pure and sincere people must be trained in order to help...in his implementation of global justice." (This process is already underway, with groups like the Imam Mahdi Scouts being trained as Mahdist cadres by Hizbullah in Lebanon.)

The rest of the document departs from this standard eschatological prognostication into paranoid, indeed bizarre, claims of the American media's support for Christian Zionism; for example, did you know that "more than 1500 TV networks, 80 000 priests [ministers that is], 200 scientific institutes and colleges as well as Hollywood" are working for and with the right-wing Christian agenda? Basic elements of Christian eschatology are misrepresented, such as the claim that "the Christian Zionist sect believes....that Christ will appear and will take the followers of this religion to heaven on a spaceship." Iranian eschatologists obviously are confusing Baptists with Heaven's Gaters. In a truly paradigmatic example of the pot calling the kettle black, this document claims that "one of the characteristics of the West in the current era is obsession with the end of time." That might have been true about 7 years ago—but today? And of course, all this ultimately goes back to the nefarious Jews and Zionists, to whom even Hollywood is in thrall. Did you know that *The Ten Commandments* and *Ben Hur* were made, and awarded Oscars, by "the illegal Zionist entity...in order to cover up its legitimacy crisis...."? Neither did I, having always thought they were part of a brilliant plot to pump up Charlton Heston's career before he began consorting with primates.

There is more here, much of it reconfiguring of Fukuyama, Huntington, Marx, and others, in order to show both the (alleged) vacuity of their ideas and how these ideas were used to forestall the victory of Islam.

Lone Wolf and Wolf Pack Mahdism

July 23, 2013: Make a New Mahdist Plan, 'stan!

Nine members of Kyrgyzstan's *Jaysh al-Mahdi*, "Army of the Mahdi," were given long prison sentences for attacks in Bishkek two years ago. The Radio Free Europe/Radio Liberty story adds that, in the 2011 firefight with state security, JAM's "leader was killed." One wishes that the Kyrgyz authorities had taken him alive, or at least squeezed more information out of his followers who were (although, to be sure, perhaps state security has more info but is simply withholding it from the press). The rare analyst who actually touches on this movement chalks it up to "universalistic jihadism" and makes no mention whatsoever of the overt Mahdism element. That's unfortunate, because Mahdist movements are qualitatively different from jihadist ones, although the two do share many aspects. Much more research needs to be done on JAM in Central Asia, and any connections it might have to Twelver Shi`i state or non-state actors, as well as to Sufi *tariqat*.

December 23, 2013: Mahdi Is Just All Wrong For Thee.

Just in time for the Christmas season comes this heart-warming tale from the Bangaladesh's *Dhaka Tribune*: "A self-proclaimed pir (religious preacher), who claimed himself to be Imam Mahdi, his son and four disciples were slaughtered in a house…last evening." Lutfor Rahman "had long been claiming…to be Imam Mahdi as well as the last Nobi [sic] (Prophet) and his residence [had come] under attack several times by extreme Islamists" from organizations like Shahshantantra Andolan, Khelafat Andolan, Khelafat Majlish and Islami Oikya Parishad. A local high-ranking police official, ironically named Mehedi [Mahdi] Hasan, said that Rahman had been arrested at least three times by police, and jailed once, in recent years for his Mahdist claims and for "hurting

religious sentiments."   Rahman was also said to have disseminating
leaflets stating that he was the Mahdi.   His recompense for this: being
tied up, mouth taped, and killed by fellow Muslims in an unspecified
manner (although I'd wager blades were involved).

Observations:

1.   While I often write on the dangers that Mahdism presents to
others—especially in macro terms, as evidenced by numerous examples
of such movements from Islamic history—this is the micro, flip-side
thereof: claiming to be the Mahdi can be hazardous to one's health.
(For two prominent 20th century examples of unsuccessful Mahdism
being a death warrant, take a look at the case of the failed Turkish Mahdi
of 1930 and, more famously, the Mahdist revolution manque in 1979
Saudi Arabia, both detailed in my first book *Holiest Wars*.)

2.   *Pir* is a Persian term for a Sufi shaykh.   I don't know Bengali, so
perhaps the term in Bangladeshi Islam has lost its mystical connotation
and simply means—as the article translates—"religious preacher."   But I
suspect Sufism is involved here, knowing that historically the Islamic
mystical orders are the primary ground whence Mahdism sprouts.

3.   The primary opposition to Lutfor Rahman's self-styled Mahdist
da`wah ("summons") came from political Islamic groups, notably ones
interested in resurrecting the caliphate ("Khelafat").   These were almost
certainly fundamentalist Sunni, as Bangladesh's 150 million population is
89% Muslim, and of that the vast majority (95% or so) is Sunni.   It's
possible that Rahman was part of the small minority of Shi`a; but, on the
contrary, he may have been Sunni—since Sunni Mahdism is quite
prevalent in Islamic history.

4.   Once again, a major news organ in a predominantly-Muslim
country demonstrates ignorance of basic Islamic doctrines and history,
in stating that belief in the Mahdi is the province of "a sect of Muslims."
No, such belief is mainstream across space and time in the Islamic

world–although articulation thereof is, obviously, fraught with danger in modern Islam.

5. Contrast the violent retribution meted out to Mahdist pretenders with that directed at false Christs in the Christian world. Men like Alan John Miller (an Australian claiming to be Jesus) and Apollo Quiboloy (a Filipino Jesus claimant), far from being eradicated, can build up movements and, presumably, make a comfortable living via messianic pretensions–whereas Mahdist poseurs are little tolerated in the ummah. The two major reasons for this, of course are that: Islamic political thought still does not draw a line between the religious and the political– so a claim in the former realm threatens the latter order; and Islamic societies are simply far less tolerant than Christian ones, whether the issue is messianism, atheism or homosexuality.

November 28, 2012: Awaited Mahdis and Mad Hatters.

With the hajj over for this year, Saudi officials by mid-November were no doubt still heaving sighs of relief that Iranian agents had not managed to stir up trouble in 2012. Then, another pesky *mutamahdi* (false mahdi) reared his mystical head, "muttering 'I'm the Expected Mahdi' while dressed in ihram and circumambulating the Ka`aba....Brig. [General] Yahiya Massad al-Zahrani, Commander of the Grand Mosque Security Forces, said the man, thought to be a psychistric patient, would be referred to the mental health hospital in Makkah [Mecca]....The man is described as a tall black male adult in his 40s." In 2011 there were at least half-a-dozen such incidents in the staunchly-Wahhabi Kingdom of Saudi Arabia–one of which is attested in an online recording wherein, between 1:57 and 2:00, you can hear a man shouting (probably into the mike on the minbar, or "pulpit") "Ana al-Mahdi! Ana al-Mahdi al-Muntazar!" ("I am the Mahdi! I am the Awaited Mahdi!" "Goo goo g'joob." OK, my translation is a bit liberal, I confess.) No doubt he, too, was hustled away to have his sanity examined (quite possibly via full lobotomy).

But at least the Saudi self-styled Mahdis are (so far) peaceful. Over across the Maghrib, in Morocco, members of a group called *Ansar al-Mahdi* ("Helpers" or "Partisans of the Mahdi") have once again been "thwarted [in] an attempt...to carry out attacks on strategic sites in the kingdom;" furthermore, "members of the cell are suspected of trying to contact with [sic] members of the Al-Qaeda international terrorist network in northern Africa." Northwest and West Africa is rapidly becoming a jihadist and Salafist nexus, home to AQIM (al-Qaʻidah in the Islamic Maghrib) in Mali, Mauritania and Algeria; *Boko Haram* in Nigeria; *Ansar al-Shariʻah* (responsible for killing our Benghazi consulate staff) in Libya. And Sufism, Islamic mysticism, is quite prevalent in the region as well—one major reason that western African and the Maghrib have seen plenty of Mahdist movements over the centuries (most notably that of Ibn Tumart's *al-Muwahhidun*, or "Almohads," a millennium ago). Currently the jihadists/Salafis and Sufis are at each other's throats—particularly in Mali and Libya. But Sufism has also been the primary ground for most Sunni Mahdist movements in history, and it is very possible that it could be, once again.

Note, too, that eschatological rhetoric and imagery is increasingly transnational and mainstream in Sunni Islam—not limited to (alleged) mental cases or to the heterodox fringes of the Islamic world. Charges that Western (Christian) civilization in general and the U.S. in particular are under the thumb of Iblis (Islam's satanic majesty) or his henchman, the Dajjal, are being disseminated by Malaysian thinkers from Pakistani sites. All of this is yet more evidence that Mahdism continues to roil the Islamic world—and may yet prove a strategic threat to extant regimes, and perhaps even, eventually, to the U.S.

April 24, 2012:   A Plague of Mahdis.

While the news headlines in recent months, as far as the Islamic world is concerned, have been dominated by the likes of the rise of the Muslim Brotherhood in Egypt, Iran's nuclear program and the civil war in Syria, the *long durée* of Mahdism continues to simmer just under the surface, sometimes bubbling up into the more mundane world of *histoire événementielle*. **Cases in point**:

1. The Mahdi is running for the Presidency of Egypt–or so one Muhammad Muhammad Musa maintains about himself. Even a self-deluded, messianic candidate might gain some electoral traction when he runs on a platform of claiming that his predecessor (Mubarak), Bashar al-Asad and the now-room-temperature al-Qadhafi are all "minions of the Deceiving Dajjal" [Muslim "AntiChrist"], however. (Special thanks to my friend Ray Ibrahim for first alerting me to this story!)

2.   Last month nine members of *Ansar al-Mahdi* in Spain, er, occupied al-Andalus, went on trial for planning jihad to spark the de-Reconquista of the Iberian Peninsula in the name of Islam. These members of the "religion of peace" believe that "any land that was once owned by Muslims shall always and forever be Muslim." Substitute "owned" with "conquered," "was once trod upon" or even, really, "touched" and you have the perfect recipe for unceasing war by Muslims against those who simply won't give back such lands–employed not just in Spain and Portugal but Palestine, India, southern Russia, the Balkans, Xinjiang, *ad nauseum*. But note that this sharp concept never cuts the other way–Christians are not allowed to demand back, say, Constantinople and all of Asia Minor; or North Africa, which was entirely Christian under the late Roman Empire.

3. Also last month, just across the Strait of Gibraltar, the Moroccan group *Yamaa Mahdaiuya* [*Jama`ah Mahdawiyah*, "Mahdist Community/Troop/Gang"] was "dissolved" by Rabat for heretical teachings but not–at least officially, or at least not yet–for promoting

jihad. Supposedly "surrounded by a halo of mysticism," members of this organization had to sell all their property and give the proceeds to the leaders—whom they also had to ask permission before having sex with their own wives. And ignorance of own's own societal history must be as rampant in Morocco as in the U.S.—at least among journalists—as the correspondent for "Morocco Tomorrow" editorializes that belief in the Mahdi "is a concept linked more to Shiite [sic] Islam than to Moroccan religious culture." Really? No. Actually, Mahdism is part and parcel of North African history in general, and Moroccan history in particular—exemplified by the perhaps the most successful Mahdist leade of all time (and a Sunni at that), Abd Allah Ibn Tumart (d. 1130), creator of the *al-Muwahhid* ("Almohad") empire, predicated on belief in him as the Mahdi.

4. The Sunni cleric Imran Nozar Hosein—born in Trinidad, educated at prestigious al-Azhar in Cairo, former diplomat and Islamic *da`i* ("missionary") in New York—recently delivered a lecture series on Mahdism, one primary presentation of which postulated that the "Arab Spring" was in reality a Mahdist one, that the uprisings across North Africa and into Syria and the Arabian peninsula presage not the advent of Jeffersonian democracy—as the Twittersphere, NPR and the "NY Times" would have it—but rather the first stirrings of a transnational Mahdist state.

Observations:

1. It may be tempting to dismiss such Mahdist-minded movements and individuals as outliers in the Muslim world; but as history's favorite mustachioed dictator once said, quantity has a quality all its own, eventually. Mahdism just keeps rearing its mystical, oft-problematic and violent head in the Muslim world, even here in the age of Twitter, the Internet and planned asteroid mining. Even if one postulates that "modernized" Muslims—member of the Muslim Brotherhood, for

example–reject out-of-hand such "outmoded" beliefs, that still leaves a substantial minority of 1.5 billion people which does not, most notably among the Salafist-minded pious in the Sunni world, to include (to name just a few) members of massive organizations and movements like Tablighi Jama`at, Deobandis, Barelvis, many Sufi orders, etc. (Of course, Mahdism is a key doctrine in all branches of Shi`ism, wherever they exist.)

2.   Mahdist movements can be peaceful and nutty (Yamaa Mahdaiuya), or violent and nutty (Ansar al-Mahdi, not just in Spain but in Iraq or anywhere else such a group coalesces). In this regard, Mahdism greatly resembles Sufism (Islamic mysticism)–which, not coincidentally, has been the germination ground for many Mahdis over the centuries. Just remember: "nutty" does **not** equal harmless.

3.   Relatedly, note how easily Mahdism elides into the irredentist Islamic jihad so beloved of modern Muslim ideologues and provocateurs. Mahdists are, in effect, the jihadists *par excellence*, with absolutely no brakes on their behavior except those which their self-styled Mahdi may apply.

4.   Note that even seemingly "moderate," Westernized, loquacious and intelligent Islamic scholars like Hosein believe in the Mahdi, promulgating and rationalizing that belief for the (Sunni) masses–in this regard playing a role vis-a-vis the *hoi polloi* rather like that of *Tablighi Jama`at,* in terms of not directly advocating jihad but preparing the way of the one who will.

October 30, 2011: Pharaoh v. the Mahdi.

My good friend, Charles Cameron–blogger and analyst extraordinaire on such eclectic topics as game theory, COIN and Mahdism–alerted me some time back to an article which claimed that Mustafa Shukri (d. 1978), former head of *al-Takfir wa-al-Hijrah* ("Charge of Unbelief and Emigration") in Egypt, had mandated that "the movement's estimated 4,000 adherents...vow complete allegiance...to Mustafa as the mahdi...." This is according to Jeffrey Cozzens, "Al-Takfir wa'l [sic] Hijra: Unpacking an Enigma," *Studies in Conflict and Terrorism,* 32 (2009), pp. 498-510. [That specific quote is from p. 494.]

Many analysts study Salafist groups such as ATWH (to use Cozzens' rather awkward acronym–which inexplicably includes both the initial Arabic definite article "al-" and the conjunction "wa"); some, albeit far fewer, study Mahdist groups (and the subset of those who actually know what they're talking about is even smaller). So it's both interesting and refreshing to see that an analyst at least mentions the two trends in the same article. However, Professor Cozzens, while he may be well-versed in Salafism/jihadism, seems woefully ignorant of Mahdism. He notes that Shukri "personally reserved the right to arrange divorces and marriages within his sect," as well as to "determine who was 'in' and 'out'...[and] who had apostatized from Islam....;" likewise, Shukri "sent 'missionaries' abroad–primarily to Saudi Arabia and Yemen–to both spread ATWH's ideology and raise funds" (p. 494). If Cozzens knew anything about the topic, he'd know that this was typical behavior of a man who deemed himself the Mahdi. The most prominent historical precedent to Shukri's behavior was that of Muhammad Ahmad the Sudanese Mahdi, who between 1881-1885 exhibited exactly the same megalomaniacal domestic (interpreting Islamic law himself; mandating marriages and divorces; etc.) and foreign (inviting other Muslim leaders to serve as his caliphs) policies. Other historical Sunni Mahdis also behaved thusly–yet Cozzens makes no connection thereto.

In the final analysis I must confess to some degree of skepticism regarding these alleged Mahdist claims of Mustafa Shukri, however. Cozzens cites no primary Arabic sources to corroborate his claim (ironically, considering that he lambastes other analysts–who allege AWTH's jihadist bent and ties to the al-Qa`idah network [AQN]–for not using primary sources) and actually adduces simply more secondary sources himself (such as David Zeidan's *Radical Islam in Egypt,* from 1999). The issue of convergence between jihadism/Salafism and Mahdism is far too important a topic to be left reliant upon a fading rabbit trail of mere secondary sources.

July 5, 2011: Prophet Motives.

Once again the staunchly Sunni Kingdom of Saudi Arabia has produced a self-styled Mahdi–this in addition the half-dozen who have already staked their eschatological claims in recent months. According to Emirates 24/7 news (citing the Saudi daily *Okaz*), on Friday, July 1, 2011, "a Saudi man mounted a prayer platform at the Grand Mosque [in Mecca]...and told thousands of worshippers that he was a prophet and their saviour before he was seized by police. The 36-year-old man, identified as Sami, waited until the Muslims finished their evening prayers...mounted the podium and delivered his brief, fiery speech. 'I am Al Mehdi Al Montathar...I am a prophet sent (by God) to save and guide you." Saudi police hustled him off for the obligatory mental exam and, one might surmise, perhaps some pedagogically-enhanced questioning.

Observations:

1. To reiterate briefly some of my previous analysis of this fascinating phenomenon of Mahdist claims in the heart of Wahhabi Sunnism:

    a) *Contra* conventional (Western) wisdom on the topic, Mahdism is not just a Shi'i belief, as any examination of Islamic history demonstrates

    b) Riyadh is paranoid about such movements, for two reasons:

        i) The attempt by Juhayman al-Utaybi and his armed followers to overthrow the Saudi regime in 1979 was a Mahdist one

ii) Mahdist Iran is KSA's greatest foe, and the Saudis lose sleep over the Iranians sparking such an uprising in the country, especially in the heavily-Twelver-Shi`i eastern provinces.

2. Too much can be made of this man's claim (even assuming that it was reported accurately by the authorities and/or Saudi media) that he is a "prophet." The Mahdi will of course NOT be a *nabi'*, or "prophet" *per se*, in the sense of bringing a new dispensation; rather, he will be the "rightly-guided one" who renews the community of Muhammad—and, indeed, expands it to cover the whole earth. But in the sense that Allah directly guides him, the Mahdi is quasi-prophetic. Also, consider that reporting that quotes him as claiming to be a prophet might simply be intended to impugn him in Muslim eyes for the heterodoxy of claiming to be another prophet post-Muhammad.

3. Mahdi claims are being made not just in Saudi Arabia but throughout the Muslim world (as per my writings, lectures and interviews) and Mahdist expectations and prognostications are proliferating even more rapidly. What is the reason for this? Possible explanations:

a) The belief (real or perceived) that the Islamic ummah is under attack by the "West," "Crusaders," "Zionists," and even Hindus— and the global dissemination of this belief via the Internet.

b) The approach of the Islamic year 1500 (2076 AD); there are hadiths (alleged sayings of Muhammad) that tell of a *mujaddid*, "renewer," of Islam who comes every century, and this doctrine has often been conflated with that of the eschatological Mahdi.

c) Iran's incessant Mahdist propaganda has increased Mahdist hopes throughout the Islamic world, including in Sunni KSA.

d) In-breeding within Islam has produced a disproportionate share of Muslims (at least vis-a-vis other societies that do not practice close-cousin marriage) who are mentally deficient and/or disturbed (on this distasteful topic, see Nicolai Sennels, "The Problem of Inbreeding in Islam," *PJ Media,* Sep. 19, 2010).

May 14, 2011: Mahdi, Thy Name Is Legion.

According to a story last week in Saudi media, mental health officials there have expressed concern that in the last year there have been multiple cases of individuals openly claiming to be the Mahdi: "three cases...in the Kingdom...occurred in under a month...[and] six cases in the Eastern Province alone in the last year" according to Dr. Muhammad al-Zahrani, head of the al-Amal Mental Health Complex in Dammam. It is unclear from this phrasing whether the total is six or nine, but the tally includes such phenomena as "a 29-year-old Saudi who earlier this month was arrested...in Qatif after voicing his claims during prayers at a mosque on Tarout Island," "a foreign man [who] snatched the microphone from Sheikh Abdullah al-Juhani, Imam of the Grand Mosque in Makkah, during Asr prayer to announce his claims," and "an Egyptian [who] was arrested at a hotel in Madina which he purportedly used as a base to acquire followers." Dr. al-Zahrani opined that delusional men such as these need medical treatment more than judicial punishment and should be hospitalized or institutionalized and "given good care until the best way to treat them is determined."

Observations:

1. Knowing full well that the eastern areas of KSA contain large populations of Twelver Shi'is, it's nonetheless striking that the bastion of conservative (some would say fundamentalist) Sunnism is witnessing such phenomena. Geopolitically, the Saudis are no doubt paranoid about the issue for two major reasons: a) memory of the failed Mahdist overthrow of the monarchy by Juhayman al-Utaybi and Muhammad al-Qahtani "al-Mahdi" in 1979; and b) concerns that Tehran is stirring the Mahdist pot in KSA's east.

2. The presence of an unidentified Egyptian trying to create a Mahdist base in Madina bespeaks the growing transnational trend within Mahdism. Iraq has three active Mahdist movements (aside from the Mahdist Lite one of Muqtada al-Sadr, the *Jaysh al-Mahdi*) on of which, *Ansar al-Mahdi*, has been accused of sending *da`is* ("missionaries") to Egypt. Might this "Egyptian" in KSA be connected to Iraqi Mahdism via Egypt? Preachers in heavlily-Shi`i Bahrain, scene of a great deal of Twelver Shi`i-Sunni conflict in recent months, have been claiming the Mahdi is near at hand to deliver them from Sunni oppression. Iran may not want an open Twelver Mahdist claimant on its own soil, but it would certainly not be unhappy with such, Shi`i or Sunni, causing problems for Bahrain, KSA or Egypt

3. KSA already seems to have a problem with "jinn possession." One might speculate as to whether this has any connection to the "mental health" of self-proclaimed Mahdis–as well as, if I may be politically incorrect, to the issue of crazed Muslim mobs killing Christians and other non-Muslims, demanding death for those who "insult Islam–the religion of peace" and "honor" killing women.

April 18, 2011: A Muslim Prophet Is Not Without Honor–Except in Somaliland.

Somalilandpress reports that a man claiming to be a prophet and the Mahdi was arrested and sentenced to two years in prison as well as a back-breaking (in the Horn of Africa) $300 fine:

A local court in the capital Hargeisa on Saturday sentenced an ethnic Somali man to two years imprisonment and $300 fine for claiming to be a prophet. Judge Abdulrashid Mohamed Hersi said Ethiopian national Sharif Ahmed Ali was found guilty of claiming prophet hood. The judicial official added he had claimed status of the Qur'anic figure al-Khidr as well as the Mahdi.... During the five-day proceedings, he pleaded innocent and denied all the accusations but the court insisted they have seven witnesses." The man carried a staff, which he claimed gave him the same powers as Musa (Moses) had had. "He also told locals he controls Mother Nature and that he will ensure it does not rain in the country for the next eight months. His words come as the region is hit by the worst drought in two decades." He was ordered fined and imprisoned. "This is the first time such case has occurred in Somaliland" and although there are no blasphemy laws "Muslims believe that prophet Mohammad is the last prophet from God. Numerous such cases have been reported in places such as Saudi Arabia, Indonesia, Pakistan and Iran."

Observations:

1. al-Khidr is a strange figure **in** Sura al-Kahf [18] who meets Moses and does some perplexing things. al-Khidr is a favorite of the Sufis (some of whom believe he never died) and of Twelver Shi`is (some of whom believe he accompanies the Mahdi—so being both al-Khidr and al-Mahdi is a two-fer!).

2. Who knew there was a WMD problem in Somalia? Good thing the court ordered that boomstick destroyed.

3. Since the chap was from Ethiopia (although, presumably, a Muslim), why not just deport him back there rather than sentence him to the hell of a Somali prison? Perhaps the judge deemed him a stooge of those perfidious Ethiopian Christians, and that a couple of years on ice (or, in the Horn of Africa case, on brimstone) would sufficiently detach him from his handlers. (IF it's only a couple of years—$300 is several years' income there, and if he can't raise the money he might never get out.)

4. If there is no blasphemy law, why is it a punishable offense to claim prophet hood? Come to think of it, this might be a good idea here in the U.S.—especially before the 2012 Presidential election, just in case Obama gets any wild ideas.

5. Even Somali news organs are now noting the "numerous cases" of folks claiming to be the Mahdi in recent years. In all seriousness: isolated incidents of such deranged individuals are indicative of very little; but a large and growing pattern of such, all with the same Mahdist derangement, is much more noteworthy.

April 13, 2011: Another Meccan Mahdi?!

As if Barack Husayn Obama's resurrection of Jimmy Carter's foreign policy wasn't enough to make you feel like it's 1979 all over again: "A man snatched the microphone at the Grand Mosque in Makkah and declared he was the Mahdi, the prophesied redeemer of Islam who is expected to come prior to the Day of Resurrection. According to eyewitnesses, the imam has just started the *asr* (afternoon) prayer when the man grabbed the microphone and made his announcement, Saudi daily "Arab News" reported. Security officers inside the mosque quickly arrested the man, who was said to be an Egyptian national in his 30s. The man was taken to the police station on the mosque premises for investigation. Initial reports say that the man was suffering from mental problems..." (According to *Gulfnews.com*).

Observations:

1. For any journalists or politicians who read this: 1979 was the year not only of the Soviet invasion of Afghanistan and the creation of the Islamic Republic in Iran, but also of the attempted Mahdist take-over of Saudi Arabia by forces loyal to the Mahdi Muhammad b. Abd Allah al-Qahtani and his *eminence grise*, Juhayman al-Utaybi. These Mahdists occupied this same Grand Mosque for some three weeks in late 1979, until killed or captured by French forces hired by the Saudis (who did not trust the incompetent Carter CIA to help).

2. Evidence suggests that this new Meccan Mahdi is a Sunni, not a Shi`i: he is in the stronghold of Wahhabi Sunni Islam, and he proclaimed himself Mahdi, not the returned 12th Imam—as would have

174

been the case if he were Shi`i (in the Twelver Shi`ism or Iran, Iraq, Lebanon, Bahrain and eastern Saudi Arabia, the Mahdi has already been here and disappeared over a millennium ago; in Sunni Mahdism the Mahdi has yet to arrive, despite false claims over the centuries by legions of self-styled Mahdis).

3.   There are several ways to parse his being an Egyptian national. This may simply be a ruse to lay blame on someone other than a Saudi. If he truly is Egyptian, perhaps the recent events there excited him so much that he decided to go to Sunnism Central and kick the revolutionary fervor up a notch—and the highest level of such in Islam is the holiest war of eschatological Mahdism. Also, as I reported on last fall (November 17, 2010), followers of Ahmad Hassan al-Yamami, an Iraqi who claims to be the "son of the 12th Imam," were arrested in Egypt. Was this Mahdi claimant one of al-Yamami's group (which would seem to put him at loggerheads with the chief of Ansar al-Mahdi), or perhaps influenced by the Egyptian branch thereof?

4.   "Suffering from mental problems" is a diagnosis that one might reasonably well apply to anyone in history who claimed to be the Mahdi—from the 11th century AD Ibn Tumart, whose followers took over most of northwest Africa; to Shah Isma'il of Iran whose fanatical Safavids followed him as the Mahdi and violently converted that country to Shi`ism in the 17th century; and to Muhammad Ahmad of Sudan whom hundreds of thousands of Sudanese revered as the Mahdi enough to kill not just General Charles Gordon and his British and Egyptian troops but scores of their fellows who did not share their Mahdist convictions.   But such mental problems—megalomania perhaps the chief of them, often accompanied by delusions of hearing the voices of Allah, the angel Jibril and the deceased prophet Muhammad telling him he was the Mahdi—did not stop these men (nor the scores of others, less successful, such as Mehmet the Mahdi in early Republican Turkey or the

aformentioned al-Qahtani) and, in fact, probably empowered them with charisma in the eyes of their followers.

5. A deluded chap temporarily pulling a Mahdist Phil Donahue in Mecca may not seem like much, but when you add this example to the scores of others in recent years it's hard not to conclude that another avenue of popular protest, alongside that calling for toppling of tyrants and more input from the Arab (and other) *hoi polloi*, that may once again emerge in the Muslim street is Mahdism. In fact, Mahdism has proved the most Islamically-legitimate means of overthrowing "unjust" and "unIslamic" rulers in both Sunni and Shi`i sections of the ummah for a millennium. The Saudis know this, courtesy of 1979; the Iranians (at least the leaders) live it. Even staid, still somewhat secular modern Turkish society has produced two men with Mahdist aspirations: Fethullah Gulen and Adnan Oktar. Mahdism is a force whose power has yet to be fully realized in the 21st century Islamic world.

January 18, 2011: Back in the Bishkek Mahdiyah....

According to a new report from *The Telegraph*, the U.S. embassy and a U.S. airbase in Kyrgyzatan were on the hit list of "a newly formed Kyrgyz militant group, calling itself Jamat Kyrgyzstan Jaish al-Mahdi, or 'the Army of the Righteous Ruler', which is dedicated to establishing an Islamic caliphate across Central Asia." Mahdists, of course, are proponents not just of a caliphate but a Mahdiyah, a divinely-guided Islamic state headed not merely by a caliph but by the eschatological Mahdi, directly guided by Allah. No word yet on whether or not Mahdist-caused explosions were accompanied by balalaikas ringing out.

Those Kyrgyz Mahdis Really Knock Me Out.

Iraq. Pakistan. Palestine. Now add Kyrgyztan to the roster of Muslim-majority states with openly declared Mahdist movements:

"The chairman of Kyrgyzstan's state committee on national security, Keneshbek Duishebaev, said a group called 'Zhayshul Mahdi' ('Jaysh al-

Mahdi,' Army of the Righteous Ruler) was responsible for a series of bombings in Bishkek, including one near a synagogue last autumn and one outside a sports complex, as well as a recent attempted bombing outside a Bishkek police station.

Duishebaev said the leader of the group, whom he identified as Sovetbek Islamov, was killed during a security operation. Duishebaev said the group has 16 members: 15 Kyrgyz nationals and one Russian. He said of those, 11 are under arrest, two are dead and three are currently being sought."

Observations:

1. "Jaysh al-Mahdi" is the same name (transposed to Kyrgyz from Arabic) as Muqtada al-Sadr's group in Iraq. This may mean some connection, but more likely it simply reflects the militant jihadistic bent of many current Mahdist ideologies.

2. Note that the targets of this Mahdist jihad have been a police station, sports complex and synagogue. Considering that of Kyrgyzstan's 5.5 million population, only perhaps 1,300 are Jews–one has to ask why this miniscule population was singled out for Mahdist violence? Christians, mainly Russian Orthodox, make up a substantial minority and would seem to be a more logical target of Islamic Mahdist wrath. Most analysts will lay the blame on jihadist and conservative Muslim rage at Israel, conveniently ignoring that Islamic teaching in general, and eschatological ones in particular, condemn Jews as minions of *al-Dajjal*, the "Deceiver" (or Antichrist).

3. One should take the Kyrgyz government claim of this group's small number with a healthy dose of skeptical salt. Governments are always loathe to give accurate numbers of opposition groups–especially eschatological ones.

4. But even if there really are only 16 active, jihadist Mahdists in this central Asian nation, it's yet more evidence that even in an

overwhelmingly Sunni context Mahdism can develop—no surprise to anyone who has studied this aspect of Islamic history.

November 17, 2010: Preach Like an Egyptian.

According to a story last week in the Egyptian news organ *al-Masry al-Youm* [*Egypt Today*], a shady Shi`i sect's members are being rounded up in that country [link now dead].   State Security "has opened investigations into 12 Shia [sic] Muslim individuals from Egypt, Morocco, Iraq and Australia arrested...on charges of 'promoting Shia doctrines, as well as 'falsifying' the Qur'an and rejecting the Hadith," thanks to funds received "from several foreign countries." The most important aspect of this story is that the sect's leader, Ahmad Hassan al-Yamami, is believed to be the Awaited Mahdi, "or expected messiah of the Shia faith."

Observations:

1. al-Yamami was the head of *Ansar al-Mahdi* ["Companions of the Mahdi"] in southern Iraq, a group that engaged in battles with both Iraqi government and American forces several times, most recently in January 2008.   I wrote about him and this movement in "The Modern Impact of Mahdism and the Case of Iraq" [a chapter in *Political Islam from Muhammad to Ahmadinejad*, Joseph Skelly, ed. (Praeger Security International, 2010, pp. 182-192)].   According to members of the group whom I contacted, they were the innocent victims of Baghdad's attacks (which government was also illegitimate, since it refused to believe in al-Yamami's claims). Regarding al-Yamami himself, I was told that he is the "son of the 12th Imam," one of five signs presaging the coming of the actual 12th Imam al-Mahdi.

2.   If the Egyptian press report (based on State Security's assessment) is correct, then al-Yamami has ramped up his eschatological claim from mere Mahdist precursor to Mahdism *per se*.

3. The presence of only a dozen supporters seems to indicate a quite marginal following for this Mahdist movement in Egypt—but its transference from Iraq to the most populous, and centrally-located, Arab Muslim country also demonstrates that Mahdism may be acquiring regional dimensions, as does the presence of believers from Morocco and, strangely, Australia.

4. Egypt is an interesting new locale for al-Yamami. Cairo's official tally of only 0.5% Shi`i population in the country is very likely far too low; furthermore, Egypt has a strong historical and intellectual tradition of Shi`ism, as it was ruled from 969-1171 AD by the Sevener Shi`i Fatimid dynasty—which in fact founded the famous al-Azhar madrasah and mosque the year after the Shi`i conquest. Thus, Egypt might be more susceptible to Shi`i blandishments than other Sunni countries (a vulnerability which the Islamic Republic of Iran may be trying to exploit: when he was in Iraq, Baghdad claimed that al-Yamami's Ansar al-Mahdi were supported by Iran).

5. There they go again: another media outlet stating that Mahdism is strictly a Shi`i phenomenon. Egyptians should know better than the ignorati at Reuters and AP. But, to be fair, perhaps the order came down from the government to refrain from reminding Sunnis that most men claiming the Mahdiyah have come from their ranks.

July 19, 2010: The Mahdi: Living on Mayan Time.

A nice Swedish chap, Mikael, emailed me, providing a link about an Iraqi fellow, Hamid, living in Stockholm who is, allegedly, the Mahdi [link now dead]. It seems that this dispensation of the world will end with its last leader, Barack Obama, on December 21, 2012 and half the world will perish as a rogue red star approaches Earth, stops the planet's rotation and, presumably, causes dogs and cats to live together before both are irradiated to death. My evangelical friends would note that the last line of the site mentions the "Luciferian knowledge" that the

Mahdi's helper manifests. At least this Mahdi isn't the typical jihadist kind that Islamic history usually throws up.

June 26, 2010: "Don't Haze Me, Bro–I'm the Mahdi!"

Recently, on *PeaceTV* (an Urdu and English TV station broadcasting from Mumbai and run by Zakir Naik, an Indian Islamist recently denied entry to to the U.K), a man claimed to be the Mahdi. What's interesting about this episode is that, yet again, a wanna-be Mahdi crops up even in a staunchly Sunni venue (Naik and his TV outlet are on record as opposing Shi`ism, *contra* his claims of inter-Muslim tolerance). Also, the willingness by even such an off-kilter Muslim to make a public claim to the Mahdiyah indicates that the traditions about the Mahdi's coming are being studied and internalized–preparing the ground for more serious, and potentially dangerous, Mahdist aspirations in the future. One does wonder, however, what happened to this poor deluded man after the cameras stopped rolling?

As disturbing as this mutamahdi is the "sister at the back," shown at 2:46 (before the clip ends at 2:49), clad in what appears to be a dusty brown, oh-so-stylish, burqa and backed by sartorially-similiar Muslimas. Of course, once the real Mahdi comes, that garb will likely be mandatory for all women.

Update: This video has been posted to a site called "Pakistan Defence Forum." There are a number of comments on it–most notably this one: "It seems false Mahdi [sic] are popping [sic] all over. Another reason to keep blasphemy laws and apply them to these clowns."

February 14, 2010: Back to the Future in Morocco?

In 1124 AD one Abu `Abd Allah Muhammad bin Tumart al-Susi, known to historians as Ibn Tumart, declared himself the Mahdi in what is now Morocco and created legions of *muwahhidun* (hence the textbook term "Almohads"), dedicated to two things: 1) belief in him as the Awaited Mahdi, and 2) *tawhid*, "unity [of Allah]," or strict monotheism, over against the perceived *shirk*, or "idolatry," of the extant Islamic rulers, the Murabits (Almoravids). Eventually the Muwahhids conquered, in the name of their Mahdi, most of the Magrhib as well as the Iberian Peninsula—and, with their intolerant and cruel Islamic agenda which oppressed and killed in particular Catholic Christians, put the lie to the tiresome myth of medieval Islamic "tolerance" in al-Andalus.

It would seem that Morocco is experiencing a case of "*deja vu* all over again," as it deals with two similar modern-day groups. The first is *Ansar al-Mahdi*: "Helpers of the Mahdi." A few weeks ago the Moroccan Supreme Court rejected the appeal of 46 members of AAM, who had been sentenced to prison for "funding terrorist operations and planning a terror campaign against the Moroccan regime." In addition, Morocco's legal system last month sentenced members of the group *Fath al-Andalous* (Reconquest/victory over Andalusia) to fines and 4-15 years prison terms for plotting terrorist attacks. Note well the group's aim, as advertised in its name: "REconquest" of Spain and Portugal. Once you go Muslim, in this mindset, you can never go back to being, say, Christian. Let us hope (and pray) that these two groups don't merge, or the 21st century version of the Maghribi Mahdi may well put the 12th century one to shame in terms of violence and persecution of Christians.

March 13, 2008: Father Knows Best (Especially When He's the Mahdi): New Iraqi Mahdist Movement.

I have been in contact with representatives of Sayyid al-Yamani, the head of the group *Ansar al-Mahdi* in southern Iraq. Herewith are 11 questions I sent them, along with the verbatim answers:

1. What is Shaykh al-Yamani's relationship to the Mahdi? "Sayid al Yamani (Ahmad al Hassan) is the son of Imam al Mahdi; Mohammed bin al Hassan (p), the twelfth Imam. He is the promised Yamani ,the messenger and guardian of Imam al Mahdi; Mohammed bin al Hassan (p). It would be useful for you to know that in the generations to come the rulers of the State of divine justice after twelve Imam Mahdi

Mohammed bin Hassan (p) each of them is Mahdi by intestate Messenger of God Mohammad (pbuh). Mahdi this title to the Imam Mohammed bin al Hassan (p), and his twelve sons, the first of whom is Sayid al Yamani (p). al Yamani true launch title Mahdi too.

2. <u>Is al-Mahdi already here on earth?</u> Yes, Imam Mahdi Mohammed bin Hassan (p) is on the earth and live among the people but most of them do not know it and don't see him, and you can in this regard review many novels, which shows this sense.

3. <u>Is al-Mahdi the same as the Twelfth Imam returned from *ghaybah* (occultation)?</u> Yes, it is quite true to say that Imam al Mahdi is the twelfth Imam Mohammed bin Hassan (p) returned from ghaybah, and also true to say that his son Sayid al Yamani (Ahmad al Hassan) also can be named Mahdi.

4. <u>Is al-Yamani's group *Jund al-Sama'* or *Ansar al-Mahdi*?</u> al Yamani group called Ansar al-Mahdi or Ansar Allah, supporters of Imam Mahdi (p) and supporters of Sayid Ahmed Hassan al Yamani; the messenger and guardian and the Imam Mahdi (p). We are unrelated to the so-called (Jund al-Sama'), and there is great difference between us. Ansar al-Mahdi say that Ahmed Hassan (p) is the promised Yamani, a branch of Imam Mahdi Mohammed bin Hassan (p) and his son , while the group Jund al-Sama' deny the existence of Imam Mahdi Mohammed bin Hassan (p) in total.

5. <u>Do al-Yamani and his group have any connection to Moqtada al-Sadr and the Jaysh al-Mahdi?</u> No relationship whatsoever between us and Moqtada al Sadr and his army Jaysh al-Mahdi, in a passage names as it is known.

6. <u>What is al-Yamani's opinion of the American-sponsored Iraq government in Baghdad?</u> The government has to be based on the principle of the Governorship of God and must derive its legitimacy from God and from Imam Mahdi Mohammed bin Hassan (p).

7. <u>What is al-Yamani's opinion of *vilayet-i faqih* in Iran?</u> Not valid as the answer became clear to you from the previous question.

8. <u>What sort of state in Iraq does al-Yamani envision? A caliphate? A Mahdiyah?</u> Government, which al Yamani see it is the government based on the principle of Governorship of God. Whatever you want to call it as the term crossing, but the lesson in reality is substance and meaning.

9. <u>What will be the Mahdi's role once he is revealed?</u> Imam al Mahdi will reveal justice and installment and will be published uniformity across the globe, and re-link the right relationship of God with humans after regrettably interrupted by the ego.

10. <u>Do al-Yamani and the Mahdi expect Sunnis as well as Shi`is to be followers?</u> Imam al Mahdi and Sayid al Yamani expect followers from all sects and religions. They're for all and from all. Their aim is to pull out the state of human rights in order to reach absolute perfection and worship to God alone, which is the real freedom.

11. <u>Is al-Yamani's group peaceful or will it wage violent jihad if need be?</u> You have to know first that al Yamani group represent the real message of all messengers and prophets of God on earth. If you look and consider the march movement of all prophets (p), you will realize that the message to heaven always pursues a peace advocacy and the one that is better, Koran says: ((Say Bring proof that you are truthful)), but you will always find that the bad governors and bad scholars and Slobs will face peaceful prophets with violence, force and displacement, and then–and only then–preachers forced to defend themselves and their faith. And to answer this question, we would say yes, the group of Al Yamani is designated to peaceful and that is all what they want from others."

Observations:

1. al-Yamani is not quite claiming to be the Mahdi, but to be his "son," "messenger" and "guardian." In terms of charismatic power in

an eschatologically-charged milieu, however, we might make note of the famous Vulcan saying "A difference which makes no difference is no difference."

2. The Mahdi **is** extant on earth and al-Yamani is in contact with him. Remember that in Shi`i Islam the descendants of Muhammad through his son-in-law and younger cousin Ali (who married Fatimah, one of Muhammad's daughters) are Imams, or rightful leaders of the Islamic world. Various Shi`i sects believe that one or another of these was (and will be) the true Mahdi; the largest group, the Shi`is of Iran and Iraq, believe that it was the Twelfth such Imam, named Muhammad, who will return at the end of time as the Mahdi. But before the Twelfth Imam went incommunicado in 941 CE (a silence lasting until today and known as the "Greater Occultation" [*ghaybah* in Arabic]), he was between 874 and 941 in a state of "Lesser Occultation" wherein he was unseen but still in contact with his followers. If al-Yamani is saying the Mahdi is here and he is taking direction from him, then the Greater Occultation has ended and something approximating the Lesser one is back in effect.

3. Ansar al-Mahdi, despite Iraqi government statements otherwise, denies any connection to the seemingly more violent Jund al-Sama' (Soldiers of Heaven) and to the Sadrist Jaysh al-Mahdi.

4. Regarding the governments in Baghdad and Tehran, al-Yamani seems to be saying "a pox on both their houses;" thus, both parliamentary democracy and the "rule of the religious jurists" are condemned as illegitimate.

5. The Mahdi's supporters will not only be from all branches of Islam but also from "all sects and religions." This is a sort of universalism not normally seen in Mahdist thought (and not at all in Salafi/Wahhabi Islam).

6. Ansar al-Mahdi–again, *contra* Iraqi government pronouncements–claims to be peaceful. This puts it at odds with both Jund al-Sama' and

with the Jaysh al-Mahdi, both of which have taken up arms against both the Baghdad government and U.S. forces.

7. It may be that Ansar al-Mahdi–the popular support for which we really have no way of knowing–will evolve into a quietist movement (as with the Mahdaviyat movement of Sayyid Jawnpuri in 15th/16th c. Gujarat, India) over time. Or frustration may boil over if the claims of al-Yamani are not recognized with the larger Iraqi society, and/or if the government tries to repress the group with force.

November 28, 2007: I Dream of Mahdi.

Mahdist movements throughout history have been characterized by dreams presaging the alleged Mahdi's appearance, whether those of the Mahdi claimant himself, his followers, or both. Such was the case with the two most prominent Mahdist movements in modern times, those of the Sudanese Mahdi Muhammad Ahmad in the 1880s and the Saudi Mahdi Muhammad Abd al-Qahtani in 1979. Usually, however, such dreams instruct folks to kill establishment opponents of the Mahdi, rather than family members. But hey, maybe the 12th Imam is getting testy after more than a millennium in *ghaybah*. According to a story out of Kuwait City [link dead], "Dhaher al-Fadhli, 47, shot and killed his 38-year-old wife Badriya, his eldest son Waleed, 21, and 16-year-old daughter Baida in December 2004, claiming he was ordered to do so in a dream by Imam al-Mahdi, the 'hidden imam' and a central figure in the Shiite faith." Also note that this story editorializes, wrongly, that the Mahdi is only a Shi`i belief.

November 3, 2007: And the Mahdis Keep Rolling Along.

2007 is turning out to be the Year of the Mahdi(s): yet another has emerged, in Indonesia, one Ahmad Moshaddeq , a.k.a. Abdussalam, has "declared himself a new prophet, replacing Prophet Muhammad" according to *The Jakarta Post*, Nov. 1, 2007. His al-Qiyadah group has existed since 2000, and is said to have 40,000 followers. Interestingly, prophet Moshaddeq has been arrested for violating Indonesia's shari`ah-based blasphemy law.

Observations:

1. Worldwide Relgious News lumps this movement under the rubric of "Other/NRMs"—"New Religious Movements," that is. While this is accurate in the case of someone declaring himself a new prophet in Islam, it is misleading in the case of someone declaring himself the Mahdi. Mahdism is quintessentially Islamic, for according to Islamic traditions the Mahdi will refurbish and reinstitute the original Prophetic teaching and practice, not bring a new dispensation.

2. Muslim religious leaders in Indonesia are already stereotyping the Mahdists as poor, dumb and probably in-bred. This is a variation on the theme of "poverty produces terrorism," and it's just as wrong about Mahdists as it is about jihadists. Historically, Mahdist claimants and their followers have often been educated and well-off, and while they have indeed tended to come from the geographical, sociopolitical or intellectual margins of Muslim societies that does not mean they were social misfits.

3. How moderately-Muslim Indonesia deals with such movements—Mahdist and heretical—will prove instructive as the U.S. starts to encounter more and more such movements in Iraq and elsewhere in the coming years.

October 17, 2007: Happiness is a Warm Gun—Unless You're The Gazan Mahdi.

Yet another Mahdist claimant has surfaced in the Sunni world here in 2007:

"Hamas Shoots Man Claiming to be Muslim Messiah

A Gaza man incurred the anger of a Hamas-affiliated preacher in Gaza Tuesday by claiming to be the Mahdi, or Muslim redeemer. The man went to the Imam to seek his endorsement and instruct him to tell

Muslims to follow his instructions. The Imam reacted by summoning armed Hamas men, who arrived and told the self-proclaimed redeemer to take back his claims. When the man continued to insist that he was the Mahdi, police shot him in the foot and then released him."

As comical and pathetic as this appears, it also corroborates my oft-repeated thesis that many Muslims have convinced themselves (or been convinced by their leaders, religious and political) that the Ummah is in such dire straits that only supernatural deliverance via the Mahdi can save it. Eventually a tipping point will be reached where a Mahdist claimant will be someone of enough stature to lead a serious movement and perhaps even be handed, or seize, the reins of power somewhere. Make no mistake, it will happen. And then it will be him and his followers doing the shooting, not the other way around.

August 4, 2007: A Mahdist Trifecta in 2007?

Two overt Mahdist claims have been made this year: a violent one in southern Iraq in January and a pacific one in India more recently. Now, according to the Dhaka *Daily Star*, just this week in Bangladesh a man claiming to be the Mahdi's top military commander was arrested:

"*So-called military chief of Imam Mahdi held*

Police detained a man, who claimed himself as the military chief of Imam Mahdi, raiding his rented house at Ganderia in the capital's Sutrapur after midnight last night. His nine followers were also arrested during the raid.

Sutrapur police said they recovered a huge quantity of books written on Imam Mahdi, the spiritual leader who, according to Muslims, will be sent by Allah to bring back justice and fairness, the so-called military chief of Imam Mahdi was identified as Luthfor Rahman Faruq, 55.

The Identity of the other detainees could not be known immediately.

'We have detained Faruq and his associates as they were giving anti-Islamic statements for the last two years' Mohammad Ali, officer-in-charge of Sutrapur Police Station, told "The Daily Star."

The OC said Faruq admitted that he has more than 300 disciples."

Observations:

1. Bangladesh is overwhelmingly Sunni, yet it is home to a nascent Mahdist movement—one looking for someone to follow as Mahdi (paging Usama....). Once again, the conventional wisdom that Islamic messianism is only operative in Shi`i areas is proved wrong.

2. Books on Mahdism are popular and dangerous and having an effect (no doubt the same is also true of Mahdist websites) on the popular imagination. (And I should add that despite the huge quantity of such books in my study, I've managed to avoid their siren call—so far, at any rate.)

3. History indicates that previous Mahdist movements have tended to erupt in two parts of the Muslim world: the Maghrib (North Africa) and the Indian subcontinent. This near-Mahdist movement fits the pattern of the latter.

4. Note that the government authorities are delegitimizing this group by accusing them of making "anti-Islamic statements"—as if the Mahdi were not an orthodox belief in Sunni Islam! More interestingly, this fits the historical pattern of previous counter-Mahdist agendas established by the likes of the Saudis (v. the 1979 al-Utaybi uprising), the Ottomans (v. the 1881 Muhammad Ahmad rebellion), and others (outlined in my book *Holiest Wars*).

Strategically, this is yet more ammunition for my argument that a substantial—yet vociferous—minority in the Islamic world, Sunni as well as Shi`i, yearns for someone to proclaim himself Mahdi.

June 22, 2007: A New Indian Mahdi?

A new Mahdi claimant has arisen in India, one "Mohammad Shakil" al-Mahdi:

"Mehdi followers arrested for instigating Muslim youths

(*UNI*, June 16, 2007)

Raisen, India: "Twelve people who were arrested yesterday for tutoring Muslim youths to wage a holy war, are followers of the controversial Mehdi sect, which believes that the 'prophet' would come to this world again when injustice increases. One of the arrested, Mohammed Shakil, claimed that he was Mehdi and would become omnipotent in a few years." The story goes on to say that while small (slightly over 100 followers), the group had members throughout India. Furthermore, after taking a "pledge" to the new Mahdi, they would be taken to meet Usama bin Ladin!

In my book *Holiest Wars* two of the eight Mahdist movements treated therein were Indian: those of Muhammad Jawnpuri in the late 15th/early 16th c. CE, and of Ahmad Barelwi in the 19th c. These new Mahdists are likely in the same tradition, although more research needs be done. **The four most striking elements of this story are**:

1. It's the second openly-declared Mahdist claim of 2007, the first being that of the Najaf Mahdi of southern Iraq in January.

2. It proves that Mahdism is NOT limited to the Middle East proper, and so confounds the conventional wisdom that radical Islamic movements are almost certainly to occur only in the Salafi/Wahhabi Arab Middle East.

3. It shows that even when Usama bin Ladin himself is not declared or considered the Mahdi (as has been done), even a self-styled Mahdi and his followers acknowledge UBL's importance!

4. Reporters [and analysts] continue to manifest a colossal ignorance of Mahdism: for example, this articles says that only a "section of Islam" believes in the Mahdi (untrue; the vast majority, both Sunni AND Shi`i, do), and it refers to the Mahdi as a "prophet" (again, untrue). [Original link is dead, alas.]

Thursday, Dec. 19, 2009: A Kuwaiti Mahdi?

Perhaps this chap was just gearing up for the Mahdism Conference this summer on the other side of the Gulf:

"Security guard goes haywire: An Egyptian security guard working at the Farwaniya Hospital has been referred to the Psychiatric Hospital for behaving abnormal, reports Al-Watan Arabic daily. The guard reportedly kept screaming that he is the Al-Mahdi al-Muntazar (Muhammad al Mahdi (the guided) is the 12th and last Imam of the Twelve, and is also known as Muhammad al Muntazar (the awaited) [link now dead]." Folks like this give Mahdism a bad name! Seriously, however, it's fascinating that an EGYPTIAN—thus almost certainly a Sunni—would have such a delusion. Perhaps Iranian Shi`i proselytizing is indeed having an effect in the Arab world!?

Ottoman Mahdism

June 26, 2013: The Rule of Three and the Mahdi.

Since today is the (alleged) 1,145th birthday of Muhammad "al-Mahdi," the (supposedly) occulted-but-not-dead-yet 12th Imam of Shi`ism, it seems a good time to comment on several recent stories about the Mahdi from Shi`i, Sunni and Sufi sources. First, the newly-elected President of the Islamic Republic of Iran–where the official religion, recall, is Twelver Shi`ism–thanked the *Imam-i Zaman*, "Imam of the Age," for his "epic" electoral victory. While this is interesting, most notably in demonstrating that Hassan Rouhani's Twelver Shi`i credentials and belief in Mahdism differ very little, if at all, from those of outgoing President Mahmud Ahmadinejad, it is in no wise exceptional–ignorant hyperventilating claiming otherwise notwithstanding. Belief in the return of the "Boy Wonder" Muhammad (died, but claimed occulted in the 9th c. AD) as the eschatological Mahdi is THE key belief of the largest branch of Shi`ism. (However, it's no more remarkable in those circles than Tim Tebow or George Bush or any of the world's other 2.2 billion Christians speaking of Jesus' Second Coming, and/or thanking him for beating the Steelers or John Kerry.) Ahmadinejad simply seems to think the Mahdi's return will be sooner, whereas Rouhani would opt for a later one, sometime in the unspecified future. An Iranian government spokesman's statement yesterday (June 24, 2013) that Ahmadinejad might return with the Imam to "work for the establishment of pure Islam" is agitating certain eschatological embellishers; but far from elevating Iran's outgoing President to the right hand of the Mahdi, it is even more likely that such a claim amounts to the establishment damning the cleric-baiter Ahmadinejad with faint praise–or mockery. Rouhani does appear moderate, or at least grounded in reality, next to Iranian Major General Muhammad Hassan Nami, who just prior to the Iranian election declared that he had procured both a picture and a voice recording of the Awaited Mahdi—neither of which has yet seen the light of day, alas.

But as I've commented many times in recent years, Mahdism is not only—or even primarily, these days—the province of the Twelver Shi`is. The Sunni world has a number of proponents of Mahdist *da`wah* ("propaganda" or "summons"), most notably the Turk Adnan Oktar who uses the pseudonym "Harun Yayha." (I went to Istanbul in 2008 and interviewed Oktar about Mahdism and several other topics, especially his Islamic Creationism.) Recently, Oktar did a TV clip entitled "If Obama Supports the System of Mahdi, the Islamic World Will Attain Peace." (No date is given for the spot, but it would appear to be from May, 2013, when Turkish Prime Minister Erdoğan was meeting with President Obama in Washingon, DC.) Oktar, doing his best Robert Palmer "addicted to love" impression (surrounded by a bevy of attractive, expressionless women), waxed eloquent about the need for not just the Islamic but the Christian world to accept the Mahdi, beginning with Barack Husayn Obama. Only in this way, Oktar opined, can peace come not just to stricken Syria but the persecuted Muslim world in its entirety. He also called on the Organization of Islamic Cooperation to "take Mahdism seriously" and accused (presumably American) Evangelicals of being pleased with attacks on Muslims, even claiming that a prominent (but unnamed) Evangelical Christian leader said that "this is what we want." Oktar's followers seem to believe that he is the Mahdi—while critics accuse him of heading a "sex cult." (Of course, Mahdism and sex are not necessarily mutually exclusive.) Perhaps Obama would make a better Mahdi than Oktar—assuming he is really out of a job on January 20, 2017.

The last recent Mahdi news comes from the world of the Sufis, or Islamic mystics–no surprise, really, since as I pointed out in my book *Holiest Wars* many Mahdist movements have arisen from Sufi contexts (owing both to Sufism's penchant for charismatic leadership, and its orders constituting ready-made battalions of potential jihadists). Just over a week ago a long disquisition was published by the Naqshbandi-Haqqani Sufi order, entitled "The Appearances of Mahdi (AS) and the Sohbets of Sheykh Effendi Concering His Arrival." (A *sohbet* is, in the original Persian, a "conversation.") "Sheykh Effendi" was Abd al-Karim al-Kibrisi who died in 2012; he was the number two man in the Naqshband-Haqqani order, behind Shaykh Muhammad Nazim al-Haqqani, based in Cyprus and still going strong at age 91. Abd al-Karim, much like his master, seems to have had a predilection for prognosticating about when the Mahdi would arrive–and being wrong. So Hoca Lokman Efendi, the new number two man in this Sufi order, wrote to allay concerns about the coming of the Mahdi. He pointed out that being obsessed with the eschatological end of the world (which will come after the Mahdi) should not overshadow one's personal concern with his own life's end. Also, the Dajjal will come before the Mahdi, but few seem concerned with determining when that will be. Lokman also blasts the Wahhabis of Saudi Arabia as one of the "two horns of Sheytan [Satan]"–and, for good measure, theorizes that the sect's founder, Ibn Abd al-Wahhab (d. 1792), was descended from some of the Jews of Medina who refused to accept Muhammad as a prophet and moved to al-Najd region. The other satanic projection, according to this Sufi leader, is the al-Sa`ud tribe, which accepted Wahhabi Islam and took over the Arabian peninsula with British help and also somehow, against all historical evidence, "brought down the [Ottoman] caliphate." And since there is no longer a political caliphate, Muslims must prepare for the arrival of the Mahdi, says Lokman, "by cleaning ourselves up, by accepting the Shariat [shari`a] and putting the Shariat into our lives, personal shariat…because there is no Khilafah [caliphate]."

Bottom-line: Within the past month, yearnings for the Mahdi have been expressed not only in the world's largest Shi`i Muslim country (Iran) but also in one of its most populous Sunni ones (and center of the largest Islamic empire ever to exist: Turkey); furthermore, one of the Islamic world's most significant transnational and non-state actors, the Naqshbandi-Haqqani Sufi order, actively promotes preparing the way for the Mahdi, as it often did in Ottoman times. This is yet more anecdotal data to support the empirical evidence garnered by Pew last year which demonstates that Mahdism, far from being an outlier Muslim belief, has become mainstream and pan-sectarian. And Mahdism, like many other facets of life, appears amenable to the "rule of three."

June 7, 2013: These Aren't the Mahdists you're looking for....

A few days ago *Arutz Sheva* (*Israel News*) ran an article by Daniel Lev under the headline "PA [Palestinian Authority] Arabs Fete 'New Mahdi,' Establishment of Calpihate" [sic]. It seems those Islamic union ultraists who are crazy for resuscitating the caliphate, collectively organized as Hizb al-Tahrir [HT] (literally "Party of Liberation"), held a rally in Ramallah, West Bank. According to Lev, HT "has its own Mahdi candidate–organization leader Ata Abu Rashta, born in Mandatory Palestine and a long-time resident of a refugee camp near Hevron [Hebron]. Speakers at the rally said that Abu Rashta, as Mahdi, would unify Muslims and establish Sharia law in countries around the world." Lev also explained, for any Mahdist-savvy ingénues, that "radical Islamists have been pushing for the reestablishment of the Caliphate– this time to be led by the all-powerful Mahdi, who will unite all Muslims and establish Islam as the dominant religion in the world, ruling for several years before the 'Day of Judgment'. Although the identity of the Mahdi is a secret, many Islamists believe that he is alive now, and several individuals have claimed the title. Many Islamists were said to have believed that Osama Bin-Laden was the Mahdi, or his right-hand man, until he was killed several years ago by U.S. forces in Afghanistan."

Observations:

1. I watched the accompanying video and while my ability to read Arabic outstrips my capacity to follow it when spoken (especially quickly, as the last interviewee did), I heard nothing from either HT representative about the Mahdi. The second speaker, Bahir Salih, did refer to Abu Rashta (HT's current leading ideologue) as "Imam," but not as Mahdi.

2. The eschatological Mahdi would, by definition, also be the Sunni Caliph–since his main task is to create a global Islamic state. Accordingly, all self-styled mahdis throughout Islamic history (at least all the ones I've studied) have thus also considered themselves to be caliphs. But very few caliphs have also attempted to claim the mantle of Mahdism. (The returned Twelfth Imam of the Twelver Shi'is would not be called "caliph" but, rather, "Imam al-Zaman"–Imam of the Age, or another equivalent title. But HT, remember, is a Sunni group.) Lev wrongly conflates the two registers, Mahdist and Caliphal–whether out of an attempt to sensationalize the issue, or from ignorance, is unclear.

3. Hizb al-Tahrir has never, in my experience and research–and I've been to two of their American conferences (the second of which I've written about at length)–articulated any Mahdist ideology or sentiment. It's quite possible, of course, that they tone down the Islamic fervor of their message here in the U.S.; but, again, that clip from the West Bank evinces no Mahdist claims, as near as I can tell.

4. Mr. Lev is correct that there are currently Islamists who think the Mahdi is extant on earth, although I would take issue with his claim that "many" believe UBL was he (some did, but not exactly legions). As I pointed out in an article last year, actual (Pew) polling data indicates that over 40% of the world's Muslims expect the Mahdi to come in their

lifetime(s). Of course, the rub comes when anonymity is sacrificed on the altar of personal Mahdist identification such that, when apocalyptic push comes to political shove, many fewer Muslims seem willing to recognize any one individual's claim to be him. But even a low percentage of 1.6 billion can represent enormous numbers of Mahdists in real terms.

5. Note that last line: UBL was deemed by some "the Mahdi, or his right-hand man" until SEAL Team Six sent him to meet the houris. The relegation of a potential Mahdi to more of a "John the Baptist" preparer-of-the-way role is a common trope in Islam, both Sunni and Twelver Shi'i. I saw the latter at work in Iran when I was there in 2008: in a number of conversations about the late Ayatollah Khomeini (d. 1989), I was told that some Iranians had thought he was the Twelfth Imam al-Mahdi but that, after he died, they realized he was probably the Imam's harbinger instead. On the other hand, dashed Mahdist expectations can cause disappointed disciples to claim that the failed figure is simply occulted, or in mystical hiding–especially if he is dead. This is a Twelver Shi'i doctrine that has worked its way into Sunni eschatological thought, and which indeed was applied to Usama bin Ladin (as I wrote about not long after his dispatch).

6. I have argued in a number of publications and lectures that groups like Hizb al-Tahrir are a greater threat to the West than ones like al-Qa'idah, because they have a long-range strategic goal of (re)Islamizing society (from the top-down, whereas the Muslim Brotherhood has heretofore preferred the bottom-up, educational approach) and not simply a tactical one of killing Americans and/or Israelis. IF HT's caliphal dreamin' were ever fused with full-blown Mahdism, then that would constitute a *sui generis* Islamic threat of a new order. HT pines for the Ottoman caliphate, but not the Mahdi—at least not yet..

Timothy R. Furnish, Ph.D.

May 15, 2013: Janissaries, Jacqueries and Jihad.

Three of my favorite Islamic world topics are the Ottoman Empire, Sufism and–of course–Mahdism. So when all three are rolled together, as they are in a book chapter by Ahmet Yaşar Ocak, I must (like Mr. Sparkle) blog on the topic or die; I can do no less! Ocak's publication from 2007, which I just recently found, is entitled "Sufi Milieux and Political Authority in Turkish History: A General Overview (Thirteenth-Seventeenth Centuries)," and found in Paul L. Heck, ed., *Sufism and Politics: The Power of Spirituality* (Princeton: Markus Wiener), pp. 165-195. Ocak's topic is the love-hate relationship between the Ottoman state and the Sufi (mystical) orders found therein. A number of Sufi orders–Bektaşis, Naqshbandis, Mawlawis (Mevlevis)–were officially sanctioned and supported by the sultans; the Bektaşis, in fact, were the official order of the sultan's shock troops, the yeniçeris or "Janissaries," such that many soldiers were members and Bektaşi shaykhs served as military chaplains. On the other hand, two more antinomian orders–the Qalandaris and Malamatis–were more often at loggerheads with Istanbul. The Qalandaris were suspect and repressed because they liked to shave their heads, faces and eyebrows; received support from the Ottomans' archenemies over in Persia, the Twelver Shi`i Safavids (because of theological similarities between Qalandari Sufism and Twelver Shi`ism); and, most damningly, because one of their shaykhs once tried to assassinate a sultan. The Malamatis were more hirsute but had in many ways a bigger problem vis-à-vis Istanbul: their shaykhs tended to want to proclaim themselves Mahdis; and this is, to put it mildly, problematic from an imperial point of view–because when someone claimed he was the Mahdi, this "implied that that political power should be vested in him, rendering the Ottoman government illegitimate and cruel" (Ocak, p. 183). Shaykhs, or tribal leaders, of other orders also sometimes declared themselves the Mahdi in Ottoman domains. Between 1240 and 1665, at least nine different Sufi or Sufi-affiliated men led major Mahdist revolts against Ottoman authority: In 1240, two Turkmen Wafa`i Sufis: Baba Ilyas-i Khurasani and Baba Ishaq. In 1416, three Qalandari shaykhs: Torlaq Kamal, Borklug Mustafa and Badr al-Din (the last "**supported by [Byzantine] Christian feudal lords who had lost their domains to the expanding Ottomans**" (Ocak, p. 187). In 1511, Shah Qulu (instigated by Safavids). In 1512, Nur Ali Khalifa. And in 1520, Shah Wali. The next century, in 1665: Sayyid Abd Allah. Those last three were unspecified Sufis who "presented themselves as *sahib al-zaman* ["Lord of Time/the Age"] and *mahdi al-dawran* ["Mahdi of the Period"] (Ocak, pp. 187-88).

Of course, it is little surprise that Sufi *mileux* are often the ground for Mahdist movements. I've remarked many times before, in various venues, that Sufis are predisposed to charismatic leadership and have a ready-made organizational structure that lends itself to mass movements, particularly Mahdism. And as Ocak observes, Ottoman Sufis (at least the official orders) were jihadistic: "[e]specially in wartime they [Sufis] were a great source of moral support for both sultans and soldiers....They gave speeches encouraging the soldiers in jihad and offered prayers for victory. At times, they accompanied the sultans on military campaigns, which spurred the soldiers to fight with greater enthusiasm" (p. 179). This was noted some years ago, too, by that great scholar of Sufism J. Spencer Trimingtham: "Evliya Çelebi [the renowned Ottoman writer] writes of hundreds of dervishes...who took part in the final siege of Constantinople" (*The Sufi Orders in Islam*, p. 240).

One final bit from Ocak, before I move on to my own analysis: while Western European jacqueries (medieval peasant revolts) are often adduced by historians and sociologists as analogous to Mahdist rebellions in Islamic lands, there is at least one major difference: the latter are not purely socioeconomic or political, but usually infused with

Islamic Sufism; and in fact "even once the movement had been repressed and its followers eliminated, their memory survived among the people as long-enduring legend" (Ocak, pp. 184-5).

Observations:

1. Ottoman problems with Sufis and even with self-styled Mahdis did not stop in the 17th century; North/East African, Anatolian Kurdish and Middle Eastern Arab Sufis fought the Ottomans at various times in from the 18th-20th centuries, epitomized by the Sufi Muhammad Ahmad of Sudan (d. 1885) whose declared Mahdism was the most succeessful. And in fact Mahdism even broke out in the Turkish Republic, as late as 1930, in the town of Menemen, as one Mehmet declared a jihad against the secular state and beheaded a police officer before the Turkish army sent him to the afterlife (see my book *Holiest Wars*, pp. 58ff). Note that the Ottoman domains were predominatly Sunni and that thus mystical Islam was being deployed, for the most part, by and against non-Shi`is.

2. Martial Sufis have lived on to fight another day–today. One prominent example is in the former Ottoman province of Iraq, where the Naqshbandi Sufis fought against the American occupiers and continue their jihad against the Shi`i regime in Baghdad as *Jaysh Rijal al-Tariqa al-Naqshbandiya*. Another is in Somalia, where for several years the pan-Sufi *Ahl al-Sunna wa-al-Jama`a* has fought against the al-Qa`ida-linked al-Shabab. In much of the rest of the Islamic world–Tunisia, Libya, Egypt, Pakistan, Afghanistan–Sufis are under attack, not from governments but from Wahhabi-Salafi Islamic fundamentalists.

3. Sufism, contra many analysts with their heads firmly buried in secular sands, is quite prevalent and influential in the modern Islamic world. According to last years's Pew study, "The World's Muslims: Unity and Diversity," some 19% of the Islamic world's populace belongs to Sufi orders, comprising over 300 million people. Also, that same study examined Muslim belief in "the Mahdi's imminent return"

and ascertained that some 42%—over 670 million—of the world's Muslims hold to it. Based on that data, the anomaly is not that Sufism ever erupts into Mahdism—but rather that it doesn't happen far more often in the modern world!

4. Note that the collapsing (under incessant Muslim attacks!) Christian Byzantine Empire was not above aiding and abetting Sufi-fueled Mahdist revolts against the Ottoman Empire—because the enemy of their enemy was their friend. Perhaps we should consider incorporating a similar approach into our geopolitics and counter-terrorism strategy.

February 19, 2013: The Mahdi v. the Wahhabis-Salafis: the Haqqani Battle of Evermore.

Frequently I analyze the historical and theological connections between Sufism (Islamic mysticism) and Mahdism; often, I discuss the antagonism between Sufism and Salafism/Wahhabism (Islamic fundamentalism, for readers from Rio Linda, the State Department or CIA). But I have never theorized that Sufi-based Mahdism might be, at least in part, a reaction to Salafism—this intriguing proposition comes courtesy of Dr. Itzchak Weismann at the University of Haifa (Israel) via a paper entitled "The Myth of Perpetual Departure: Sufis in a New (Age) Global (Dis)Order," which he was kind enough to let me read ahead of its upcoming publication in Itzchak Weismann, Mark Sedgwick and Ulrika Martensson, eds., *Islamic Myths and Memories: Mediators of Globalization* (Farnham, Surrey, UK: Ashgate, forthcoming).

His paper deals with the Haqqaniyya branch of the Naqsbhandiyya Sufi order, whose "teachings combine the rejection of Western civilization, nostalgia for the lost Ottoman caliphate and unbridled animosity to the Islamic fundamentalist trend with the the cultivation of Western discipleship, interest in New Age culture and **a belief in the imminent appearance of the awaited one—the Mahdi**" [emphasis added]. The Haqqani founder, Muhammad Nazim `Adil al-Haqqani, was born in 1922 in Turkish Cyprus and claims familial connections with both the Qadiriyya and Mevleviyya ("Whirling Dervishes") orders. His early education was a blend of tradition Islamic religious studies and secular science–a degree in chemical engineering from Istanbul University–while later he became a Sufi adept and started his own branch of the Naqshbandiyya. Shaykh al-Haqqani is a firm believer in using the latest media to advance his particular Islamic message, and is unique even in Sufi circles for his frequent and vituperous condemnations of Salafism/Wahhabism as not just "the archenemy of Sufism" but "a disgrace to the Muslims, and the cause for the militant image that is now associated with Islam in the West"–to which he links his particular (and rather fluid) "apocalyptic vision." Shaykh al-Haqqani's son-in-law and "deputy" in the Western Hemisphere is Hisham Kabbani (born in Lebanon, 1945) who also was trained in both Islam and science (chemistry degree). He has founded a number of Sufi centers in the U.S. and, like his mentor, rails against Islamic fundamentalists while appealing to non-Muslim Westerners under rather New Age auspices disseminated via the Internet–including aspects of Shaykh Nazim's Mahdist prognostications. Dr. Weismann notes that Nazim al-Haqqani's eschatological warnings are rooted in the same Islamic angst that arose, in modern times, with the Six Day War of 1967 and were further ramped up by the "Mahdist" occupation of Mecca's Grand Mosque in 1979. (I explored the effects of both the Six Day War, and the Juhayman al-Utaybi uprising, on Islamic eschatology in my 2001 doctoral dissertation, "Eschatology as Politics, Eschatology as Theory: Modern Sunni Arab Mahdism in Historical Perspective," pp. 1-52 and pp. 243-248) but adds that al-Haqqani is, however, "unique among the Mahdists" in that he opposes Sunni fundamentalism. And, unlike them (although Weismann never actually states this), al-Haqqani's Mahdist views have changed over the years. Almost a quarter-century ago, he wrote that the Mahdi was "living in solitude in a cave in the Rub` al-Khali desert in Arabia" (as per A.J. Quinnell's 1981 novel *The Mahdi*) but that they were in contact and the Mahdi would appear "soon," following a U.S.-USSR nuclear war that would enable the Dajjal to conquer the whole world except for Mecca, Medina and Damascus (as per some hadiths)—after which Jesus, the Mahdi and their followers would defeat him (helped afterwards by radioactivity-soaking jinns!). In later versions, his apocalyptic scenario replaced "godless" Western materialism and Communism as the enemies of Islam with the Wahhabis-Salafis, so that by the early 1990s he was lecturing that Westerners would come to believe in the Mahdi more than even Arab Muslims and that when the Mahdi came, he would behead Wahhabi scholars. A few years on, as the Christian millennium approached, the Shaykh envisioned the U.S. in an even more favorable light, as a global bringer of peace. Here in the early years of the 21st century, Shaykh Kabbani has taken up the eschatological prognostication mantle while retaining its core anti-Wahhabi/Salafi element, according to Dr. Weismann—who also maintains that the "underlying motivation behind" the Haqqani Sufi eschatological paradigm is "the militant Islamist threat" and thus that this "apocalyptic myth…amounts to a call to the foremost Western powers and especially the U.S. to join hands with the spiritual forces of Sufism in a common struggle against worldwide 'Wahhabism' and establish…a new(-age) global order."

In sum, Weismann sees the two Haqqani Sufi leaders as reimagining Mircea Eliade's "myth of eternal return" for the modern age of globalization—which has caused so much *sturm und drang* for the Islamic ummah in particular—primarily as a reaction to their co-religionist Wahhabi and Salafi rivals: The Mahdi **will** come to vindicate the Sufis, devastate the Islamists, convert the West and create (with a little help from his Muslim prophet friend, Jesus) a global Islamic state prior to the End of Time.

Observations:

1. This Haqqani Sufi Mahdism is but the latest example of the historical Sufism-Mahdism nexus–but at least this one is peaceful (so far), unlike many manifestations thereof: the 19th c. Sudanese Mahdi Muhammad Ahmad; the short-lived (literally) Turkish Mahdi Mehmet, 1930; the al-Qahtani-al-Utaybi Mahdist revolt in Mecca, 1979. Note, however, that while the Mahdi's followers are to exhibit a pacific belief in him, the Mahdi himself will be quite ferocious once he appears, particularly toward Wahhabis-Salafis.

2. This is SUNNI Mahdism, for the Haqqaniyya *tariqa* ("order") is a Sunni one–once again disproving the persistent conventional wisdom that Mahdism is a Shi`i phenomenon.

3. Ironically, considering the Sufi-Salafi/Wahhabi acrimony, al-Haqqani engages in the same sort of "newspaper exegesis" as do the latter–and which is almost certainly borrowed from American Protestant eschatologists such as Hal Lindsey.

4. Along with deploying Mahdism as an anti-Wahhabi/Salafi salient, the other major innovation of Shaykh Nazim is his using the belief as a hook to attract Westerners to Islam via the latter's attraction to "New Age"-style mysticism. (For an example of how this may be working–albeit probably not in the way either Shaykh Nazim or Shaykh al-Kabbani intended–see the new rap song and video by The Underachievers, called "The Mahdi." Lyrics such as "I'm...Soldier of the Father/But ain't no Christian" might be edifying to the Sufis, but the incessant usage of the "n-"word appears rather novel in Mahdist discourse.)

5. Does expressing the hope that the Mahdi will come and decapitate Wahhabi scholars indicate that Shaykh Nazim al-Haqqani feels the Sufis are losing the global *da`wah*, and that the only recourse he

sees is divine intervention?   If so, this Sufi Mahdism is profoundly
morbid, not hopeful.

6. The worldwide leader of the Haqqani Sufi order is not afraid to
blame fellow Muslims–Wahhabis and Salafis–for the "militant image" of
Islam regnant in the West (and, indeed, globally).   One may safely
surmise he knows more about Islam than John Brennan, Eric Holder
and even Barack Husayn Obama.   Perhaps the current US
administration could learn something from Shaykh Nazim.

7. This Sufi Mahdism is eerily similar to the Twelver Shi`i brand
espoused from Qom and Tehran, *mutatis mutandis*.   In particular, both
expect that when the Mahdi/Twelfth Imam (re)appears, he will humble
(to put it mildly) the Sunni fundamentalists.   Is a de facto Sufi-Shi`i
alliance over against the Wahhabi-Salafi-AQN front out of the question,
then? Perhaps Ahmadinejad should have traveled to Cyprus to meet the
Haqqani shaykh, rather than to Egypt to shake hands with the Muslim
Brotherhood President Morsi.

8. Ultimately, while Weismann presents substantial and compelling
evidence that the Haqqaniyya order's leadership is utilizing Mahdism as
both a shield and sword against Sunni fundamentalists, I remain, at this
juncture, merely "almost persuaded" that such has been conclusively
proved.   But certainly this brilliant analysis reminds those of us who
follow Mahdism to look for similar trends in other Sufi orders across the
globe. According to the enormous Pew study from 2012, "The World's
Muslims: Unity and Diversity," belief in the imminent coming of the
Mahdi (and Jesus) is rampant in the Islamic world (some four in ten
Muslims expect the Mahdi in their lifetime). Mahdism, whatever milieux
whence it springs, remains a powerful Islamic doctrine, as it has been for
at least a millennium.   And with superb studies like Weismann's
available, no one will be able to say that they were not apprised of
Mahdism's potential–for good or evil. What Weismann shows is that

these Naqshbandi-Haqqani shaykhs, as their predecessors did in Ottoman times—and as Turkish neo-Sufis like Fethullah Gűlen and Adnan Oktar still do, today—look for the Mahdi to come and fix the the religious and political dispensation.

[For any readers who don't know, "The Battle of Evermore" is a Led Zeppelin song about an apocalyptic battle which draws heavily upon the imagery of Tolkien. Find the post-Zeppelin performance by Jimmy Page, Robert Plant and–appropriately!–a bevy of North African musicians.]

U.S. Policy toward Islamic Eschatological Movements

January 16, 2013: Brennan and CIA: All Eyes and No Sight When It Comes to Islam.

Since President Obama nominated his current chief counter-terrorism advisor, John Brennan, to be the next CIA director, criticism has focused on Brennan's alleged Bush administration involvment in "enhanced interrogation techniques" and rendition, as well as his shaping of the current administration's extensive terrorist-killing drone program. But while important issues these are largely tactical ones–and much more problematic, strategically, is Brennan's worldview toward Islam which, in effect, is the Obama administration's position writ large: generally, "describing our enemy in religious terms" is wrong and counterproductive; specifically, "nor do we describe our enemy as 'jihadists' or 'Islamists' because jihad is a holy struggle, a legitimate tenet of Islam, meaning to purify oneself or one's community, and there is **nothing holy or legitimate or Islamic** [emphasis added] about murdering innocent men, women and children."

Brennan's view has been encapsulated for some time in the CIA's "Political Islam Strategic Analysis Program" [PISAP] which is described on the agency's website thusly: PISAP "was established in 2004 in recognition that forces that have have not traditionally been studied, in a comprehensive manner, by the Intelligence Community needed to be examined as they affect the national security interests of the United States. The effort does not focus on Islam as a religion or on the worldwide Muslim community; rather, it examines those organizations that use religion for political purposes and use religious ideology to attempt to change the existing political, social, or economic order...."

So according to the next CIA director, and the analytical arm of his agency, Islam *per se* is off-limits as a subject of study, yet the Islamic concept and 1,400-year-old politico-military policy of jihad **is** Islamic and fair game–except when a noted non-Muslim like John Brennan says it's not?

Brennan's misapprehensions, or misrepresentations, of jihad have been meticulously documented and critiqued already, most notably by the very able and knowledgeable Patrick Poole at *PJ Media*–so there is no need for me to revisit that ground except to note the following: if violent jihad has no legitimacy in Islam, then why are 31 of 51 FTOs (Foreign Terrorist Organizations) on the State Department list Islamic? And why do such groups invoke, as both justification and motivation, the jihad-waging examples of not just "prophet" Muhammad but (if they're Sunni) the first four caliphs, the Abbasid caliphs, Salah al-Din and the Ottoman sultans or (if they're Twelver Shi`i) Ali, Husayn, the Safavid shahs and the "martyrs" of the modern Islamic Republic of Iran?

John Brennan, according to his bio, has a M.A. with a specialization in Midde Eastern studies from the University of Texas-Austin; speaks Arabic; and was the station chief in Saudi Arabia in the 1990s. Unless UT's academic program is far less rigorous that those of us in the field have been led to believe, Brennan would have had to study some Islamic history, and thus would know full well the quintessentially Islamic nature of jihad, as well as its supreme importance in Muslim religious, military and political history. (For Allah's sake, the Ottoman Empire officially issued a fatwa [Turkish "fetva"] of jihad against the World War I Allies in 1914!) Assuming that this is the case–then why does he pontificate so ahistorically and inaccurately? Some think that this is part of a clever strategy by the Obama administration both to 1) drive a wedge between jihadists and the rest of the world's Muslims, and 2) force (or at least entreat) Muslims, especially within the U.S., to re-think their own religion's doctrines, starting with the thorny jihad one–and, ultimately, to disown it. So our only options would seem to be that this administration's counter-terrorism policy-makers–which is, *de facto* if not *de jure*, an anti-ISLAMIC terrorist agenda, since we don't have legions of Predators spanning the globe and launching Hellfire missiles at congeries of "right-wing extremists," soccer hooligans or Tea Partiers (at least not yet)–either are woefully ignorant of Islamic history and doctrines, OR that they are, on the contrary, well-informed about them but intentionally duplicitious for strategic reasons.

Since the first alternative is simply beyond the pale of logic (as well as being too horrible to contemplate), let us accept *arguendo* the second–which is hugely problematic in its own right. To gauge this, let us see how the perspective of John Brennan and the CIA's Directorate of Analysis would work (or, more accurately, not work) when applied to Mahdism, Shi`ism and the Islamic Republic of Iran [IRI].

Several analyses of belief in the Mahdi and its effect on the policies of the IRI have been done–most notably my "A Western View on Iran's WMD Goal: Nuclearizing the Eschaton or Pre-Stocking the Mahdi's Arsenal," and Mohebat Ahdiyyih's "Ahmadinejad and the Mahdi" (*Middle East Quarterly*, Fall 2008) as well as Charles Cameron's take on the importance of Mahdism in general as a topic of analysis (*zenpundit.com*, August 27, 2009). Rather less academic, but more recent, is Hosam Matar's "The Mahdi and Iran's Foreign Policy," which ran on the English site of the Lebanese daily "al-Akhbar" on January 11, 2013. Mr. Matar makes a number of valuable observations about Mahdism among the ruling clique in Tehran (and Qom), most notably: that the ruling ayatollahs and politicians view their state as needing to be created in the (imagined) image of the the future, post-occultation Mahdist kingdom (as I wrote about five years ago)–whether passively (the traditional view) by waiting on Allah to make it so, or actively (the Khomeinist position), in which "believers must strengthen their faith individually and socially, promote Islam, and build the necessary power to prepare for his return" (quite likely up to, and including, nuclear weapons—as I expounded upon in my aforementioned article.) Matar also observes that this view is not limited merely to the upper echelons of power in Tehran: "since Iran is the world's leading Shia [sic] power, many Iranians expect that it will play a major role in preparing for the Mahdi and in his subsequent activity. This belief renders Iranian Mahdism enormously significant in global politics."

But if anything Matar understates the issue, by positing Mahdism as purely an Iranian and Twelver Shi`i phenemenon—which it most decidely is not. Of the world's 200 million or so Shi`is, Twelvers do comprise the majority—but in addition to Iran they are a majority in Azerbaijan, Iraq, Bahrain and (almost certainly) Lebanon, as well as constituting significant minorities in Afghanistan and Pakistan. Furthermore, there are several other major branches of Shi`ism besides Twelvers: Isma'ilis, or Seveners; Zaydis, or Fivers; Alawis; and Druze. Although none of these sects has the same messianic expectation as the Twelvers (and the numbers pertain to how many "Imams," or divinely-guided descendants of Muhammad through Ali and Fatima, are legitimate), they are nonetheless in varying degrees open to eschatological suasion in general and Iranian influence in particular—the Zaydis of Yemen and the Alawis of Syria foremost among them.

Furthermore, Mahdism is also a very real concern in the majority Sunni branch of Islam, as evidenced by the legion of Sunni Mahdist claimants and movements that has surfaced over a millenium or more of Islamic history, and by the continuing outbreak of such efforts today. Considering, then, the strength of Mahdism in both Shi`i and Sunni Islam, the major modern manifestations would include, at a minimum:

- Mahdism is the operative ideology in the world's foremost state sponsor of terrorism: Iran.

- At least half-a-dozen self-styled mahdis have proclaimed themselves publicly in staunchly Sunni Saudi Arabia in the last several years (and the Kingdom was the locale for the last overtly militant Mahdism in the Sunni world: 1979's Mahdist occupation of the Great Mosque in Mecca).

- Iraq is home to at least four organizations claiming to be preparing the way for the Mahdi, either peacefully (*Ansar al-Mahdi*; *Jaysh al-Husayn*) or violently (*Jaysh al-Mahdi*; *Jund al-Sama'*).

- Another violent eschatological group, *Ansar al-Mahdi*, is bedeviling Morocco.

- Muslim Brotherhood-dominated Egypt, in the last year, has seen a chap proclaiming himself Mahdi and running for President as well as the presence of *da`is* ("missionaries") from Iraq's Ansar al-Mahdi in Cairo.

- The Turkish Creationist and promoter of (peaceful) Mahdism, Adnan Oktar, continues a torrent of publications and lectures; many of his followers believe that he himself is the Mahdi.

- The Zaydi "rebellion" in Yemen has as one of its aims the re-establishment of a Shi`i polity in the northern part of the country, as well as the resurrection of the Fiver Shi`i Imamate—at least as a religious institution.

- The Nurbakhshi neo-Sufi and Mahdist sect of extreme northern Pakistan "has been targeted for conversion by the Twelver Shi`is [of Iran] in their quest for demographic and regional expansion" (Shahzad Bashir, *Messianic Hopes and Mystical Visions: The Nurbakhshiya between Medieval and Modern Islam*, University of South Carolina Press, 2003; p. 286).

- Rural Iran itself is also home to "a phenemenon referred to popularly as the 'thirteenth imam'" which "although anathema in official and mainstream Twelver Shi`ism...has nevertheless persisted...." and "could gather a nucleus of antiestablishment supporters" (Farhad Kazemi, "Ethnicity and the Iranian Peasantry," in Milton J. Esman and Itamar Rabinovich, eds., Ethnicity, *Pluralism and the State in the Middle East*, Cornell University Press, 1988, pp. 201ff).

This wide range of Mahdist organizations, both Shi`i and Sunni and stretching from the Maghrib to South Asia, is **utterly incomprehensible** if approached from the myopic vantage point of John Brennan or the CIA's PISAP program—since few of these movements is overtly political, yet many of them espouse violent jihad. In fact, *many Mahdist movements in Muslim history were apolitical right up to the point at which they flipped a switch and transmogrified into violent political revolutions*—a point which cannot be scientifically determined but which can be at least estimated if one studies ISLAM's doctrines and history rather than ignores them. And just how is "us[ing] religious ideology to attempt to change the existing political, social or economic order" to be differentiated from the intrinsic and general Islamic imperative to "command right and forbid wrong" as well as the more specifically Mahdist focus on socioeconomic justice—unlesss one studies the banned topic of Islam as a religion? DCI-designate Brennan's dismissal of jihad as both "Islamic" and "legitimate," whether one deems it fatuous or fiendishly Machiavellian, blinds him to this inconvenient but supremely important historical truth: that since jihad has been both "Islamic" and "legitimate" for most Muslims over the the last 1,434 years, perhaps it would behoove us to stop denying that and find allies in the ummah for whom it is also "holy"—or, conversely, ones for who jihad has been ruled out as illegitimate and who can make the case more convincingly than a US government official who is (presumably) Catholic. (Brennan's telling Muslims what is and is not "legitimately Islamic" makes about as much sense—and carries as much weight—as our Episcopalian Attorney General Eric Holder doing so.)

Islamic groups who consider jihad "holy war" and are willing to engage in it against Salafis, or "fundamentalist" Sunni Muslims (which includes al-Qa`idah in all its manifestations), would include several Sufi orders: the pan-Sufi *Ahl al-Sunnah wa-al-Jama`ah* which has been battling *al-Shabab* in Somalia for several years; the Sanusis in Libya; the Qadiris in Mali; any number of tariqat (Sufi orders) in Egypt. Islamic sects that, conversely, have indeed ruled out violent jihad as a doctrine are in the minority (and generally deemed heterodox by mainstream Muslims) but can, at the very least, offer alternative views; these would include most notably the Ahmadis and Isma'ili Shi`is, as well as some other Sufi orders.

But a U.S. intelligence community that looks only at non-religious aspects of the Islamic world (note how oxymoronically that reads!), striving to find only secularist allies therein, renders itself—no matter how many satellites, reconnaissance drones, data-sifting software programs and even HUMINT assets it employs—"all eyes and no sight" (*Troilus and Cressida*, Act I, Scene 2). Brennan's insistence on ignoring the realities of Islamic doctrine and history, even if feigned, keeps us blind to all else that moves to our benefit in the world of Islam.

August 19, 2011: Promoting the Mahdi at Lackland Air Force Base.

Today I have an article running over at *Family Security Matters* about classes being presented on Islam by the Turkish Mahdist followers of Harun Yayha at Lackland Air Force Base in Texas (the U.S. Air Force's only basic training base): "Promoting Islam at Lackland Air Force Base."

Mahdist Mélange

January 5, 2013: A Mahdi by Any Other Name—Would Still Kill the Jews?

Now that the Mayan Non-Apocalypse has come and gone with nary a whimper, it's time to return attention to the strain of apocalyptic thought that potentially could produce a bigger bang: the Islamic kind. Predictions, and warnings, of the Mahdi's appearance continue to proliferate in both major sectarian branches of Islam, as well as in several major areas of the Islamic center.

In the Twelver Shi`a world:

1. The Karbala (Iraq)-based *Shafaqna Shi`a News Association* recently has been running a three-part series on "Signs of the Reappearance of Imam Mahdi." The first installment, as well as the second, discussed the astronomical signs that allegedly will precede and/or accompany the Mahdi's return. The third focused on the Mahdist precursor figures, the Sufyani and the Yamani—the former a "type" of the Dajjal, or Islamic anti-Christ; the latter an End Time good guy (for Muslims) whom Shafaqna earlier (in 2012) had already seen portents of in the ongoing Hawthi Zaydi (Fiver Shi`i) rebellion against the Sunni regime in Sana`a, Yemen.

2. For the better part of a decade, there has been an active Mahdist movement in Iraq whose leader, Ahmad al-Hasan "al-Yamani," claims to be the very aforementioned eschatological figure from southwestern Arabia. They are called *Ansar al-Mahdi* ["Helpers of the Mahdi;" henceforth AAM] and run a website as well as publish, every few months, a rather lengthy broadsheet called "The Mahdi Times." The latest edition, from November/December 2012, is largely concerned with the group's establishment of a branch in Egypt-the Sunni Arab

world's most-populous country-and the (alleged) government opposition thereto. A few notable points: the Egyptian opposition to al-Hasan's messianic *da`wah* is referred to as "Yazidi" (a pejorative term in Iraqi and Iranian Shi`ism for the heteoodox beliefs of some Kurds) and/or "Salafi" (Sunni fundamentalist); only a few of AAM's members are said to know Arabic, thus indicating most are not from Egypt or Iraq; there is at least one American, Joseph McGowen, among the AAM–perhaps helping explain why, when government security forces accosted AAM over alleged visa irregularities, the American embassy is said to have helped; at least one Egyptian TV station would regularly attack AAM (before it went off the air); and al-Hasan claims that his father is the occulted 12th Imam, Muhammad b. al-Hasan, which would mean he was sired by a five year-old boy who had been born in 868 and assumed *ghaybah* ("occultation") in 873 (unless he somehow reached to puberty, and beyond, in that mystical state).

In the Sunni world:

3. Another Mahdi-related figure (sometimes seen as a forerunner, other times as a successor) is *al-Qahtani*. Heretofore the most prominent such was Muhammad Abd Allah al-Qahtani (d. 1979), the putatative "mahdi" held up as inspiration for the abortive coup against the Saudis led by Juhayman al-Utaybi in 1979. Now, however, another–and, thankfully, more pacific–Qahtani has been identified: he is Fethullah Gülen, the exiled-to-America neo-Sufi Turkish leader of a massive global charter school system This is according to a man whom some consider to be the Mahdi himself, Istanbul-based Adnan Oktar. (And in fact it's not overly cynical to observe that since Oktar and Gülen are in many ways rivals for the mantle of the late Ottoman/early Turkish Mahdist thinker Said Nursi, the former's relegation of the latter to a supporting role is quite astute in Mahdist circles.)

4. While Gülen and Oktar are peaceful Sunni Mahdists, and al-Yamani seemingly a nonviolent Shi`i one, at least one prominent Sunni cleric links the Mahdi not just with jihad but, indeed, with genocide: Egypt's Mahmud al-Masri, in a recent religious diatribe, opined that either the Mahdi will wipe out the Jews of "the Zionist entity" when he comes, or that this will happen right before he appears; only the Jews of Isfahan will survive to become followers of the Dajjal until they are killed along with him (a standard Sunni eschatological calumny, indicting both Jews and Twelver Shi`is). "Ultimately," says al-Masri, "not a single Jew will be left on the face of the earth." This view of the Mahdi as the "terminator" of Israel and the Jews echoes that coming out of Ahmadinejad's Iran—with important exceptions.

Observations:

1. Arab Shi`i Mahdism had been largely bottled up in Iraq by Saddam Hussein (brutally, no doubt); the U.S. invasion and toppling of the secular dictator has, among many other unintended consequences, let the Mahdist jinn out of the Ba`athist bottle.

2. Western fears of a Cairo-Tehran Pan-Islamic axis are greatly exaggerated. Those who espouse such are ignorant of the current Egyptian anxiety about that country reverting to its Fatimid past, when a (Sevener) Shi`i minority regime lorded it over the Sunni majority. Both the Muslim Brotherhood [MB] and al-Azhar (Egypt's, and indeed the entire Sunni world's, pre-eminent religious institution) share this disquiet about Shi`ism (and, thus, about Iran).

3. But while Egypt is leery of Shi`ism and, presumably, its attendant (and integral) Mahdism, al-Masri's screed is clear evidence that Salafi Sunnism has room for strong eschatological belief. And recall that the Salafis are the junior partners of the MB in the ruling al-Nur party there—so any MB politicians who don't already adhere to Sunni Mahdism as a core doctrine are likely to be exposed to it by their coalition partners.

4.   Note that these examples of strong Mahdist belief are manifesting not in the heterodox, Sufi-infused "peripheries" of Islamic civilization–Senegal, say, or Indonesia–but rather in the very central regions of the old Muslim empires: Iraq, Egypt and, a bit later chronologically (thanks to the Byzantines), Turkey. This demonstrates, once again, that analysts and historians who scoff at Mahdism as a mainly marginal belief system are deluding themselves (and others).

October 31, 2011: Delayed Mahdification.

Last year I was asked, by the *Washington Times*"to opine on the anti-terrorism fatwa that had just been released (March 2010) by the Pakistani-born, London-based Muslim cleric Dr. Tahir al-Qadri. Since al-Qadri is a Sufi of the Qadiri order and a Barelvi to boot–Sufis are Islamic mystics while Barelvis are quasi-Sufi venerators of Muhammad; both groups are despised by Wahhabis and their South Asian analogs, Deobandis–his 600-page fatwa would have about as much effect among non-Sufis and non-Barelvis as a papal encyclical would for Southern Baptists.

I recently discovered that al-Qadri also lectures on the Mahdi! He has put out a book and a DVD set that explicate the hadiths (alleged sayings of Muhammad), over against "people who claim to have seen Imam Mahdi...or are waiting for his arrival [who] are misleading the ummah [Islamic community]." According to al-Qadri, the Mahdi will be born in Medina two or three centuries before *Yawm al-Qiyamah* ("Day of Resurrection"), and at some point in his life will conquer al-Quds (Jerusalem) then live to the age of 80 and die. As for dates, al-Qadri's exegesis leads him to the conclusion that the Mahdi will be born in the year "204"–but that since the Sunni hadiths do not provide more specific data than that, his birth year could be 2204, 3204, or 10,204 (Paul Muad'dib, anyone?).   On   the   other   hand,   al-Qadri rebukes (modernist) Muslim scholars who would conflate the Mahdi

Timothy R. Furnish, Ph.D.

with the centennial *mujaddid*s ("renewers" of Islam) predicted by other hadith to come every 100 years—mainly on the basis that such such misguided Mahdism allows for *mutamahdi*s, or "pretenders."

Observations:

1. The first of Ramadan, 2204 AH (After Hijrah) will be 8 August 2760—so the Obama Administration can safely kick this Mahdist threat down the road to the George Prescott Bush Administration and beyond.

2. al-Qadri retains the Sunni belief in the Mahdi yet moderately (and conveniently) chides those Muslims, both Shi`i (Ahmadinejad) and Sunni (Adnan Oktar of Turkey), who believe in the Mahdi's imminent appearance.

3. al-Qadri also adduces a Mahdi who will conquer Jerusalem for Islam—but, again, not before the 28th Christian century, thus disappointing not just Hamas but also the entire U.S. State Department.

4. The Mahdi for al-Qadri is not simply a reformer or refurbisher of the ummah, but rather a concrete historical leader who will unite the planet under one (Islamic) banner some several centuries before the final end; but, again, his coming is at best so far in the future that al-Qadri effectively neutralizes the issue for Barelvis and at least some Sufis.

October 30, 2011: The Mahdi from Another Planet.

Anyone who's interested in Islam and Mahdism but hasn't read *Dune* really should. Even if you're not as fanatical about the "Duniverse" as me (I've read not only *Dune* but all five of Frank Herbert's sequels as well as the many prequels and sequels written by his son, Brian Herbert, in tandem with Kevin Anderson), at least read the original novel. As Orson Scott Card points out: "Remember that Herbert wrote Dune in the 1960s, before the first oil embargo, before any Islamist government was ever formed. Whether Dune had any causal influence on the rise of Al Qaeda [sic], Herbert certainly did a superb job of predicting the rise and power of such an ideology. I would be surprised if there were not, among the followers of Osama bin Laden [sic], at least a few readers of Dune for whom this book feels like their future, their identiy, their dream. In other words, Herbert got it horribly right." Exactly right. The only thing lacking in Mr. Card's astute analysis is the importance of the Islamic messianic imperative in the novels.

Now comes the astronomical revelation that not just the future, but space, might belong to the Mahdi: "desert planets like the one depicted in the science fiction classic 'Dune' might be the most common type of habitable planet in the galaxy" (*space.com*, Sep. 1, 2011). Let's just hope and pray that Louis Farrakhan isn't right about the Mahdi having a functioning starship.

Sep. 22, 2011: The Mahdi Went Down to Georgia....

Little did I know that only 100 miles or so from where I live in Georgia (USA, not the former USSR), there are concrete—well, granite—signs of the Mahdi's coming. East of Atlanta the so-called "Georgia Guidestones" were erected in 1980, funded by a still-unknown, allegedly-Neo-Rosicrucian benefactor (perhaps Ted Turner, but my money is on Umberto Eco). These enormous slabs are engraved, in eight different languages, with rather anodyne rubrics on how to achieve an Age of Aquarius, er, Reason.

Now, over three decades after their construction and emplacement, Mr. Van Smith claims to have ascertained the real reason for this "modern Stonehenge:" serving as a harbinger of the imminent coming of the Mahdi! (See *vanshardware.com*, Sep. 16, 2011.) According to Smith, the Georgia Guidestones are somehow linked to the Burj Khalifa in Dubai, the world's tallest building, in pointing to the Mahdi's arrival. Smith also weaves into his conspiratorial apocalyptic narrative the usual suspects: Freemasons (of course!), the Dajjal, the "Eye of Providence" on the dollar bill and a recently-discovered comet. In a bit of a twist, however, Smith downgrades the Mahdi to the level of having "occult puppet masters pulling his strings"–so that "World War III [would] be waged in order for the Mahdi to ascend to his global throne, with the ultimate resolution being the destruction of the West: the United States, Great Britain, Israel and their closest allies must be toppled, with billions of human lives extinguished." (The end goal is a reduction of the planet's population to only 500 million, in order to fulfill the Guidestones' secular commandments to live in harmony with nature. I think I've read this story already–Tom Clancy's *Rainbow Six*.)

Smith yet again demonstrates the inaccurate understanding of these matters evinced by many armchair eschatologists: he thinks that only "Shiite[s]" (sic) believe in the Mahdi (actually, many Sunnis do, as well, and the belief more often manifests in Sunni venues); he claims that Iran's eschatological video "The Coming Is Upon Us" set a date for the Twelfth Imam's reappearance (it did no such thing, as I pointed out in my article on the topic); and he thinks that only recently have "Shiite leaders" begun equating the Dajjal with Freemasonry–but in fact this exegetical trope has been around for decades. At least he didn't claim that the Mahdi plays the fiddle....

June 8, 2011: This Terrorist is Toast!

Herewith a mash-up of several eschatologically-minded stories from the news in and about the Islamic world:

1. An Indonesian Muslim thinks he is the Mahdi with "power to reposition the moon, sun and stars."

2. Usama bin Ladin resurfaced last week–in a piece of British toast:

How very boring and Euro-centric of UBL. At least God, when He manifested on *The Simpsons*, told Homer He was off to appear in a tortilla in Mexico ("Homer the Heretic" episode).

3. According to the most recent End Time prognostication over at Mahdiunite site, the Mahdi will return on Friday, July 28, 2023 at 2:45 PM on the roof of the Ka'bah in Mecca and, simultaneously, Jesus will reappear in Damascus.

Other than this being exactly a 100 years after the official dissolution of the Ottoman Empire and the declaration of the Turkish Republic, I don't know why this date (1445 A.H.) should hold any special significance for Muslims.

But I guess it depends which side of the eschatological toast you prefer to butter. In Bin Ladin's case, I believe the Navy SEALS added quite a bit of raspberry jam–right up there near the top.... And, as the SEALs are reported to have said upon storming the Abottabad compound, paraphrasing Dr. Peter Venkman from *Ghostbusters*: "this dude is toast!

March 9, 2011: Who's Your Mahdi (Daddy)?

It seems Mahdism is not just for male Muslims anymore. According to a poster to the online fatwa factory of "Islamweb," "I saw a woman on television claiming that she is pregnant and carrying the Mahdi; is she telling the truth?" The virtual mufti replied "The Mahdi can be known only through the signs that are mentioned in the prophetic Hadeeths [sic] and he will be known only after his emergence. Therefore, the claims made by some women that they are expecting Mahdi are false and nonsensical." Said mufti goes on to blame belief in the Mahdi for "laziness" and "passivity" among Muslims–guess he's never heard of the rather energetic jihads waged by the 12th c. followers of Muhammad Bin Tumart, the 19th c. ones of Muhammad al-Mahdi of Sudan and, just 30 years ago, those of Muhammad al-Qahtani in Saudi Arabia. Too bad, as well, that this inquirer did not identify his location and which TV show featured the woman claiming such an intemperate conception. But the very claim is yet more evidence that Mahdism is a growth industry (no pun intended) in the Sunni world (for the Twelver Shi`i 12th Imam will not be re-born).

December 15, 2010: Mahdi You Can Drive My Car

Of course, as Allah's Rightly-guided One, he can drive any car he damn well pleases—especially his own! Acccording to an Islamic blogsite "cars will be one of the technical vehicles available in the time of Hazrat Mahdi...and...these will have headlights and interior lighting. It appears from the information provided in the hadith that the headlights of Hazrat Mahdi's (as) car will also shine brightly." How this blogger gets that out of the rather laconic (Shi`i) Hadith by al-Numani that "his [the Mahdi's] steed will shine like the full moon" is beyond me—but then, I'm just an ignorant Christian, er, dhimmi. [Original link has disappeared; reposted at *harunyahya.com*.]

October 12, 2010: The Mahdi from Kashmir.

One of the commentators at the Islamic online think-tank Grande Strategy claims to have seen the Mahdi, or at least a Mahdi "prototype," in his recent post "To the Unknown Mujahid, May We Never Forget You." This near-Mahdi experience was alleged to have happened back in 2001, right after the U.S. invasion of Taliban-ruled Afghanistan. The commentator was in the Faisal Masjid (presumably the huge Faisal Mosque in Islamabad, Pakistan) "doing special war prayers for the Taliban in Afghanistan" (how moderate of him) when "at one point, a CIA operative showed up, pretending to be Italian" (and who must have been at least a station chief, if not the CIA director himself, because "one day, we did not have those prayers and the next day we found out that it was because the CIA requested that we don't pray against them.") However, he and his brethren soon defied the CIA directive and returned to war prayers (in a religion of peace?); furthermore, between sessions of invoking Allah's wrath upon the infidel Americans, they soon noticed something striking about the chap teaching Arabic classes in the mosque:

" This particular class was being taught by a man, the like of whom I had never seen before, nor since have ever seen again. When you reach a certain level of spiritual enlightenment…sometimes you can 'see' or 'feel'… the 'noor' [Arabic *nur*, "light"] or 'aura' or 'spiritual light' of another… This man did not have a glow–it was like a 1000 watt halogen lamp…. I checked myself by discretely asking a few other brothers… and they too confirmed. [H]e was tall, bearded, wore a military camo jacket and in all his manners was as if he had walked out of the 1st century Hijri. He spoke English well enough that you could tell he was well-educated and belonged to a noble family. He was from Kashmir…. Some close relatives of his were also senior officers in the Pakistan Army. He was obviously a mujahid, although… one that was fighting against India and in Kashmir and had nothing to do with the Afghanistan war…. Your average jihadi does not have this noor. Some even have a black aura, i.e. they are doing something very wrong. This man was special in a very real way but when you try to describe why, you are found wanting. I knew his name then, but… I can't remember it now…. I later found out that he was taken by the Americans…. I have no idea… if he is dead in a ditch or in Guantanamo bay or some place worse. I would like to put this in the record that if we ever manage to establish an Islamic state insh'Allah, it should be a top priority to have this man released insh'Allah….Why? Because I believe…<u>that if he is not the Mahdi himself or one of his men, at the least he is the precursor to the kind of men that would make up the army of the Mahdi</u>. Or for those who do not believe in the Mahdi, he is the category of men that can save us from our present circumstances. A prototype to our success…. Disclaimer: I <u>don't</u> want to claim that he is the Mahdi."

As to the reasons for this posting, the anonymous Grande Strategist says this is "information that could be useful for the Muslim world" which could "be lost forever if something happens to me"–although "not intending this as a farewell address, I fully intend to live long…and see the tables turn [sic]…."

Observations:

1. "Grande Strategy" appears to be a Pakistani, and most likely Sunni, forum (although it is registered in Bellevue, Washington). Once again, the lingering conventional wisdom (both scholarly and popular) that only Twelver Shi`is believe in a coming Mahdi is demonstrated to be wrong.

2. The purveyors of this site appear to be educated, articulate chaps—so the prejudice (again, both scholarly and popular) that only ignorant *fellahin* ("peasants") believe in such an eschatological figure is demonstrably false.

3. A Kashmiri Mahdi or *mujaddid* ("renewer" of Islam) might be problematic, because several hadiths state that the Mahdi must be an Arab, like Islam's founder, Muhammad. (This was one of my criticisms of the otherwise-entertaining fiction book from 1999 by Margo Dockendorf, *The Mahdi: A Millennium Thriller*—she has the Mahdi coming from India.)

4. The Mahdist "glow" or "aura" attributed to this unknown Mahdist mujahid sounds like that claimed by Mahmud Ahmadinejad in his initial U.N. speech in 2005. Sunni hadiths about the Mahdi do not predict such a phenomenon—but representations of the Shi`i imams regularly portray them thusly. And, interestingly enough, this puts the allegations that Ahmadinejad may think that he is the Mahdi in a whole new light.

5. One has to wonder just how powerful the Islamic deity is if his "rightly-guided one"—or even an epigone thereof—can be taken prisoner by an infidel Christian power. Again, the thesis that the U.S. invaded Iraq to gainsay the Mahdi's coming-out party has been advanced before, by both Ahmadinejad and Muqtada al-Sadr. But does it not occur to these chaps that such a claim simply make Allah look impotent? On the other hand, perhaps the Marines at Gitmo have been briefed that the

Mahdi is under their care; this might at least explain why American military guards, most of whom are Christian, have been ordered to "revere" the Qur'an there.

6. This Grande Strategist wants to bring back the caliphate (as he, or someone on that site, has advocated at length previously)–and thinks this quasi-mahdi may be just the chap to head it up, or at least to help build it.

7. The author carefully avoids a categorical claim that he saw the Mahdi in Islamabad–but he comes very, very close to doing so. And his willingness to do so now, some eight years later, another bit in the growing pile of evidence that even educated, Sunni Muslims have convinced themselves that the plight of the ummah is so dire that only the Mahdi can save it. This will become an increasingly problematic factor in global geopolitics as the 21st century advances, especially as 2076 AD (1500 AH) appoaches, since Mahdist expectations increase at the turn of every Islamic century.

8. If he does come from Kashmir–will he be a Led Zeppelin fan?

April 15, 2010: Der Mahdi?

Today Daniel Pipes posted a long, and positive, review of Jeffrey Herf's book *Nazi Propaganda for the Arab World* which uses as source material "summary accounts of Nazi shortwave radio broadcasts in the Arabic language" in the 1930s and 1940s which were aimed at turning Arabs against the Jews and promoting Islam as compatible with National Socialism and Hitler's geopolitical aims. I hope to read the book myself soon, but in the interim this particular aspect of Herf's book, as reviewed by Pipes, struck me: "Specifically for Shi'ites [sic], the Nazis hinted at Hitler being the awaited Twelfth Imam or the Muslim eschatological figure of Jesus, who will fight the anti-Christ (namely, the Jews) and bring on the end of days." If Indy had just known, maybe he wouldn't have hated Nazis so much….

April 19, 2009: al-Mithrandir?

My interest in Christian and Islamic eschatology is perhaps only rivalled by my fascination with all things Tolkien. So when I see comments on a site stating that "Dajjal is Sauron, Imam Mahdi is Gandalf and Aragorn is Christ" my interest is piqued, to say the least. The comment comes from a site entitled "The Arrivals," on youtube, which appropriates scenes and characters from *The Lord or the Rings* as types for Islamic eschatology. Not all of the 50 videos seem to work, but check it out. The larger issue is whether Tolkien's archetypes, which arise out of a Christian and European context, work for Muslim propaganda. As someone who's studied both realms, I think the answer is a resounding "no."

April 13, 2009: You Should Be Dancin', Yeah–Like the Mahdi!

A video purporting to be of the Mahdi, moving ecstatically while on the *hajj*, has been posted (see *abovetopsecret.com*, April 9, 2009). I'm not sure the old Patrick Swayze or Michael Jackson would give this routine their imprimatur, but, hey, if you'd been in stasis for over a millennium, you'd probably want to cut lose with some eschatological moves, too! Seriously, the bigger issue is that, once again, someone in the Muslim world claims to have seen the Mahdi, in at least some kind of action.

January 16, 2009: Hamas Promotes the Mahdi?

Last year, on the Ides of March, I commented on the Palestinian cleric–`Isa Badwan–whose claim that the Mahdi had been born in 2004 in the Palestinian territories was carried on Hamas' *al-Aqsa TV*. Comes now an article ("Palestinian Journalist and Intellectual Criticizes Hamas TV Report of Mahdi's Birth & Prediction of Conquest of Rome") by an expatriate Palestian intellectual, Ahmad Abu Matar, criticicizing elements of Hamas for allegedly fostering such Mahdist beliefs among the Palestinian masses; Abu Matar mocks not only Badwan–"Since, as most Palestinians are surely aware, the city of Gaza's territory is only 45 square kilometers, it is highly possible that the awaited Palestinian Mahdi, who has already been born, lives within a few meters of the Israeli soldier Gilead Shali"– but also Iraq's Muqtada al-Sadr, for claiming the U.S. invaded Iraq in order to identify and capture the Mahdi.

Here's an interesting, related question: will the Mahdi join a local pack or den of the Hizbullah-run Mahdi Scouts? Look for pack branches in the Palestinian (Sunni) territories of the Lebanese (Shi`i) Mahdi Scouts to be formed any day now.

December 21, 2008: Our Man from Qahtan.

Last week I received the following email (name withheld at my discretion) from a Muslim purveyor of my site:

"Dear Dr. Timothy Furnish,

I have always been fascinated by the concept of the Mahdi. I was mindlessly surfing the web and sort of stumbled on your site. It does not surprise me at all that you are a Christian and yet you are very interested in what goes on with my religion. I am Muslim, Sunni of the Shafie mazhab and belief in the Mahdi had always been an article of faith for my family.

It used to distress me that there are a lot of Muslims who have never heard of the Mahdi. or the Dajal or the second coming of Isa bin Maryam. And there are people who are adamant that the Mahdi will be Isa bin Maryam–but I guess it is too late for them to understand. I have been fortunate to have all these information as a youngun and to have it consolidated again in my old age.

Many people believe that the Mahdi is already here–I for one. You know so much about my religion and I'm sure you know that hadith by the Prophet (s.a.w) something to the effect that the deen (Islam) will be revived every 100 years. The prophet was born in 570 CE (some say 571 CE) and there was a 900 years gap between him and Isa bin Maryam.Would you think it is too far-fetched if the Mahdi had been born in say 1970/1971 CE (dates which are pretty close to 12 Rabiulawal–the Prophet's birthday in Islam). He would be about 40 years old in 2009–I reckoned his age at the time of his "baiat" is calculated by the Islamic calendar.

There are several curious features about 2009. The middle of Ramadan 2009 could fall on a Friday and wukuf of the Hajj 2009 could also fall on a Friday. It will be a winter Hajj -remember the hadith about the Black army and crawling in snow to join them? (27th.December 2009 will be 10thMuharram 1431). And the black army from Khorasan-call them Taliban or terrorists, but they will emerge from Afghanistan (Khorasan of old) and it is interesting how the Afghans had never been conquered by non-Muslims and they have always been mostly Sunnis.

I never believed Osama is the Mahdi–but he could well be the man from Qahtan. There are so many teams working very hard to find the Mahdi-search & destroy teams all–and they will never ever find him, that is Allah will conceal him until the great baiat [ba`yat, or "loyalty oath"].

You probably already know that when he comes-some Muslims will turn against him and become disbelievers while some non-Muslims will accept Islam from him. I only wish that there were more Muslims who were interested in watching out for him...

Best wishes,

XXXXXXXXXXXX"

Observations:

1. My correspondent is Sunni–yet more anecdotal evidence that Mahdism is an issue not just in Shi`i areas like Iran and Iraq. Although having my site stumbled upon while someone is "mindlessly surfing the web" amounts to damning with faint praise–or praising with faint damns, methinks.

2. This reader believes not that the Mahdi is coming but that he is ALREADY HERE!

3. She references a hadith recounted by Ibn Majah that advises going to the Mahdi even if it requires crawling on ice or snow, and also that the family of Muhammad's house will suffer afflictions until delivered by "a people...from the East bearing black banners." Her interpretation of this is it applies to the Taliban of Afghanistan. This might make President-elect Barack Obama's proposed surge in Afghanistan a bit more problematic.

4. "I never believed Osama is the Mahdi—but he could well be the man from Qathan [sic]." What she means is the man from Qahtan. As David Cook points out in his superb book *Studies in Muslim Apocalyptic*, "the Qahtani...in all likelihood is a figure older than Islam and represents the messianic hopes of the South Arabian tribes....As the Mahdi traditions became the standard ones in Islam, there were attempts to connect the Qahtani with him in some way....For this reason he is glossed as the brother of the Mahdi, though whether the relationship is a blood relationship or a religious one...in unclear....At any rate, he is specifically said to be no less important than the Mahdi...ruling for 20 years and dying a violent death....." (pp. 179-80). So Usama bin Ladin, according to this representative of the Sunni street, is perhaps the Mahdi's brother?!

5. My interlocutor not only believes the Mahdi is here on Earth, but that "search & destroy teams" are gunning for him. Presumably these are American and/or Israeli ones. And presumably their intell is as bad as that we had about Saddam's WMDs....

6. "I only wish there were more Muslims who were interested in watching out for him..." She should have seen the masses at Jamkaran this past summer, pining for the Mahdi's coming. Again, this is yet more anecdotal evidence that the Islamic Republic of Iran's attempts to use Mahdism as a way to gain leverage in the Sunni world are not without cause.

April 17, 2008: Mahd[i] about Obama.

As we're all painfully aware of by now, some of Barack Hussein Obama's liberal legions of supporters harbor messianic expectations about him–and I'm not referring just to journalists. Over on the other side of the political spectrum, there are evangelical Christians who have seasoned their eschatological stew with Mahdist spices, and in fact kicked things up a notch by claiming that the Mahdi of Islam will be the Antichrist of Christianity. It was probably inevitable that these two ideological currents would eventually flow together, as evidenced by emails to my website recently:

"Barack HUSSEIN is probably Islam's mahdi.....1400 year old Islamic prophecy says this mahdi will be named HUSSEIN...I have reference for this... The masses have called Barack Obama the messiah.... Say he walks on water, the chosen...etc... The entire world is for Obama...looks like anti Christ to me... And the mahdi to muslims....

This 12th imam named HUSSEIN will promise peace, unity, brotherhood hood and the kingdom of god on earth. OBAMA HAS PROMISED THIS TO AMERICANS...while he gives all America's money to the U.N. And Muslim nations...Obama plans for USA to enforce the U.N.s law forbidding defamation against religions...This will stop the real truth about Islam lies and will cause persecution and death among Christians, etc...This man is not what he appears to be and America will know it soon...Not to mention the fact Obama was a Muslim when he was 6 to 10 years old ...and even took the shahada recently in the presence of a newspaperman....Taking the shahada is the only requirement to become Muslim. And Obama knows this ...He wears Muslim garb.. And.. His so called church is pro Islamic and and anti-white, anti-American and anti-Christian...."

There you have it. A vote for BHO is a vote for the Mahdi.

March 14, 2008: Istanbul or Constantinople? Nobody's Business but the Mahdi's!

Last month, on Palestinian *al-Aqsa TV*, Imam `Isa Badwan gave an interview in which he stated that the Mahdi had been born in the Palestinian territories four years ago. How did he know? Because "someone who is well known and whom I trust...told me that" a newborn baby spoke and said "I am the man who will be killed by the Antichrist." Badwan went on to say "the coming of the Antichrist will be preceded by the conquests of Rome...and Constantinople....These places will be conquered only by the righteous Mahdi. The Mahdi is from Palestine...."

Observations:

1. Islamic traditions say that Jesus spoke in the cradle, not the Mahdi; none of the three major compilers of hadiths about the Mahdi (Abu Da'ud, Ibn Majah, Ibn al-Tirmidhi) says that the Mahdi will do so. Perhaps some of the commentators say this. Or perhaps beliefs about Jesus have been transferred, in popular Islamic thought, onto the Mahdi.

2. The aformentioned compilers also say nothing of the Dajjal (which should be translated "the Deceiver," not really the "Antichrist") killing the Mahdi; and most commentators on Islamic eschatology have said, rather, that Jesus will kill the Dajjal, not that the Dajjal will kill the Mahdi.

3. Of course the Mahdi's conquest of Rome and Constantinople was a common trope before 1453 AD among Islamic eschatologists. But the Sunni Muslim Ottoman Turks took the former Christian imperial capital in that year, presenting something of a dilemma for Mahdists who cling to this tradition. As I observe in my book *Holiest Wars* (p. 29, note 103): "For this to make sense in the modern world, the Muslim eschatologist must posit, as many Muslim fundamentalists...do, that the current government of Turkey is un-

Islamic and deserves defeat, and that is major city Istanbul should be called by its former Christian name."

4. Mahdism is alive and well not only in Shi`i Iraq but in Sunni Palestine!

December 17, 2009: "Boss, Boss: De Mahdi, De Mahdi!"

Two months ago ABC News reported that in Muslim-majority Russian Daghestan Qur'anic verses in Arabic were appearing on a 9-month old boy's legs. Thousands of Muslim pilgrims were flocking to see this "miracle," no doubt at least in part because "A Muslim imam who visited... had a more apocalyptic take on the situation, saying, 'It is written that the closer to the end of the world, such signs will appear on a person's body.'" A Muslim blogger commenting on this was even more specifically eschatological:

"This is possibly a Sign from Allah announcing the birth of Al-Mahdi, either: (a) the Mahdi was born when this Russian baby was born, or (b) the Mahdi has just been born now when appearance of these verses has been publicized and the Russian baby is 9-months old (the period of normal pregnancy, meaning the period from conception of a baby to his birth). However, this boy most likely is not Al-Mahdi. So, if this is true sign about the birth of the Mahdi, we can expect the Mahdi to become the leader of Muslims within the next 30-40 years. Most Hadiths indicate that the Mahdi will be 40 years old."

[And for those of you who don't remember late-1970s TV: the title to this blog refers to "Fantasy Island"–that pre-KHAANN! vehicle for Ricardo Montalban. His sidekick, Tattoo, got very excited on sighting the arriving plane—the sign of kicking off the episode.]

October 3, 2006: If the Dajjal is here, can the Mahdi be far behind?

Ayman al-Zawahiri last week is said to have referred to Pope Benedict XVI as *al-Dajjal*, "the Deceiver"–the Islamic equivalent of the

Antichrist who, according to the Hadiths (traditions), will lead the forces of evil and battle both the Mahdi and Jesus before the end of time.

Is this just al-Zawahiri pushing propaganda buttons for his jihadist brethren, or does al-Qa`idah's number two man have an eschatological mindset? My money's on the latter, since as I point out in my book *Holiest Wars* there are jihadists convinced that Usamah bin Ladin is the Mahdi.

Modern Turkish Mahdism

March 26, 2014: I'm Not the Mahdi–Now $%*# Off!

Many analysts and journalists who cover the Islamic world focus on the likes of al-Qa`idah ["al-Qaeda" for those of you from Monkey's Eyebrow, KY; abbreviated to AQ] and the Muslim Brotherhood [MB]. Far fewer spend much time on an equally important Islamic movement: that of the Turkish neo-mystic Fethullah Gülen. (For a rough metric of the relevant interest in these three, try a Google search for each and you'll find the following results: AQ, 107 million; MB, 86 million; Gülen, 1.3 million.)   Such relative disinterest is unfortunate, because this Turkish-American movement (Gülen has lived in Pennsylvania since his eviction from a much more secular Turkey in 1991) is important on three levels: 1) Mahdism; 2) global educational reach; and 3) within Turkish politics.

In terms of Mahdism, both Gülen and another prominent, albeit much more idiosyncratic, Turkish religious leader named Adnan Oktar, are devotees of the late Turkish mystic mystic Said Nursi (d. 1960), known to his followers as "Bediüzzaman" (Arabic *badi` al-zaman*, "wonder of the age"). Nursi in his writings stressed the compability of Islam with modern science and education, and advocated "jihad of the word" over "jihad of the sword." Nursi very likely considered himself to be *a*, if not *the*, Mahdi–tantamount to the Islamic *mujaddid*, "renewer," who is predicted in some hadiths to come every century.   That would seem to be the same view that Gülen holds of himself, as evidenced by an interview in "Today's Zaman" last Friday: "I am not claiming to be the Messiah or Mahdi; I am just an ordinary man…." He continued: "Some circles have attributed similar remarks to Bediüzzaman in the past. They exploited his comments and views on the return of the

Messiah or Mahdi, arguing that he considered himself the Mahdi or Messiah." And Gülen reiterated his denial: "On this matter, I follow in the footsteps of Mevlana [the Sufi mystic Jalal al-Din Muhammad Rûmi, d. 1273 AD]. I am not claiming to be the Messiah or Mahdi." Also like Nursi, Gülen is an Islamic mystic but holds no formal membership in any of the hundreds of *tariqat*, or Sufi orders.

His educational system, however, is pedagogically and religiously a mixture of Nursi's ideas and Gülen's own thought, with a dose of Naqshbandi Sufism–specifically, the need to be involved in politics–thrown in. (On this topic, see Erol N. Gulay, "The Gülen Phenomenon: A Neo-Sufi Challenge to Turkey's Rival Elite," in *Critique: Critical Modern Middle Eastern Studies*, Vol. 16, No. 1, Spring 2007, pp. 37-61.) The "Gülenistas" have created perhaps the world's largest charter school system, which as of 2012 was also the largest such system in the United States, numbering 135 schools and 45,000 students. Although the schools in America are said by administrators and proponents to be STEM-oriented ones that eschew Islamic indoctrination, critics are doubtful. Overseas, particularly in Muslim-majority countries, Gülen schools unabashedly teach Islam–but a neo-Sufi, indeed kinder and gentler version of that faith than is disseminated by the Wahhabis and Salafis of Arabia or the Deobandi-influenced Taliban of South Asia.

Politically, the ruling AK Party of Turkey–particularly its leader and the current Prime Minister, Recep Tayyip Erdoğan–has increasingly been at loggerheads with Gülen and his people, accusing them of constituting a "deep state" which wields the real power behind the scenes. The actual reasons for this split between two erstwhile allies are byzantine (pun intended), but seem to center around who has more power in Turkey; view of and relations with Israel vis-à-vis other Muslim states; and the profits from Turkey's gold-for-oil trade with Iran.

Observations:

1. As I've remarked before, I'll take any day, and twice on Friday, a Mahdi or Mujaddid who states that "the conquest of the world will be achieved, not on the back of a horse, a sword in the hand, a scimitar at the waist" but rather by "penetrating into people's hearts with the Qur'an in one hand and reason in the other" (Gulay, p. 42)—as has Gülen. This IS truly moderate Islam, and far from lumping Gülen's people in with the jihadists we should be encouraging the spread of his charter schools across the Islamic world, with their Sufi Lite message of educational, not bloody, jihad (which, really, is tantamount to *da`wah*, "proselytization").

2. However, also regarding these charter schools and their place in the U.S. (or any other non-Islamic society): great scrutiny should be applied to them here, to ensure that they stick to teaching science, technology, engineering and math and do not attempt to inculcate Islamic values among the 99.4% of the U.S. population that is non-Muslim. If they can do that, let them operate. If not, shut them down more quickly than Duke in this year's NCAA tournament.

3. Regarding Turkey's internal politics and this Erdoğan-Gülen struggle—I don't have a dog in that fight, but it looks increasingly as if the latter is the only force that can prevent the former from asserting neo-Ottoman-style authoritarian power. A Gülenized Turkey might become the first truly moderate Islamic state; certainly the Gülenists are much more likely to drive such a result than the poseur moderates like the Muslim Brotherhood.

Today's post title comes from Monty Python's brilliant 1979 satire of messianism, *Life of Brian*—specifically, the scene "I'm not the Messiah!"

March 11, 2012: The Soporific Mahdi?

A prominent Turkish Muslim theologian and writer, Hayrettin Karaman, just a few days ago wrote about the Mahdi in the Turkish newspaper *Today's Zaman*. The piece was entitled "Is the Islamic world waiting for Mahdi?" Karaman disagrees with an unnamed "Muslim intellectual" that only the eschatological Mahdi could create peace and a "just order" and that the establishment of any "new caliphate" prior to the Mahdi's arrival would inevitably transmogrify into a "distorted" brand of a "modern administrative system." On the contrary, Karaman Bey argues that such "passively awaiting the Mahdi and expecting everything to be accomplished by someone else while doing nothing contradicts Islamic principles," and thus that Muslims need to "shake off this lethargy and learn to ensure harmony between modern and Islamic ideas."

Observations:

1. Who is this Muslim thinker that advises waiting for the coming of Islam's primary messianic figure before engaging in political activism? I would very much like to know, but the article does not say.

2. Karaman is painting all Muslims who believe in the Mahdi as quiescent quislings to the idea of (re-)creating the Caliphate–a common criticism levied by Sunni opponents of Mahdism, but one that is not always accurate. It is entirely possible to yearn for the coming of the Mahdi and yet simultaneously also take steps to (re-)Islamize society, install a (more) Islamic government and/or politically unify disparate Muslim states. The historical existence of many Sufi-oriented Mahdist movements in centuries past demonstrates that this is the case in the Sunni world; the ongoing attempts by the Islamic Republic of Iran to "prepare ye the way for the Mahdi" and to establish the Twelfth Imam's state in microcosm there shows that Twelver Shi`is also can walk and chew Mahdist gum at the same time.

3. Relatedly, that Mahdism lulls Muslims to sleep and makes them passive, otherwordly dreamers is an old criticism by Sunni clerics–but one which runs counter to countless historical examples of Sunni and Shi`i activism, political agitation and jihad.

July 10, 2010: Somebody's Comin'....

To paraphrase Dr. Peter Venkman's jail cell singing scene from *Ghostbusters: somebodies*, that is–at least according to Adnan Oktar, a.k.a. Harun Yahya: Jesus and the Mahdi will both return in the 21st century (my money's on 2076, which is not only the American Tricentennial but the year 1500 AH in the Islamic world). Oktar, by the way, is a prominent Turkish Mahdist and anti-Darwinist, whom I interviewed two years ago. Some Turkish followers think he himself is the Mahdi.

April 6, 2010: The "Soft" Mahdism of Neo-Ottoman Expectations.

Much virtual ink has been spilled, recently, about the global Islamic movement headed by the Turkish expatriate Fethullah Gülen (who, two years ago, was ranked the world's #1 public intellectual). Many analyses are positive, whether intensely or mildly so; others, on the contrary, portray Gülenists as crypto-Islamists threatening not just Turkey but the United States. I'm still forming my opinion of this movement, but at this juncture I tend to side with those who see the Gülenists as neo-Ottoman Sufis (or perhaps neo-Sufi Ottomans?) rather than as Muslim Brothers with moustaches. One important aspect of Gülenist ideology that often gets missed by commentators is its *sub rosa*, "soft" Mahdism, which derives from Fethullah Gülen's own personal adherence to the teachings of Bediüzzaman Said Nursi (d. 1960) as elucidated by Zeki Saritoprak, chair of Nursi Studies (no kidding!) at John Carroll University in Cleveland. Nursi was a late Ottoman/early Turkish Republic Islamic thinker and writer who was heavily influenced by Turkish Sufism. And Sufism, with its mystical and charismatic proclivities, has always been quite susceptible to Mahdist trends–Nursi's Sufi leanings being no exception. He did, however, differ with traditional Sunni Mahdist thought on some levels: for example, according to Zeki Saritoprak, "we may say...that in Bediüzzaman's view every age has its Mahdi," from which "it is understood...that the Mahdi

239

is not an individual." Most importantly, "he [Nursi] does not consider the Mahdi to be someone who will set everything in order…with the sword. He sees him [the Mahdi] as a normal human being and great reformer" who will "revive the Sunna of God's Messenger" and whose "service will become increasingly brilliant until the start of the 16th century of the Hijra, following which an evil movement will gain dominance" ("The Mahdi Question according to Bediuzzaman Said Nursi," conference presentation, 1995). But Nursi's thought seems to exhibit some cognitive dissonance on the topic of the Mahdi: while in some writings he stresses the non-individual concept of the Mahdi as almost a Star Wars-like "force" rather than a person, in other places Nursi does admit that "the Great Mahdi expected at the end of time is the last of the Mahdis and reformers."

Observations:

1. Nursi's/Gülen's pacific Mahdism is a welcome break from the normal martial messianic view of the Mahdi espoused in many Sunni, and some Shi`i, sources (and embodied by any number of self-styled Mahdis over the last millennium of Islamic history); however….

2. This same view of the Mahdi as an apolitical *mujaddid*, "reformer," who exists in every age also allows for relative ease in donning the mantle of the Mahdi by a sufficiently self-assured, pious and charismatic Muslim leader–as may very well be the case with Fethullah Gülen himself, or with another prominent, Nursi-influenced Turkish Mahdist, Adnan Oktar (whom I interviewed, in Istanbul, in 2008).

3. The 16th Islamic century begins in 2076 AD. Thus, Said Nursi and, presumably, his disciple Gülen both see the first three-quarters of the 21st century as a period of increasing Mahdist, and almost certainly Turkish, influence. Will the Mahdi restore the Ottoman caliphate before the American tricentennial?

4.   Someone, somehow, needs to ascertain the extent to which neo-Ottoman Nursian Mahdism influences the ruling AK Party in Turkey. It may be that Turkey's soft Mahdism proves more problematic to the West, in the long run, than Iran's harder version.

January 3, 2009: Show Me the Mahdi?!

In November, 2008 I was in Istanbul interviewing Adnan Oktar, a.k.a. "Harun Yahya," about his ideas of Mahdism and Pan-Islamic unity. (Interview segments are available on *youtube* as "An Interview with Mr. Adnan Oktar by Timothy Furnish.") Of course this necessarily entailed a discussion of his views of Darwinism v. Islamic Creationism.

Iraqi Mahdism

August 30, 2012: Senior Iraqi Politician: The Mahdi Hates the Kurds and their Ways.

Yesterday the Iraqi Kurdish media outlet *Rudaw* ("The Happening") ran a fascinating, and rather disturbing, article entitled "Shia Leader: The Awaited Imam Mahdi Will Fight the Kurds." The "Shia leader" in question is a former Majlis (Parliament) member and senior figure in the Islamic Supreme Council of Iraq (formerly the Supreme Council for the Islamic Revolution in Iraq, or SCIRI), Jalal al-Din Ali al-Sahgir (or "Sagheer"). ISCI (or SIIC) is the second-largest party in the Iraqi Majlis, holding some 52 of 440 seats, and is quite powerful in Basra and southern Iraq particularly via its armed Badr militia. So when al-Sahgir speaks on Mahdism, it's worth weighing his words.

According to *Rudaw*, back on August 10 al-Saghir delivered a *khutbah* ("sermon") in Baghdad's Buratha Mosque (of which he is the imam) in which he speculated that recent political events in Syrian Kurdistan might be signs of the impending arrival of the 12th Imam al-Mahdi–especially, eschatologically, if an earthquake were to strike there, and Turkish troops were to move into the Cizre/Malikiyah area; al-Sahgir also is said to have mused that Syria would fracture into five polities, including a Kurdish one which would be obliterated by the Turks. He also, allegedly, referred to Kurds of Syria and Iraq as *mariqah* or *maraqah*, "renegades" or "heretics," whom the Mahdi will combat, along with "converted Shia"–but claimed subsequently to have meant the "Kurdish autonomous region" and not the Kurds themselves. According to Professor Nawzad Koshnaw, Arabic professor at Salahaddin University in Erbil (Iraqi Kurdistan), al-Sahgir's employment of *mariqah* is tantamount to *khawarij*, the "outsiders/rebels" in the early history of

Islam whom the fourth Sunni Caliph (and first Shi`i Imam), Ali, fought against–and thus al-Saghir clearly implied that "the Kurds are deserting the laws...of the Iraqi government, and therefore Imam Mahdi will appear and fight the Kurds."

Observations:

1.   Modern Iraqi Mahdism has, heretofore, been largely a phenemenon manifesting among *outré* groups there: Ahmad al-Hasan's *Ansar al-Mahdi*, the late Abd al-Zahra al-Qar`awi's *Jund al-Sama'*, or Mahmud al-Hasani al-Sarkhi's *Jaysh Husayn*, as well as (albeit probably more politically and less eschatologically) Muqtada al-Sadr's *Jaysh al-Mahdi*. Now, however, a mainstream Iraqi politician is espousing Mahdist views–and not just pious ones reflecting some far-off, future hope but beliefs working eschatology into the modern political scene in the Middle East. When George Bush ordered the U.S. military into Iraq to take down Saddam, had none of his advisors ever apprised him of the apocalyptic attitudes prevalent in Twelver Shi`ism–or the dangers of letting the mahdist jinn out of its secular, Ba`athist bottle?

2. Ali al-Saghir not only advances ambiguous apocalyptic auguries–he identifies one particular group, the Kurds, as enemies of the Mahdi. Most Kurds are Sunni Muslims, and some (particularly in Iran and even some in southern Iraq) are even Twelver Shi`i. Nonetheless, Imam al-Saghir feels no qualms about singling them out for Mahdist opprobrium–primarily, it would appear, not on religious grounds but on a political one: insufficient loyalty to the post-Saddam Iraqi state.

3. The leadership of ISCI/SCII has, since the group's founding with Iranian supervision in 1982, been not just pro-Iranian but pro-*vilayet-i faqih* ("rule of the [Shi`i] jurisprudent," Khomeini's signature political concept). In the Islamic Republic of Iran adherence to this concept has been largely equated with loyalty to the Tehran regime itself. Iraq, however, does not have Twelver Shi`i clerical rule–at least not yet. Is

al-Saghir signaling that this is the direction in which Iraq's government must go, by his lights? Even more troubling, are his Mahdist critiques of the Kurds a way for him to preemptively rule out an entire ethnolinguistic group from political legitimacy—and thus to set the stage for their purging, or worse, should clerics like himself seize power in Baghdad?

Take a look at al-Saghir's own website (if you can read Arabic), among which the interesting articles/lectures include the likes of "Who Are Yajuj and Majuj?" (The Islamic equivalents of Gog and Magog described in the Bible in Ezekiel chapters 38 and 39, as well as Revelation chapter 20.)

October 22, 2011: Lies, Damned Lies, and Mahdism.

It's probably a good thing that U.S. forces are totally leaving Iraq by the end of this year—because now even Iraqi members of Parliament are not only lying about our role there and in the world, but about the reason we invaded in the first place. Iraqi MP Maha al-Douri spoke in Tehran last month and spewed the following prevarications about the United States:

1. *We are trying to "annihilate Islam."* Really? Look, lady, if the U.S. wanted to annihilate Islam, we could certainly do it much more easily and cost-effectively than the death-of-a-thousand-cuts approach pursued in Iraq and Afghanistan. For a clear, albeit horrific fictional example, see Tom Kratman's book *Caliphate*, pp. 170-172. But of course such is not even remotely a consideration—unless you're a truth-challenged Muslimah legislator.

2. *Massive conversions to Islam are taking place all over the world.* Not really. Anecdotally, while conversions to Islam are all the rage among the media in Eurabia, the U.S. and Canada, much less attention is paid to the conversions to Christianity in sub-Saharan Africa and China. And in Twelver Shi'ism Central itself, Iran, it seems that conversions to Christianity are a major issue. Empirically, there is just as much data

that can be adduced showing Christianity winning the conversion battle as can be in favor of Islam. At worst, it's a draw. And since Christians outnumber Muslims worldwide some 2.2 billion to 1.5 billion, that demographic equation won't be changing any century soon.

3. *Islamic terrorism is a false charge "implanted in the mind of the world" by America.* At the risk of Clintonism, "that depends on what your definition of 'implanted' is." It is, after all the (Hillary) Clintonian State Department's list of foreign terrorist organizations that shows 58% (28 of 48) to be Islamic in motivating ideology, methodology and goals—while Christianity, which has some 600 million MORE adherents than Islam, has NO groups on the list (the Continuity Irish Republican Army [IRA] and Real IRA are Irish nationalist and only incidentally Catholic; by the same token, I excluded a number of groups from the Islamic category—such as the Popular Front for the Liberation of Palestine, the Kurdish KGK/PKK and the Iranian Mujahadin-i Khalq, because they are nationalist much more than religious).

4. *Americans "planned and executed the 9/11 attacks...."* Who knew Iraqi Mahdists could be 9/11 Truthers? If that absurd contention really needs refutation—beyond basic knowledge of the events, the current geopolitical situation and logic—such was provided several years ago by *Popular Mechanics.*

5. *America is fighting "all the Islamic leaders."* This would be news to the Sultan of Oman; rulers of Egypt, Tunisia, and Algeria; Kings of Morocco and Saudi Arabia; Presidents of Nigeria and Indonesia; Prime Minister of Turkey; new leaders of Libya; and, most tellingly, the current Prime Minister of al-Douri's own country, Iraq. Perhaps "it depends on what her definition of "Islamic,' is"—which must be something along the lines of "anyone allied with Iran," in which case the list grows rather thin.

6. *The U.S. has been warring on Muslims in order to "prevent...any Islamic awakenings in preparation for the advent of the Mahdi;" and in fact "when the Imam al-Mahdi appears.... America will fight him and this is the reason for its war and occupation of Iraq."* As I've noted before, more than once, both Muqtada al-Sadr (he of *Jaysh al-Mahdi* fame, in Iraq) and Ahmadinejad have advanced this claim previously. But this is the first time that an elected member of the Iraqi government has done so.

Observations:

1. Is this *taqiyah* (religously-sanctioned lying allowed within Islam) or simple stupidity? It's hard to believe that anyone could look at U.S. actions over the last few decades and make these fatuous claims, but the same beliefs are held, *contra* all logic and facts, by too many on the American Left. Either way, I would wager that Sayyida al-Douri's views are not unique to her among Iraqi Shi`is; let's just hope that they are a minority view among them, and particularly among Iraqi legislators. But I wouldn't bet on it.

2. Although the MEMRI translation and transcript never points this out, al-Douri is speaking not just on Iranian TV but LIVE FROM TEHRAN (the opening screen shot is of an unidentifiable, because the images are too small, venue; but "Tehran" in Arabic script is clearly visible). How long will Iraq survive as a quasi-democratic, pseudo-ally of the U.S. when its leaders are trotting off to the Islamic Republic of Iran to osculate the ayatollahs' derierres?

3. And speaking of derierres, as our troops exit Iraq it's certainly notable that they are being rhetorically kicked in that part of their anatomies by al-Douri. Like Mark Twain said, the difference between a dog and a human is that if you feed the former, he won't bite you. But this Iraqi wench certainly proves the truth of Twain's adage.

April 8, 2008: Iraqi Mahdism.

My article on Iraqi Mahdism, "Will Iraq Stoke Flames of Islamic Messianism," ran this week at *PajamasMedia*.

October 3, 2006: The Methodist and the Mahdi.

From *The Times* of London this morning: "The followers of Moqtada al-Sadr believe that U.S. invaded Iraq to prevent the return to Earth of their sect's messiah-like figure, the Mahdi, or 12th imam [original link is dead].

Hojatoleslam al-Sadr claims that his militia is preparing for the day when the Mahdi, the last direct descendent of the revered Shia figure Ali, reappears. Shia believe that the Mahdi, who disappeared in 868, will bring justice to Earth.

At a prayer service in the central Iraqi city of Kufa on September 15, the cleric told a crowd of thousands that the Americans were collecting a dossier on the Mahdi to prevent his return. 'Did you ever ask yourself about why all of this, the bloodshed and the prisons? Why are the brothers fighting each other for a political game planned by the Americans? This all happened because they (the Americans) are waiting for the Mahdi. This planning started ten years ago. They have a big file for Imam Mahdi and they just need his picture to complete it.'

Hojatoleslam al-Sadr and his advisers are convinced that the Americans want to destroy Islam and stop the Mahdi. 'The Americans are trying to hijack Islamic movements. They think that these are serving the Mahdi's interests. Whatever they did in Afghanistan and Iraq are all attempts to hijack the Mahdi's return.'"

Sound familiar? Check out my detailed take on this from *FrontPageMag*, in a symposium entitled "Ahmadinejad's Armageddon (Sep. 4, 2006)."

TV Eschatology

March 17, 2015: Red Heifers and Red Herrings: *Dig* Leaves Islamic Apocalyptic Activism Buried.

As if I don't get enough eschatology in my day job—now I'm immersing myself in the topic by night, once weekly, with the new TV show *Dig*. An FBI agent stationed at the U.S. consulate in Jerusalem gets embroiled in a nefarious eschatological plot, led by a mysterious Orthodox rabbi and a Protestant minister, to hotwire the apocalypse via a red heifer and 13-year old holy child who may or may not be the clone of Jesus. The usual tropes appear: Peter Connelly almost became a Catholic priest before joining the FBI—but now is having an affair with his boss and brooding over the death of his daughter; Tad Billingham is not just a Protestant cult leader but, of course, merciless and conniving (is there any other kind of fundamentalist Christian?); the Israeli cop chain-smokes, wisecracks incessantly, gruffly orders around subordinates—and has an uncle who knows all about the Urim and Thummim. And the red heifer connection between Old Testament Judaism and fundamentalist Christian eschatology has been ripped from modern news stories.

There are a few twists: a Jewish faction seemingly working to stop (or perhaps hijack?) this attempt to move the apocalyptic needle is called the Essenes—but I wonder whether the modern descendants of those who wrote the Dead Sea Scrolls would have Special Forces-level military training? The U.S. Ambassador, revealed as part of the plot, spends her time in the Jerusalem consulate rather than the actual U.S. embassy over in Tel Aviv. Peter's dead daughter appears reincarnated in a young American archaeology student whom he meets—the night before she is brutally murdered.

Of course, the most striking aspect of *Dig* is that it posits a Jewish-Christian cabal trying to spark the coming of the Jewish Messiah/the return of Jesus–or at least the apocalyptic conditions for that to happen. There are "Christian Zionists" who believe the Temple must be rebuilt so that Jesus can come again (even if the Antichrist has to dwell in it first); there are also some Jewish groups, such as the "Temple Institute," which wish to do so–although for non-Jesus-related reasons. (There is even one Muslim group, that of Adnan Oktar of Istanbul, which promotes a Third Temple on the Mount alongside the Dome of the Rock and al-Aqsa Mosque.)

But in the modern world, the only folks actively attempting to hotwire the apocalypse are Salafi (fundamentalist) Sunni Muslims, most notably ISIS (ISIL/"Da`ish") and *Jabhat al-Nusrah*–as I have explained before, in various venues. ISIS in particular, in the many issues of its *Dabiq* magazine–named after the northwestern Syrian town where hadiths say the great victory of Muslims over Christian forces will occur–trumpets its firm belief that the pre-Mahdi End Times are upon us, and that its actions are helping to realize the eschaton.

Regarding eschatology, the media often write as if the Evangelical Christian view were that of all Christendom (as with, prominently, creation v. evolution). But the mainstream Christian view is not one of knowing with certainty when the End will come–much less triggering it. Regarding Jesus' discourse on the End of the Age in Matthew 24 and Mark 13, the *Lutheran Study Bible* says the following: "No one knows when the events Jesus prophesied will take place; therefore, Christians are to focus on the work He has given them" and quotes St. Augustine's admonition "Let no one then search out for the last Day, when it is to be; but less us watch by all our good lives, lest the last day of any one of us find us unprepared" (LSB, p. 1687). The Roman Catholic *New Testament of the New American Bible* speaks likewise of the Matthew text:

"The vigilant waiting…does not mean a cessation of ordinary activity and concentration only on what is to come, but a faithful accomplishment of duties at hand, with awareness that the end…will entail the great judgment…" (p. 110). Perhaps the best summation of the historical Christian position on the eschaton is found in the *Orthodox Study Bible*, in commentary on II Peter 3:10-12, which describes Christ returning: "Christians can actually hasten the coming of that day. How? Through evangelism…prayer…and repentance and obedience" (p. 1695). *Not* by rebuilding the Temple, killing anyone–even Islamic terrorists–or electing the right folks into office.

Dig is a fun show, and having been to Jersualem thrice, I particularly enjoy identifying all the scenes shot in place where I've been. But I hope it doesn't refocus the media's and public's attention away from the apocalyptic cult that really should concern us: ISIS.

February 23, 2010: Hastening the Messiah's Coming? Glenn Beck Gets Mahdism Wrong.

It has become conventional wisdom among American conservatives–both political and theological–that President Ahmadinejad and a certain segment of the Iranian government wishes to hasten the coming of the messianic figure in Islam, the Mahdi (the returned 12th Imam for Iranian Shi`is). I am not sure that this view is correct, based as it is on serial misunderstandings (if not outright misrepresentations) of Twelver Shi`i history and doctrines. Glenn Beck, for example, on his February 5, 2010 show, covered this topic and–as usual, unfortunately–got quite a few things wrong:

1. The belief that the 12th Imam will return "soon" is not really typical of all Twelver Shi`is.

2. Most Iranian (and Iraqi and Lebanese) Shi`is do NOT believe that the Mahdi's return can be "hastened," but will take place in Allah's good time and on his schedule, irrespective of human wishes. But yes, some few do believe in such hastening.

3. Beck says "12ers are so dangerous that...the Ayatollah Khomeini banned them." He's very wrong here and seems to be conflating the Hojjatiyeh organization's members with Twelver Shi`is as a whole–this is akin to confusing all Christians with, say, snake-handlers or Pentecostals who speak in tongues. The Hojjatiyeh (more properly, the *Anjuman-i Hujjatiyeh*) was an organization that was created in the 20th century to re-convert Baha'is to Shi`ism (Baha'ism having begun in the 19th century when a certain Persian chap declared himself the already-returned Mahdi–and this of course was, and is very much still, anathema to mainstream Shi`ism). And it was banned by Khomeini in 1983–but not because of any specially fervent Mahdist beliefs, but simply because its founder and leaders looked askance at the clerical rule system that Khomeini had originated and imposed.

4. Beck states that "the Twelvers believe that they have to wash the world in blood to hasten the return" of the Mahdi. While there might be SOME, both lay and clerical, who believe this, it is NOT a staple of the belief system of Twelver Shi`ism. Beck has been drinking too deeply at the alarmist, frankly ignorant well of the fiction author Joel Rosenberg. A more correct assessment would be that, like Christians, most Twelver Shi`is believe that the world will be in a state of violent chaos before the return of their messiah figure–but that is a far cry from saying that believers must initiate such violence to "hotwire the apocalypse."

I applaud Beck for actually delving into the religious beliefs of Ahmadinejad and the clerical rulers of Iran, and not applying only a political lens to examine what's going on in Tehran and Qom. However, his inaccurate, wildly-alarmist "analysis" does as much harm as good, and allows critics to dismiss his views. [Note: I have offered to appear on Beck's show to correct some of these inaccuracies, but despite contacts with his producer my offer has been, so far, rejected. It would seem Mr. Beck is more interested in heat than light on this topic.]

In a related story...during the sermon this past Sunday at church I was reading II Peter (our interim pastor is a wonderful man but he does tend to ramble), specifically 3:10-12:

"But the day of the Lord will come as a thief in the night, in which the heavens will pass away with a great noise, and the elements will melt with fervent heat; both the earth and the works that are in it will be burned up. Therefore, since all these things will be dissolved, what manner of persons ought you to be in holy conduct and godliness, looking for and hastening the coming of the day of God...." [NKJV].

The *Orthodox Study Bible* (which I love, although I am Lutheran) has the following notes on that passage:

"Christians can actually hasten the coming of that day. How? Through evangelism...prayer...holy living...and repentance and obedience...."

Neither Orthodox theology, nor that of any other Christian branch or denomination, encourages violence as a means to hasten Jesus' return–in fact, quite the opposite. (How could they, when Jesus' entire life was one of resisting and eschewing violence–quite unlike that of Muhammad or the prototypical Shi`i Imam, Ali?) Nonetheless, while many Muslims (Sunni as well as Shi`i, for the doctrine exists in Islam's larger branch, as well) share with Christians this view of peacefully hastening the coming of the deliverer, it is also undeniably true that an influential minority within each major branch of Islam–some hard-core ayatollahs, as well as some apocalyptic-minded Sunni jihadists–DO believe in "hotwiring the apocalypse."

Now remind me again which is the "religion of peace?"

June 16, 2007: Leaving Facts Behind: Tribulation Force on Glenn Beck.

Last night Glenn Beck had on his TV show three prominent fiction authors who deal with eschatology: Joel Rosenberg (*Epicenter*), Jerry Jenkins and Tim LaHaye (the *Left Behind* series). While I appreciate the fact that someone in the mainstream media (Beck is on CNN "Headline News") is at least talking about eschatological motivations affecting modern events, it's very disappointing that he featured three self-styled "experts" on CHRISTIAN eschatology and did not bother to bring on someone well-versed in ISLAMIC eschatology–which would have made sense, considering that the bulk of the discussion centered around the Middle East and in particular the end of time obsessions manifested by President Ahmadinezhad of Iran. If anyone knows Glenn Beck, suggest he read my book on the topic of Mahdism. The most egregious oversight was the ignorance of the fact that belief in the coming of the Mahdi is strong in BOTH Sunni and Shi`i Islam, not just in the latter–as these "experts" seemed to think.

Joking with the Mahdi

April 21, 2014:   Even Reverend Lovejoy Has His Ecumenical Limits....

First Church of Springfield (marquee creator courtesy of says-it com).

October 11, 2011:   The Mahdi, R.I.P–He Didn't Even Have Time to Bleed.

The CIA confirmed Tuesday that a drone killed the 12th Imam last Thursday. The CIA waited for the results of DNA testing to confirm that the 12th Imam, known as the Mahdi was dead. The CIA report contained few details. The Mahdi, known as "the secret Imam" was hiding in an undisclosed location when a missile from a CIA drone struck the building; he died instantly. It was not immediately clear if the Mahdi was the intended target but it was clear that the Mahdi is confirmed dead. Unconfirmed reports from the White House indicate that President Obama may be preparing an apology for the death–which may be accidental, but a spokeswoman from the administration would neither confirm nor deny.

Observations:

1. The "undisclosed location" was either Jamkaran, Iran or Sa`ada, Yemen. Considering the Mahdi before he went back to Allah appeared to be relatively clean and well-groomed, it was probably the former–which at least has running water.

2. It is unclear where the CIA obtained baseline genetic material for comparison, but anonymous intell community sources have indicated possibilities include the Aga Khan, Barack Obama and Viggo Mortensen.

3. Official Iranian news outlets have released statements claiming that the man actually killed was not the 12th Imam al-Mahdi but either one of his "body doubles" or, alternatively, a Zionist impostor. Or possibly George W. Bush with a beard.

4. President Obama, reading from a prepared statement after this announcement, expressed his personal condolences to all 1.3 billion Muslims in the world and said that, had it had been up to him, the Mahdi would not have been killed but rather brought to the U.S. in order to replace Joe Biden as his running mate in 2012.

5. Sunni eschatological groups have claimed that the man killed was not the Mahdi but rather the Dajjal, whom the heretical Twelver Shi`is mistakenly were following.

August 5, 2007: A Fourth Mahdi Claim in 2007?!

Yet another Mahdi claim has surfaced, this time among the predominantly-Sunni Kurds, according to *Newsmax*:

"An Iranian Kurdish group whose fighters have clashed frequently with government forces in Iran has sent its top leader to Washington, D.C., to seek assistance from the United States government.

Rahman Haj Ahmadi, president of the Kurdistan Free Life Party (PJAK), told NewsMax in an exclusive interview that he hoped to meet with senior administration officials to discuss the situation inside Iran and how the U.S. could help the opposition....

'Iranian President Mahmoud Ahmadinejad says he is waiting for the *badieh zaman*,' the legendary 12th imam of Shia Islam whose return brings justice to the world.

'We also believe in the badieh zaman,' he chuckled. 'For us, he is George W. Bush' [link now dead, alas]."

It's an open question whether Mr. Bush will be able to retain his membership in the Methodist Church, however.